Dनिरा B. Ward

NCSW President, 1981–1983

THE
SOCIAL WELFARE
FORUM, 1982/1983

To the Reader

This combined volume represents a first for the National Conference on Social Welfare. It includes papers selected by the Editorial Committees for both the 109th and the 110th Annual Forums of the NCSW. Part I includes papers from the 109th Annual Forum held in Boston, Massachusetts, April 25–29, 1982. Part II includes papers from the 110th Annual Forum held in Houston, Texas, May 22–25, 1983. NCSW regrets the delay in publication of this combined volume and extends appreciation to its members and subscribers for their patience and understanding, as well as to the authors whose papers were selected for inclusion. It should be noted that the titles of authors as used in this volume reflect their positions at the time their papers were presented at the Annual Forum.

National Conference on Social Welfare

THE SOCIAL WELFARE FORUM, 1982

PART I

OFFICIAL PROCEEDINGS, 109TH ANNUAL FORUM
NATIONAL CONFERENCE ON SOCIAL WELFARE
BOSTON, MASSACHUSETTS APRIL 25–28, 1982

Foreword

THE 1982 *Social Welfare Forum* will be remembered as a weather bell, sounding the challenges, the uncertainties, and the issues faced by the social welfare community as the nation pushes forward into the last twenty years of this century.

Dorcas R. Hardy, Assistant Secretary for Human Development Services, U.S. Department of Health and Human Services, speaking at the opening session of the 109th Annual Forum made it clear in her presentation, "The Social Role of Government in a Free Enterprise System," that the present administration believes fundamental changes should be made in government's approach to social welfare, that to bring about a vital and healthy economy and the jobs it would create is the most significant action that the federal government could take to assist the poor in moving out of poverty. She maintained that the administration will continue to shift responsibilities from the federal to the state government for more of the operation of programs, that individuals, families, and communities should be the primary sources of assistance, and that governmental assistance will be available to the most needy. Assistant Secretary Hardy indicated that we must find new methods for planning, better targeting of limited federal resources, and more effective, forthright methods for evaluation of our efforts. The address clearly led into and set the tone for this year's theme: "Fiscal Cuts and Social Costs: Analysis and Action." The presentation angered many, was thought-provoking to some, and agreed with by a few. It is in the spirit of the rich heritage of the National Conference on Social Welfare that all views be heard and that those speaking as federal administrators in office make clear where they stand. Therefore, we present Assistant Secretary Hardy's paper* to you as one vision of change and new direction.

Topics addressed at the Forum included: child welfare, criminal justice, income maintenance, health policy, domestic economics, women's rights, international social welfare, mental health, minorities, refugees, social policy, practice, the private sector, and voluntarism.

Elliot L. Richardson presented to the participants his perspectives on the growth and changes in social welfare policy and the need for a continued national policy albeit changed from the past. The Whitney M. Young, Jr., Memorial Lecture was given by John E. Jacob, President of the National Urban League. In a moving and eloquent speech he called on the social work community to remember what has been accomplished, what is yet to be done, and not to be deterred by those who would seek quantum leaps back in time.

Ronald B. Dear requested that his objection to the inclusion of this paper be noted since he feels that there is misrepresentation of data in the article.

These and many other stimulating presentations were made at this Forum. They offered new approaches to thinking, facts on what is happening in social welfare today. The Editorial Committee is pleased to present this representative sample of papers, from among many given at the 109th Annual Forum. It is perhaps more fitting than we know that this Forum, at this time in our history, was held in Boston, Massachusetts—a city in a section of the country rich in its willingness to stand during difficult times.

The members of the committee were: Ronald A. Feldman (chairperson-elect), George Warren Brown School of Social Work, Washington University, St. Louis; Esther Wattenberg, Assistant Director, School of Social Work, University of Minnesota, Minneapolis; Ronald B. Dear, School of Social Work, University of Washington, Seattle; Jane Collins (Program Committee Representative), Director, Department of Clinical Social Work, Denver Department of Health and Hospitals; Charlotte Nusberg, Senior Program Specialist, American Association of Retired Persons/International Federation on the Aging, Washington, D.C.; Mark Battle, School of Social Work, Howard University, Washington, D.C. We appreciate the consultation of John E. Hansan, Executive Director, NCSW, and we are deeply indebted to, and appreciative of Maureen Herman, Program Director, NCSW, for her able staff assistance, as well as the editorial assistance of Charles Webel of Columbia University Press.

It is our distinct pleasure to serve the members of the National Conference on Social Welfare, and we hope you find this volume beneficial.

WILLIAM T. RAY, JR.
Chairperson,
Editorial Committee

National Conference on Social Welfare Distinguished Service Awards

THE NATIONAL CONFERENCE on Social Welfare Distinguished Service Awards for 1982 were awarded to the following:

ROGER N. BALDWIN, who, as staunch defender of the Bill of Rights for all Americans and as founder and executive director of the American Civil Liberties Union, devoted his life to assuring freedom of speech and freedom from oppression and injustice for all people as guaranteed by the Constitution of the United States; and, who as a social worker, teacher, court probation officer, civic activist, and civil rights advocate gained national and international prominence for his unyielding fight for individual freedom and for voluntary association and against exploitation and poverty.

To Roger N. Baldwin, a continuous member and supporter for seventy-four years, the National conference on Social Welfare pays tribute.

CHARLES I. SCHOTTLAND, who has had a major impact on national and international social welfare policy; for his leadership in the development of the Social Security program in the United States; for his pioneering efforts to make social planning and social administration significant components of social work education; and for his leadership as Commissioner of Social Security, as Principal Advisor to the U.S. Delegation to the United Nations Social Commission; and as President of the National Conference on Social Welfare, the National Association of Social Workers, the International Council on Social Welfare, and for his active participation in numerous other social welfare organizations; and for his contributions as caseworker, administrator, educator, lawyer, author, statesman, and as advocate for the social well-being of children, families, and older citizens of the United States and the world.

NATIONAL CONFERENCE ON SOCIAL WELFARE DISTINGUISHED SERVICE AWARDS, 1955 – 1982

1955   EDITH M. BAKER, Washington, D.C.
      FEDELE F. FAURI, Ann Arbor, Mich.
      ELIZABETH WICKENDEN, New York
1956   TIAC (Temporary Inter-Association Council) PLANNING COMMITTEE, New York

1957   THE REVEREND MARTIN LUTHER KING, JR., Montgomery, Ala.
       WILBUR J. COHEN, Ann Arbor, Mich.
1958   THE HONORABLE JOHN E. FOGARTY, R.I.
       LEONARD W. MAYO, New York
1959   ELISABETH SHIRLEY ENOCHS, Washington, D.C.
       OLLIE A. RANDALL, New York
1960   LOULA DUNN, Chicago
       RALPH BLANCHARD, New York
       HELEN HALL, New York
1961   THE HONORABLE AIME J. FORAND, R.I.
1962   JOSEPH P. ANDERSON, New York
       THE ATLANTA *Constitution*, Ralph McGill and Jack Nelson, Atlanta,
       Ga.
       CHARLOTTE TOWLE, Chicago
1963   HARRIET M. BARTLETT, Cambridge, Mass.
       ERNEST JOHN BOHN, Cleveland
       FLORENCE G. HELLER, Glencoe, Ill.
       Special Award: Television Documentary, "The Battle of Newburgh,"
       IRVING GITLIN and the NATIONAL BROADCASTING Company, New
       York
       Special Citation (Posthumous): ANNA ELEANOR ROOSEVELT, "First
       Lady of the World"
1964   DR. ROBERT M. FELIX, Bethesda, Md.
       Special Citation (Posthumous): JOHN FITZGERALD KENNEDY, "Man
       of Destiny"
1965   JAMES V. BENNETT, Washington, D.C.
       SIDNEY HOLLANDER, Baltimore
       CORA KASIUS, New York
1966   REPRESENTATIVE WILBUR D. MILLS, Ark.
1967   THE HONORABLE HUBERT H. HUMPHREY, Washington, D.C.
       PLANNED PARENTHOOD—WORLD POPULATION
       Special Awards (Posthumous):
       HOWARD F. GUSTAFSON, Indianapolis
       RUTH M. WILLIAMS, New York
1968   LOMA MOYER ALLEN, Rochester, N.Y.
       KENNETH BANCROFT CLARK, New York
1969   THE HONORABLE ELMER L. ANDERSEN, St. Paul, Minn.
       HARRY L. LURIE, New York
       IDA C. MERRIAM, Washington, D.C.
1970   No award
1971   SAM S. GRAIS, St. Paul, Minn.
       DOROTHY I. HEIGHT, New York
1972   WHITNEY M. YOUNG, JR. *(Posthumous)*

1973 WINSLOW CARLTON, New York
      THE HONORABLE JAMES CHARLES EVERS, Fayette, Miss.
      JOE R. HOFFER, Columbus, Ohio
      NATIONAL COUNCIL OF JEWISH WOMEN, New York
1974 ASSOCIATION OF AMERICAN INDIAN SOCIAL WORKERS
1975 MITCHELL I. GINSBERG, New York
1976 BERTRAM S. BROWN, M.D., Rockville, Md.
      THE HONORABLE BARBARA JORDAN, Washington, D.C.
      THE HONORABLE WALTER F. MONDALE, Washington, D.C.
      WILLIAM A. MORRILL, Washington, D.C.
1977 ROY WILKINS, New York
1978 COY EKLUND, New York
      VERNON E. JORDAN, JR., New York
      CYNTHIA C. WEDEL, Washington, D.C.
1979 JAMES R. DUMPSON, New York
      GISELA KONOPKA, Minneapolis
      NORMAN V. LOURIE, Harrisburg, Pa.
      GEORGE M. NISHINAKA, Los Angeles
1980 *Special Citation (Posthumous)*: JUSTICE WILLIAM O. DOUGLAS
      DOUGLAS A. FRASER
1981 EVELINE M. BURNS, New York
      LOIS AND SAMUEL SILBERMAN FUND, New York
      NATIONAL URBAN COALITION and M. CARL HOLMAN, President,
      New York
1982 ROGER N. BALDWIN *(Posthumous)*
      CHARLES I. SCHOTTLAND, Tucson, Ariz.

Greetings to the Conference from President Ronald Reagan

I AM pleased to send greetings to members and guests of the National Conference on Social Welfare as you gather for your 109th Annual Forum.

Americans enjoy virtually unparalleled opportunity to lead fulfilling lives, ensuring their own well-being and contributing to the welfare of others. We owe this good fortune to the enterprise of those who have come before us and to the blessings of our land and our liberty.

Our government, like our people, remains committed to aiding those who need our assistance and to helping all Americans help themselves. Dedicated volunteers and professionals like yourselves help carry forth and renew that commitment.

I send my best wishes for the success of your Forum. Working together, we can continue to improve the quality of life for all Americans.

Contents

The Social Role of Government in a Free Enterprise System

I. ALAN PIFER

To SOME people, it will seem quaintly anachronistic to reexamine the legitimacy of social intervention by our national government here in 1982, as our complex, highly developed society moves on toward the end of the twentieth century. Wasn't that issue settled once and for all back in the 1930s, or if not then, certainly in the 1960s and 1970s? Yes, we thought so, but new political currents, of which the present administration is representative, have reopened the question and restored it to the national agenda.

The present administration has proposed as a broad goal for the nation a drastic reduction of the federal social role, to be achieved through budget cuts, deregulation, and a transfer of responsibilities to the states and the private sector. Just what the prospects are for passage of the full program is as yet unclear, but the first steps have certainly been taken. My purpose here is to offer a context for thinking about federal social role in today's circumstances — an effort that, perhaps, can clear away some of the misleading rhetoric that has obscured understanding of why there came to be such a phenomenon in the first place and why there must continue to be, if we are to remain a strong, secure, and stable nation.

NATURE OF THE SOCIAL ROLE

First of all, what do we mean by the federal social role? Normally, we conceive of this as compromising only those programs that provide direct services or cash or in-kind benefits to designated beneficiaries — programs which have as their general purposes the promotion of human development, the alleviation of misfortune, or the easing of social tension. Such programs have developed over a long period of time and have been added to by nearly every administration in this century, although we tend to associate them particularly with the New Deal and Great Society eras. They cover such areas as health, welfare, education, equal opportunity, housing, income security, nutrition, job training, and aid to the handicapped. Some of them are aimed at the poor, while others are available for all who qualify, regardless of income. Some require matching funds at the state or local level, some do not. Within them, varying amounts of administrative responsibility are delegated to the states or localities. Taken

ALAN PIFER is President, Carnegie Corporation of New York.

together, they free the private enterprise system from having to assume responsibility for such major tasks as income redistribution, social insurance, and the provision of social services—tasks for which the system is ill-suited and which would divert its energies from its classic economic function of producing goods and services for puchase.

There are, however, many additional activities of the federal government that we do not ordinarily think of as being part of its social role and that have a far greater impact than those I have just mentioned. Here would fall such matters as protection of the environment; tax policy; fiscal and monetary policy; the construction of highways, dams, harbors, airports, and sewers; aid for public transportation; much of the regulatory function, such as enforcement of the pure food and drug laws; agricultural price supports; the provision of investment incentives; immigration policy; and energy policy. All these activities have a great bearing, directly or indirectly, on fundamental social matters, such as where people live, how they support themselves, how large their income is, and what the quality of their lives is.

The true social role of government, therefore, is very wide and penetrates into the remotest corners of our daily lives in ways that are so familiar to us we are scarcely conscious of them. In view of this, the currently popular call to "get government off our backs" seems rather ludicrous. Equally nonsensical to me is the assertion that the taxing power of the federal government should never be used to promote social change. Willy-nilly, the federal government is in the business of influencing social change every minute of every day. To eliminate its social role—its responsibility to promote constructive social change—would be to eliminate a vast part of its *general* role and would take us back to the earliest days of the republic when we tried, unsuccessfully, to govern ourselves through a loose confederation of the states. It was not without reason that the founding fathers, in setting forth the prescription for the successor federation, wrote:

> We the People of the United States, in Order to form a more perfect Union, establish Justice, insure domestic Tranquility, provide for the common defence, promote the general Welfare, and secure the Blessings of Liberty to ourselves and our Posterity, do ordain and establish this Constitution for the United States of America.

In these words they authorized—indeed, mandated—a purposeful social role for the federal government.

ORIGINS AND GROWTH

It is true to say, however, that throughout the first century and more of our history as an independent nation, this mandate was largely ignored. Almost immediately after the Union was consummated, a deep split developed between those who wanted a relatively powerless central government—the Democrats, led by Jefferson—and those who wanted a strong one—the Federalists, led by Hamilton. In due course, the Jeffersonian view prevailed, with the result that we experienced a long succession of intentionally weak and often ineffectual national administrations. This had its moments of disaster, as when we got into a war in 1812 for which we failed to arm; but on the whole, the agrarian society of those days drifted along without much need for a strong government in Washington.

An exception, of course, was the gathering crisis over the issue of slavery. As this deepened and sectional strife became increasingly bitter, it became more and more obvious that the problem could no longer be left to the states but would have to be dealt with by the national government. Fortunately, there came to the surface of our political life at that juncture a remarkable leader in the person of Abraham Lincoln, who understood that the power available to the federal government had to be used forcefully to save the Union. A great war, costing half a million American lives, was then fought to achieve that purpose.

Despite the Civil War and its aftermath in the three notable postwar amendments to the Constitution—the Thirteenth, abolishing slavery; the Fourteenth, giving the former slaves citizenship; and the Fifteenth, giving them the right to vote—which collectively seemed to have set the stage for a massive federal intervention in behalf of black people, such an undertaking did not materialize. Mounting resistance in the South and a loss of will in the North soon ended that possibility.

There followed, then, thirty to forty more years during which the concept of negative government prevailed. In the economic realm, laissez-faire reigned supreme, and in the social realm, social Darwinism was the gospel of the day. Together, these two philosophies were sanctified into something close to a religion by the professional and propertied classes and invested with a range of allegedly moral and ethical qualities that could excuse even the most callous disregard of the rights of others or the suffering of the underprivileged.

Nonetheless, in the observance of this quasi religion there was considerable discrepancy between dogma and practice. The federal government, in fact, intervened on numerous occasions to promote the interests of businessmen and farmers and occasionally to regulate the excesses of unrestrained free enterprise, as with passage of the Interstate Commerce Act of 1887 and the Sherman Anti-Trust Act in 1890. Other notable federal social interventions in the Civil War and postbellum years were: the granting of 50 million acres of public lands to the railroad companies; the Homestead Act of 1862, which helped to open up the West; the Morrill Act of 1962, which did so much to promote the growth of higher education; the Hatch Act of 1887, which established agricultural experiment stations; and finally, the Reclamation Act of 1902, which made possible the development of a huge agricultural industry in the West based on irrigation.

By the end of the nineteenth century, the doctrines of laissez-faire and social Darwinism were under heavy attack for several reasons. First, a public awareness had begun to develop of their extremely unethical character when measured against religious and humanitarian ideals. Second, a new school of theorists—economists, sociologists, political scientists, and philosophers—had arisen to question the scientific basis of these doctrines. Third it had become apparent to thoughtful people that the doctrines were harmful to the public welfare and ineffectual in dealing with the new problems of a rapidly urbanizing and industrializing society, with its attendant problems of social unrest. Finally, people began to see that, in a democratic society, government should not be the master but the agent of the people. The use of governmental power to promote the common good through social intervention was, therefore, a justifiable form of self-help and not a form of paternalism. Herbert Croly expressed this idea persuasively in his book *The Promise of American Life*, which became widely influential after its publication in 1909.

In these new perceptions was born the notion of the general welfare state, a concept that, with the exception of the period of so-called normalcy from 1921 to 1932, would hold sway for the next eighty years—right down to the most recent presidential election. No longer, men and women began to see, did they need to accept passively the dictates of blind economic forces or the cruel tyranny of a social system which eulogized selection of the "fittest" for reward, even if this had to be at the expense of the weak. They could use democratic government as a deliberate instrument to reduce injustice and guarantee at least minimal social and economic security to every American.

This vision, which began to take legislative shape during the progressive era, in particular during the presidencies of Theodore Roosevelt and Woodrow Wilson, matured in Franklin D. Roosevelt's New Deal, Harry Truman's Fair Deal, John Kennedy's New Frontier, and Lyndon Johnson's Great Society. Expanded in each of these administrations, as well as in the Nixon presidency, in response to new social needs and expectations, the general welfare state was reformist rather than revolutionary in character. Its underlying purpose was to rescue our capitalist economic system from its own excesses and weaknesses through the institution of social controls and a program of social amelioration. Accused at various times of fostering "creeping socialism," it was, on the contrary, inherently antipathetic to a collectivist philosophy and steadfastly devoted to preservation of private ownership of the means of production.

One could, in fact, say of the general welfare state that its greatest triumph has been the safeguarding of private initiative over three quarters of a century of worldwide turbulence, marked by two great wars, Communist revolution in a number of countries, and the adoption of state ownership in many others. In 1937, after the worst of the depression crisis was over, Franklin D. Roosevelt said: "Action was necessary to remove the sore spots which had crept into our economic system, if we were to keep the system of private property for the future. To preserve we had to reform." Indeed, reform and social amelioration as an alternative to revolution have been the hallmarks of the general welfare state from its inception to the present day—a fact that has always made the conservative distrust of the very idea of a federal social role difficult for me to comprehend.

To sum up, we can see certain broad trends in our roughly two centuries as an independent nation. From the early years until about the end of the nineteenth century, except for the Lincoln period, a weak, negative concept of government triumphed. But after that, in response to the needs created by changing conditions, such as the closing of the Western frontier, mass immigration, industrialization, and urbanization, there gradually developed the full-blown general welfare state. It should be noted, of course, that this happened not as the result of some sort of left-wing conspiracy but with the enthusiastic concurrence of the vast majority of the American people.

A REVERSAL OF DIRECTION

In view of this history, how are we to interpret the election of 1980 and all that has happened since? Does it signify a true reversal of direction—a fundamental rejection by the American people of the general welfare state? Or are the efforts of the present administration no more than a brief aberration, a quixotic tilting at windmills that will look progressively more and more absurd as time goes by? Can we, indeed, even if we yearn nostagically to do so, actually move back toward the "golden age" of Herbert Spencer and William Graham Sumner? Or will such an effort quickly fall victim to the same economic, social, and political realities that caused the development of the general welfare state in the first place?

I do not believe that any of us can tell yet exactly what the future is going to bring, but I do think we can note some straws in the wind.

First, no definitive evidence has emerged thus far to suggest that there really is a broad popular wish to see the general welfare state severely curtailed—especially as it benefits the great middle class, which it does to a remarkable extent. On the contrary, when the administration tried in 1981 to reduce Social Security benefits, the outcry was instantaneous and politically decisive. And it is having a similar problem with student aid. There will be other outcries like these when middle-class interests are affected. Budget cuts, therefore, have had to be made at the expense of those who can least well defend themselves. But even there, in the current round of budget negotiations, the administration is encountering stiff opposition in Congress.

Second, the present administration, if we are to judge by its public statements, is the most ideological one we have had in a very long time, and its policies reflect such an approach. The American people, on the other hand, historically have always been skeptical of ideology and more impressed by pragmatic approaches to issues of the day. Tempers rise, and voices become shrill at times. Demagogues and ideologues flit across the scene peddling their wares. But, in any event, decisions in our mixed economy as to what government will do and what private enterprise will do generally reflect political, economic, and social realities rather than ideological purity. Our history shows this, and there is no reason to think that American attitudes have changed. I believe, therefore, that as the impractical and ill-considered nature of much of the administration's program gradually becomes clear to the public, the program will begin to fall of its own weight. Indeed, this is already happening.

Third, Americans are beginning to wake up to the inequitable consequences of the tax and budget cuts already enacted, to say nothing of the proposals for further cuts in 1982. According to a recently released report of the Congressional Budget Office, the average net *loss* in 1983 from 1981's cuts in benefit programs for households with incomes under $10,000 will be $240. At the same time, the average net *gain* for households with incomes over $80,000 will be $15,120. Furthermore, says the report, about 40 percent of the total savings from cuts in social programs will come from benefits received by families in the lowest income category—those under $10,000—and over two thirds of the savings, from reduced benefits for families earning less than $20,000. How, people are asking, could anything as blatantly unjust as this have happened? How can we reconcile traditional American concepts of fairness and concern for misfortune with policies such as these?

The administration admits that the effect of its program will be to increase income disparities between the rich and those less well off, but it claims that this will spur economic growth, which in turn will benefit everyone. Many Americans, however, are increasingly skeptical of this. In particular, they see few of the benefits of economic growth trickling down to those at the bottom of society—those without skills, those who are victims of discrimination, those who are handicapped, and those who need protection. Historically, few of the benefits ever trickled down to the unfortunate, and they are even less likely to do so in the future in view of the way our technologically driven economy is evolving. This is becoming steadily more apparent.

But what about the "safety net" offered by the administration and its call for an increase in private charity? Will these not, between them, make a broad social role by government unnecessary? Unfortunately, it does not seem so. The safety net that has been offered turns out to be primarily a net for the middle class, not for the poor and the working poor, for whom the cuts in social programs already made have been a disaster. As for private charity, studies are showing clearly that, vital as it is in so many ways, it is a woefully inadequate substitute for governmental assistance.

Fourth, it is becoming obvious to many that the attempt to steer the nation back toward an earlier age is utterly at cross purposes with the thrust of some powerful new social and economic trends that have greatly changed our society in recent years. One can mention here, among others, the rising significance of energy costs in all our lives, the massive movement of women into the labor market, the elimination of low-skill jobs through increased automation, the continued deterioration of our great metropolitan centers, the large-scale immigration of Caribbean and Latin peoples, the trek of Americans to the Sunbelt, the decline of the old industrial heartland of the Northeast and Midwest, the development of new regional inequities, and, finally, the enormous transfer of public and private resources to the elderly. Trends such as these have confronted us with social needs and problems of staggering proportions, the solutions to which have become increasingly a public, and thus a collective, responsibility and that make a vigorous social role by our national government mandatory whether we like it or not.

Lastly, more and more Americans are beginning to wonder what will be the likely consequences of the reduced federal social role as it relates to investment in people—fewer dollars for maternal and child health, less for the education of the disadvantaged, less for the prevention of infectious disease, less for nutrition, less for job training, less for graduate study, less for science education, and so on. The litany continues. Given these cuts, will the nation, they ask, somewhere down the road have a prime-age population strong enough, healthy enough, well-enough educated, and well-enough trained to earn the national living in a fiercely competitive world? Will it be able to defend the nation against a powerful enemy that has not neglected investment in its people? Will it be able to support an ever-growing proportion of the elderly? Some people, indeed, are beginning to wonder whether one day we will not all look back at the neglect of human capital formation in this era—a fault, incidentally, not confined entirely to the present administration—as the greatest disservice that has ever been done to this nation.

I do not, therefore, in the light of this growing awakening, believe that there is going to be a permanent reversal of direction, the sustained reduction of the central government's social role, that some of our fellow Americans seem to want. The pendulum has been swinging in their direction, but unquestionably it will swing back. We must only hope that it does so before lasting damage has been done to the nation's future.

Let me make it clear that there is no valid argument for leaving the federal social role totally undisturbed. On the contrary, there is everything to be said for a systematic examination of it by the Congress to be sure that the activities that fall within it are ones that really must be performed at the national level and that they are being performed as efficiently and economically as possible.

Nor is there any argument to be made that the federal government should accept the entire responsibility for the social welfare of the nation. Its role should be selective. We certainly do not want a vast, stifling federal monopoly over social programs. There should be ample room for initiative and experimentation at the state and local levels, and the federal government should encourage this. Pluralism of this kind is a source of national strength.

Furthermore, it is obvious that the sheer magnitude of the social welfare task puts it well beyond the capacity of the federal government to perform alone, however much money is appropriated for the purpose. The states and localities as well as the business sector and voluntary organizations must, of course, all play their part.

Additionally, it has to be recognized that some federal social programs, because of entitlement and indexing provisions, are close to getting out of hand. These programs must be brought under control, first to ensure that funds are available for those who need them most—the poor, the handicapped, children—and second, to keep the costs of such programs from bankrupting the nation.

In this regard, it must be noted that in the decade of the 1970s federal outlays for the elderly—chiefly tax-free Social Security, veterans and civil service pensions, and Medicare payments—increased from 13.0 percent to 27.5 percent of the budget. According to one estimate, at the present annual rate of increase, they will amount to an incredible 35.0 percent of the budget by the turn of the century; and twenty-five years after that, an even more incredible 65.0 percent. To continue down that road is madness.

Finally, one must not gloss over the fact that public resources may very well be more limited in the future than they have been in the past. We will have to learn how to use what we have to better effect.

Having offered these disclaimers, however, I must state my unequivocal view that a sharp reduction of the social role of the federal government is clearly not in the interests of the nation. Looking back over the past two decades, we have seen that it is myth, not fact, that federal social programs for the most part failed. On the contrary, they greatly reduced poverty, hunger, malnutrition, infectious disease, and infant mortality—the last of these by 50 percent. They increased equality of opportunity for minorities and women. They made health care much more widely available. They gave dignity and opportunity to many of our fellow citizens. Yes, in these and other ways they accomplished a great deal. Looking forward, we can see many pressing social problems, some new, some old, that demand the nation's attention. Why, we may ask, as we face these problems, should we abandon a public policy approach that achieved so much? Why not simply correct its evident faults and press ahead?

THE NEW FEDERALISM

To reduce the federal social role, the administration has offered the nation two courses of action. The first is simply to so restrict the funds for certain programs that they cease to be viable. The second is to hand over a number of federal responsibilities to the states under arrangements that will see an eventual phasing out of both federal funding and control. While this has a certain superficial attractiveness, it makes me extremely uneasy.

What we shall see, I fear, if certain federal programs are turned over to the states, is that many of them will drop the programs altogether and, if given half a chance, will divert the funds to other purposes, such as tax relief and public works. Other states will cut back the programs drastically by limiting eligibility and reducing benefits. A few states with a strong social conscience will do their best to continue the programs and maintain eligibility standards and benefit levels, but they will soon face an influx of desperate people from states where benefits are too low to get by on or are nonexistent.

This is known as "voting with your feet," but I would submit that the last thing we want in the national interest is an army of latter-day Okies moving around the country hoping somehow to escape the misery at home and find a slightly better life for themselves somewhere else.

The proponents of the New Federalism claim that none of this will happen because reapportionment and the Voting Rights Act have created new constituencies for social programs in the states. The fact is, however, that the people who make up these constituencies, presumably blacks, Hispanics, Native Americans, the poor, and the handicapped, are still a minority of the population in nearly every state, and their political leverage continues to be severely limited. We were able to institute these programs at the national level because previous administrations and Congresses, having a broad perspective that transcended a particular state or region, had the vision to see that a national interest was involved. It was the failure of some of the less enlightened states to have such a vision in regard to such critical matters as the promotion of equal opportunity, education of the disadvantaged, the elimination of hunger, the provision of decent housing, and so on, that brought the federal government into the picture in the first place.

If the New Federalism does go forward, it is my belief that little will have changed from those earlier days. A few states may have developed a somewhat greater degree of social conscience, but in many respects the nation is likely to be right back where it was. Hunger and malnutrition, discrimination in employment, unequal opportunity, grim poverty, and a host of other social ills may well reappear in many places, and if this is the case, we shall all be losers.

What will be different this time, however, is the way that people who are treated unequally will feel about their situation. T. H. Marshall, in his 1949 Alfred Marshall Lecture at Cambridge University, discussed the development of three aspects of citizenship: the civil, the political, and the social. What we have seen here in the United States in the past two decades is a burgeoning of the third aspect, a flowering under federal leadership of the idea of social rights. This time, therefore, people are going to be angry not only about the reality of their condition but at having been deprived of what they had come to regard as rights guaranteed to them by their national government. Here surely is the stuff out of which bitterness, alienation, and social unrest are born.

The proper social role of our national government could not have been a more timely subject for discussion at the 1982 Annual Forum, for it gets to the very heart of the controversy raised by the policies of the present administration. If we believe that the development of people—*all* people, whatever their economic status, physical or mental characteristics, sex or color—is our highest priority, because it is fundamental to economic growth and to national security, and if we believe that equity among individual Americans on a national basis is the *sine qua non* of a workable society, then we must favor strong participation by the federal government in meeting the nation's social needs. The issues, in that case, will be how to make the federal role efficient, how to make it operate in such a way that the states, the localities, the business community, and voluntary organizations will be encouraged to do their part, and how to keep the costs from getting out of control. These are scarcely small issues, but they are not insoluble.

If, on the other hand, we are not particularly concerned about the prospect of social unrest ahead, if we do not fear the consequences of reduced investment in people for economic growth and national security, if equity on a national basis is not high on our agenda, and if we believe that the workings of a free market economy can take care of most of the nation's social ills, with perhaps a residual role for state and local government, then we will have little desire to see the federal social role maintained. This basically is the issue now before the nation, and on its outcome will depend the nature of American society for many years to come.

I have recalled the historical legitimacy of the social role of our national government, of the pragmatic necessity for it and of its broad sweep. I have also suggested that although this role is currently under attack, it is, in my opinion, unlikely to disappear.

I have a clear faith that once our present national state of confusion over what the federal government should be doing in the social arena has passed, there will be much to look forward to. Through a wise and skillful exercise of federal executive and legislative power, we have the ability to ensure that every American child has a chance to reach his or her true potential, that discrimination against any person on account of race, sex, or cultural background is eradicated, that the hungry are fed and the handicapped cared for, that every family has a decent place to live, that minimum standards of health care are available to all, and that the elderly are protected. All of this we can do, and we can do it with the resources that will be available to the nation, without sacrificing either our security or our economic growth.

In the quest to reach these goals, the business community and voluntary sector and the states and localities will be essential partners of the federal government. Indeed, the construction of that partnership—now in jeopardy—has been one of the great achievements of recent decades. Let us, then, not hold back from using our national government for broad social purposes in the mistaken notion that to do so is somehow wrong. Government at the national level is not an alien institution to be reviled or ridiculed. It belongs to us—all of us—to use as we will. We must use it intelligently and purposefully to realize at long last the great promise that has always been present in American life.

II. DORCAS R. HARDY

THE REAGAN administration is making a fundamental departure from the recent past in the conceptualization of the federal role in regard to social services. For decades, the trend has been to assign to the federal government an ever-expanding responsibility for identifying the needs for social services and then planning, funding, and monitoring programs to meet those needs. Most frequently the needs and program responses were organized around special populations. The past two decades have witnessed a rapid expansion of the federal role and federal expenditures for social services and the proliferation of those categorical approaches. Between 1950 and 1980, federal social welfare spending jumped from $20 billion to $300 billion. That is a fifteen-fold increase and seven times more rapid than the rate of inflation during that period.

This administration is committed to expanding the state and local responsibility for all facets of planning and implementing social services while simultaneously reducing the federal role. As part of our strategy, the administration is utilizing a block grant approach which provides state and local decision-makers the flexibility to continue the categorical approaches of the past or as they seem to prefer, to develop new consolidated approaches to meet social service needs.

The philosophy of this administration in the formulation and implementation of social service legislation and programs is based upon the principle that the well-being of the public is primarily a responsibility of individuals, families, and the communities in which they live. When social services are needed, they are best defined and administered through public or private institutions at the level closest to the problem—state and local governments, area agencies on aging, and local community-based and private voluntary organizations. The role of the federal government in meeting social service needs is:

1. To adopt and implement national policies or programs aimed at promoting economic growth and prosperity and thereby reducing the need for social services.
2. To target federal budgetary support toward those most in need.
3. To address those social service needs that cannot be implemented at the state level and that require interstate or national orientation for effective operation. The federal government will not abandon its leadership role in such important areas as child abuse, child welfare, aging services, and services for the developmentally disabled.

DORCAS R. HARDY is Assistant Secretary for Human Development Services, Department of Health and Human Services, Washington, D.C.

It may be somewhat surprising that in describing the federal role in social services our top priority is to adopt policies and programs aimed at promoting economic growth. I believe that it is economic growth within the free enterprise system that creates real job opportunities which allow individuals and families to become and remain economically and socially self-sufficient. In the process, economic growth reduces the size of the poverty population and the need for, and costs associated with, social services. Economic growth, therefore, is both a remedial and a preventive strategy that can continue to benefit many millions of needy Americans.

There is a growing body of empirical evidence that demonstrates this strong positive relationship between economic growth and reductions in poverty rates in America.[1] In many respects the new data confirm our common-sense knowledge that when the economy is growing there are more job opportunities and more income is earned by more people.

What we may see as common sense today was not recognized as such in the 1960s. In those days, we feared that the so-called culture of poverty locked poor parents and their children into a permanent vise of poverty. Now we find this is not the case. Poverty is not a permanent phenomenon. Individuals and their families move above the poverty line, sometimes temporarily, but many times permanently. Even more encouragingly, children of the poor often perform much better than their parents. Eighty percent of the new households these children form are above the poverty level.[2] The American system does indeed allow substantial mobility.

In addition to confirming the not-so-obvious relation of economic growth to poverty rates, the new analyses have generated new data on the magnitude and selectivity of the impact of economic growth on poverty. The official government data indicate a significant decline in the poverty rate from 22 percent of the population in 1959 to 12 percent in 1979.[3] Keep in mind that the official definition of poverty is based only on cash income, does not include in-kind benefits, such as food stamps, and is adjusted for inflation annually.

Economic growth during 1959–79 proved to be a powerful vehicle for millions of Americans to rise from poverty and to become economically and

[1]*Donald Winkler and W. Douglas Morgan, "A Decline in Poverty in the United States, 1959–1974,"* Review of Social Economy, *October 1979, pp. 159–72; James Thornton, Richard Agnello, and Charles Link, "Poverty and Economic Growth: Trickle Down Peters Out,"* Economic Inquiry, *July 1978, pp. 385–94; Barry Hirsch, "Poverty and Economic Growth: Has Trickle Down Petered Out?"* Economic Inquiry, *January 1980, pp. 151–63. For a critical review of these studies, see Edward Cohen, "The Impact of Economic Growth" (unpublished staff paper, Office of Human Development Services, 1982).*

[2]*Frank Levy, Clair Vickery, and Michael Wiseman,* The Income Dynamics of the Poor *(Washington, D.C.: U.S. Department of Labor, Manpower Administration, 1977). Available from National Technical Information Service, Springfield, Va. 22151.*

[3]*Bureau of the Census, U.S. Department of Commerce Current Population Reports, Consumer Income Series P-60, No. 130, "Characteristics of the Population Below the Poverty Level: 1979."*

socially self-sufficient. It has been found that a 10 percent increase in the gross national product (GNP) or median family income will reduce the poverty rate by 10 percent to 16 percent.[4] At the same time, it appears that reducing poverty through welfare is far less efficient than reducing it through economic growth. Increasing welfare by 10 percent would reduce the percentage change in poverty by at most 8 percent, depending upon the category of the household.[5]

Clearly, reduction of poverty through economic growth rather than welfare is to be preferred, not only because economic growth is more efficient, but because it meets individual goals for self-sufficiency. Welfare, on the other hand, constitutes a form of dependency. We can all agree that most of our nation's poor would prefer jobs to welfare.

I do not intend to overwhelm the reader with statistics. My point, however, is that economic growth, and not social programs, accounted for the greatest part of our success in reducing poverty rates over the past two decades. If the primary social role of government, then, is to promote economic growth, its second important social role, as noted earlier, is to target its social welfare resources to the neediest in the most efficient and effective manner.

One of the contributions of recent research is the finding that as the poverty rate declines, the impact of economic growth on the poverty rate diminishes.[6] The reason is that economic growth seems to benefit some categories of the poor more than others. As the beneficiaries of economic growth move out of poverty, nonbeneficiaries, such as households headed by the elderly poor and females with young children, comprise a larger proportion of the remaining poor.

Many of these families and individuals will continue to require assistance beyond what the private sector can offer. It is clear that government has assumed and will continue to assume a responsibility for improving the life circumstances of the neediest in America. America will not turn her back on the poor. The issue then becomes one of how do we best allocate social welfare resources to benefit the most needy and promote their self-sufficiency.

Government-supported social services must be reserved for those in greatest need. These resources cannot be viewed as an entitlement to all, or even as a primary resource. Why? First, because there will never be sufficient federal resources to meet the need; and second, because, in all honesty, we have to admit that government-supported efforts may represent the most costly, least efficient, and perhaps least humane response to many of the problems that social services typically address.

So how do we go about targeting? For one thing, we need to be more sensitive to the differences among the categories that comprise the poor. Strategies effective for one group may not be effective for another. Self-sufficiency itself may not be a realistic objective for some categories of the poor.

---

[4]*See Cohen, "The Impact of Economic Growth."*
[5]Ibid.
[6]Ibid.; *Thornton, Agnello, and Link, "Poverty and Economic Growth."*

Services may be more or less effective in addressing different problems or categories of need. The targeting of social welfare resources in the 1980s to the special categories of the poor unaffected by past efforts will constitute a great challenge to the social welfare leadership and to the state and local officials who will make the fundamental decisions on the allocation of resources.

The third major social role of government is leadership to ensure that national problems and national priorities are given attention. The Reagan administration has a continuing commitment to focus attention on national problems such as child abuse and the inappropriate placement of children in institutional care. We will continue to support effective developmental programs for children such as Head Start. The special needs of the elderly, the developmentally disabled, and Native American populations will receive national attention. The Office of Human Development Services will continue to be the focal point of national concern for the vulnerable members of these populations.

These, I believe, are the key features of the social role of government and the powerful impact of economic growth on poverty. What, then, has been the impact of the billions of dollars spent by the federal government for in-kind transfer programs, particularly during the past decade?

In constant dollar terms, the expenditures for food stamps, housing subsidies, and Medicaid alone increased fourteen times between 1959 and 1975, to over $14 billion.[7] These and similar transfer programs brought benefits to the poor which are not reflected in the poverty rates because the official poverty definition includes only cash income and not in-kind benefits.

Confirming previous studies, the Census Bureau recently reported an analysis which placed a value on certain major in-kind benefits directed to the poor, including Medicaid, food stamps, and housing supports. Had these benefits been counted in determining poverty rates, only 6.4 percent of the population would have been below the poverty line in 1979, instead of the 11.0 percent reported under the all-cash definition of poverty.[8] Thus a plausible case could be made that as a result of the combined effects of economic growth and transfer programs, poverty in contemporary America has been drastically reduced.[9]

Turning now to the social service programs my office is responsible for, we can ask the same questions about impact. But putting today's social services into proper perspective requires some historical background.

One point to bear in mind is that, in the public's mind, as well as in the minds of legislators, the provision of social services is closely tied to serving

[7]*Morton Paglin, "Poverty in the United States: A Reevaluation,"* Policy Review, *Spring, 1979, pp. 7–24.*

[8]*Department of the Census, reported in Washington* Post, *April 15, 1982, p. 1.*

[9]*James A. Kissko, "Poverty Trends Reconsidered,"* Human Development News, *April, 1981, pp. 2, 4.*

the dependent poor. Large-scale federal support for social services has been justified primarily by the needs of the poor, particularly welfare recipients, for special assistance directed at reduction of welfare dependency and an increase in self-sufficiency.[10]

To what extent have these federal-supported social services been effective in reducing dependency and increasing self-sufficiency? What evidence is there that the billions of dollars spent for social services have had the desired impact?

I asked these same questions when I assumed my office in 1981. I have concluded that we know very little about what we have accomplished with the billions of dollars directed, with the very best of intentions and the highest of hopes, to social services for the poor.

One of the few methodologically sophisticated evaluations of the effectiveness of social services in reducing dependency was completed by the General Accounting Office (GAO) in 1973.[11] GAO set out to determine specifically whether the services provided to welfare recipients helped them to achieve self-support or reduced dependency. GAO concluded: "Social services had only a minor impact on directly helping recipients to develop and use the skills necessary to achieve reduced dependency or self-support. Therefore, one of the goals for the services that they help people get off welfare has not been achieved."

The cumulative impact of this and similar critical studies[12] of the effectiveness of social services has been to foster an antievaluation bias within the social service field and to force a fatalistic consensus that the benefits of social services have not been demonstrated and possibly cannot be demonstrated. Congress appropriated few dollars for social service evaluation, and federal agencies, including my own, avoided the larger, empirical evaluation issues while using evaluation funds for studies designed more to avoid controversy than to get at the facts.

Social service providers joined in resisting efforts at evaluation of client outcomes while arguing that the benefits of social services are real but perhaps not measurable. This disregard for evaluation which could document the effectiveness of social services now weighs heavily on all segments of the social service field as we confront the reality of tight fiscal constraints.

I believe that the lack of evidence regarding the value and effectiveness of our social service efforts is the single most important reason that federal, state, and local legislators are unwilling to appropriate as many dollars to social services as in the past. As resources tighten, I believe that decision-mak-

---

[10]*Comptroller General of the United States,* Report to Congress—Social Services: Do They Help Welfare Recipients Achieve Self-Support or Reduce Dependency? *(Washington, U.S.: General Accounting Office, 1973).*

[11]Ibid.

[12]*Joel F. Handler and Ellen Jane Hollingsworth,* The "Deserving Poor": A Study of Welfare Administration *(Chicago: Markham, 1971), see particularly pp. 127–28, 184, and 207.*

ers at all levels are becoming increasingly impatient with our anecdotal and naïve explanations that our programs do much good but in ways that we cannot seem to measure. I also believe that the majority of the American public are becoming equally uneasy about our inability to demonstrate concrete results for our expenditures of tax dollars.

I believe that the major issue today is not how many federal, state, and local dollars are going into traditional social services. The more basic issues are: What are the benefits or outcomes that the poor receive as a result of the servicesf? Do the benefits justify the costs?

I do not believe that currently we can say with any degree of confidence what services are most effective in improving the life situations of the poor in general, much less the various categories of the poor. There are, of course, exceptions, such as Head Start, which has demonstrated its effectiveness as a child development program over a long period of time. Not so coincidentally, Head Start enjoys strong bipartisan support in Congress. Even under the present fiscal constraints, both the Reagan administration and Congress supported an increased allocation of resources to Head Start in 1982. Other social service programs should be able to justify their effectiveness in the way that Head Start has.

My office is facing the issue of evaluation of effectiveness with new enthusiasm. We sponsored in Boston, prior to the meetings of the Annual Forum, a symposium on evaluation to learn of current methods that states are applying to obtain this information. My hope is that we can help find the answers to questions such as what services or mixes of services are both effective and cost-effective in improving the life situations of our clients. I know that state and local decision-makers and program managers are eager to have these answers too. We all share the same desire to use our resources in ways that will bring the greatest benefits to our clients.

What, then, is the social role of government in a free enterprise system? The primary social role of government is to promote economic growth. This creates jobs through which many of the poor become socially and economically self-supporting. Economic growth also provides the revenues for both the private sector and government to provide for the needs of the poor who are relatively less affected by economic growth.

The second important social role of government is to target its social welfare resources to those in greatest need so that they can derive the greatest improvements in their life situations from the resources available. In this process government has a responsibility to ensure that the resources are applied effectively and efficiently. Where resources are applied to activities with little or no demonstrable impact, government may seek alternative ways of targeting the resources to make a greater impact on the lives of those in need.

The third social role of government is to provide leadership and focus to important national issues and concerns. The special needs of vulnerable populations will continue to receive national attention as we work with local and state decision-makers who target resources more effectively.

What, then, does the future hold for the nation's social welfare? I believe the future is bright. Our national experience in reducing poverty overall during the past two decades should offer great encouragement to those who have strived to reduce poverty and its attendant problems. A federal policy, such as the one in operation, which emphasizes the need for economic growth, offers great promise for further sizable reductions in the poverty rate and a sharp reversal of 1981's increase. After a decade of economic stagnation, stable economic growth with a low rate of inflation is the probable outcome of the government's innovative program to promote economic growth.

Signs of real progress on the economic front are appearing. In January of 1980 the consumer price index rose at an annualized rate of 18.2 percent. Two years later, in January of 1982, the rate of inflation had been cut to 3.5 percent.

We are also in the advantageous position of having identified and differentiated the needy population with a level of sophistication impossible in the 1960s. Using our new knowledge, the problems of people in need can be met by improved targeting and more innovative application of our resources to benefit the poor.

I recognize that we are all being asked to digest a number of changes and new realities in a short period of time. The new focus on the bottom line of social services is just one, albeit crucial, challenge facing the entire social service field. A second challenge results from the transfer of the primary responsibility for direction of social services from the federal government to state and local governments.

We also recognize that adapting to change and meeting the challenges are essential to our development as individuals and our evolution as a discipline. My hope is that social workers as individuals, social welfare agencies, and the professional schools are prepared to meet these challenges and to help the social services field evolve.

I assure the social work profession that my office stands willing to assist in meeting these challenges. Our desire is to cooperate to ensure that social services remain an integral part of the nation's rejuvenated social welfare strategy.

Social Welfare in a Reactionary Age

THE WHITNEY YOUNG, JR., MEMORIAL LECTURE

JOHN E. JACOB

IT IS a great honor to be asked to deliver the Whitney M. Young, Jr., Memorial Lecture. Whitney was known and beloved by those of us in the social work profession, as by all Americans who value social justice and moral decency.

When I started my Urban League career, Whitney was guiding the Urban League movement to new heights of relevance. It was Whitney who blazed the trail for the entire profession by wedding service delivery to forceful advocacy. And it was Whitney Young who clearly set forth before the nation not only the facts of black disadvantage, but the ideas and programs to overcome that disadvantage.

For a time, Americans made progress in dealing with the curse of racism, discrimination, and poverty. Thanks to a generation of black people who would not meekly accept second-class status in their native land, and thanks to millions of white citizens who refused to live the lie of racial supremacy, segregation was dismantled. Laws were passed. Programs were started. Poverty was reduced. Opportunities opened.

Change came to America. Not enough and far too slowly. But change came. Some black people were allowed up the winding stairs to the upper rooms of opportunity. But millions of others were still locked in the cellars of poverty. A beginning was made, but only a beginning.

Whitney Young was an architect of that new beginning for America. He helped draw up the blueprints for change, but he was tragically taken from us at a crucial moment. He was spared the bitter knowledge that our new beginning was crumbled; that the house of equality and justice was turned into a split-level affair, with beautiful rooms for the affluent and broken-down hovels for the poor.

Our split-level society is being split even wider today, for instead of following Whitney Young's prescription for a domestic Marshall Plan that would wipe out poverty and revive our cities, our nation is taking a different, bitter medicine. We have gone from a domestic Marshall Plan to benign neglect

JOHN E. JACOB is President, National Urban League, Inc., New York.

and now to the New Federalism. We have gone from national measures to deal with national problems to states' rights. We have gone from public solutions to private burdens, from food stamps to surplus cheese lines, from rights to charity.

In Whitney's day a growing consensus of Americans accepted the idea that poverty is not the result of specific local experiences or individual faults, but the result of national economic malfunctions and a national history of discrimination. Today, I believe that consensus, though weakened, is still strong. But it has been challenged by a new view that is, in my opinion, based on a gross distortion of reality.

It is a view that says government takes too great a portion of our national resources, and interferes too much in our daily lives.

It is a view that says we should transfer greater power and authority to local governments who are supposed to be, as the phrase goes, closer to the problems. And we should rely on free-market solutions to economic problems and individual charity for social problems.

It is a view championed by the administration, which has successfully dismantled many vital federal programs and reversed the trend toward greater equality.

It is a view cloaked in phrases like "supply-side economics," "individual responsibility," and "New Federalism." But those phrases are a fig leaf to hide the brutal reality that its policies will drive millions of people into poverty, cause millions more to slide from poverty into total deprivation, and create an unbridgeable gap between the rich and the poor.

It is happening now.

Almost ten million people are officially counted as unemployed. Another six million are not counted as unemployed, but they are working part time while trying to pay full-time bills. Millions more are not counted as unemployed because they have given up. The jobs are not there, and they no longer look for work that does not exist.

Many social workers see the results in their agencies. There are few experiences as damaging to self-esteem and to an individual's sense of worth as prolonged unemployment. Study after study demonstrates how even small increases in joblessness result in more crime, alcoholism, drug abuse, child abuse, divorce, bad health, and mental problems. We will be paying for this recession far into the future.

The administration is firm in its determination to stay on its chosen course. That firmness will mean new draftees into the army of the poor. Three million more people were added to the poverty rolls in 1981, just as their safety net was being drilled full of holes.

Meanwhile, the affluent got more. Add up the tax breaks and take away the federal spending cuts, and see how the gap widens between the haves and the have-nots. Families with incomes above $80,000 will wind up with an extra $15,120, families under the $10,000 level will lose $240.

In a burst of candor, David Stockman, Director of the Office of Management and Budget, admitted in 1981 that all the talk of "supply side" was just talk; that the administration's program was nothing more than old-fashioned, trickle-down economics. That kind of honesty is refreshing. It should be applied to the particulars of the administration's program, too. For example, its tax program is based on the idea that cutting taxes will make people work harder, therefore increasing productivity.

Apparently, people who earn six-digit salaries need further incentives to work hard. But what about poor people? What about low-income workers? It is heartening to see that the administration realizes that, however lazy the wealthy may be, the work ethic is still strong among our poor. That must be the reason it so severely penalizes the working poor.

Through its welfare and food stamp cuts and its punishing new eligibility standards, the administration sharply increased the marginal tax rate on low-income workers. Millions of people who clung to the work ethic and who labored at low-paying jobs while surviving through small welfare benefits and food stamps now lose those survival payments. They lose Medicaid coverage, too.

It makes more sense for many of them to quit work and become totally dependent. The administration punishes those whom it should be helping. It hurts those who are trying to lift themselves out of poverty by their own efforts and hard work. It makes a mockery of America's values of fair play, opportunity, and a chance to make it on one's own.

I have been talking about this new hostility toward the poor in terms of the administration's program, but I want to make it very clear that today's new meanness is a bipartisan affair. The administration proposes, but the Congress disposes—and Congress has shamed itself by not resisting the excesses in the war against the poor and by going further than the administration in some respects. So there is enough blame to go around; enough to tar both parties and both ends of Pennsylvania Avenue.

When administration officials and Congressmen of both parties boast of the cuts in social spending, they remind me of terrorists claiming responsibility for a bomb attack on innocent people. The victims of the budget cuts are our clients—the poor and the disadvantaged who come to social work agencies in search of help. They are the people who are losing food stamps, losing Medicaid benefits, who are forced off the welfare rolls or whose small benefits are being cut. It is they whose job training programs are ending, whose public housing rents are being raised, whose school lunches are being cut.

It is our clients who are being forced to pay for a so-called economic recovery program that has not produced recovery. We can track the dollars. We can see how cuts in social programs are balanced by tax breaks for the wealthy or for new weapons we do not need, weapons like the multimillion-dollar tank that breaks down after sixty miles, the MX missile that has no home, or the B-1 bomber that will be obsolete a few years after it is produced.

It is our clients who will lose in whatever tradeoffs are made to revive the old states' rights. The negotiations with the governors on the New Federalism are temporarily suspended. The governors did not want to get stuck with welfare, even though Washington would take over Medicaid. But it is likely that some form of New Federalism will come out of this mess—new block grant programs to replace present categorical grant programs that have proved effective.

If the New Federalism gets off the ground—and it will if we do not fight it—then the clock will be turned back to the time when poor people and minorities were abandoned to the tender mercies of state governments that did not care, that were in the grip of local power elites, and that drove the poor beyond their borders.

It has been argued that today's state governments are more efficient, more democratic, and more concerned about the poor. Maybe. The record certainly does not show that.

When a state like Mississippi has a welfare standard of $120 a month for a family of four it is hard to be convinced of the fairness of the states. When no state has a welfare standard equal to the inadequate official poverty line, it is hard to believe poor people will get a fair shake from their states. And when state budgets are tightened, it is hard to believe that block grant money will not be used to cut taxes or repair highways instead of for job training, welfare, or food stamps.

The significance of the New Federalism lies in its attempt to reverse a half century's progress toward a more just and equitable society. Together with budget cuts and program eliminations, it accelerates the massive transfer of resources from the bottom part of our society to the top.

Today's policies drive a deep wedge into the heart of American society, dividing the classes and the races. Black, Hispanic, and Asian Americans have borne the heaviest burden imposed by the budget cuts and the federal withdrawal from its responsibilities. They are disproportionately poor, and bear a disproportionate part not only of the budget cuts, but also of the effects of this depression.

In May of 1982 the Labor Department said: "Blacks are 10 percent of the population, but 20 percent of the unemployed and 40 percent of the discouraged workers." Officially, black unemployment is at 18 percent; the true figure would be closer to 30 percent. In some inner-city neighborhoods black youth unemployment is far above two thirds.

Blacks are a third of all the poor.

Two out of five black children are growing up in families that are poor.

The typical black family earns less than the government itself says is necessary for a minimum adequate standard of living.

So there is a depression going on in black America today, a raging depression the likes of which other Americans have not seen since the 1930s. And as that depression hits more and more black people with greater and greater force, their government is cutting back virtually every program they need to survive.

Black people are America's barometer. Whenever the pressure on us increases, we can be sure that it will affect others too. And when it does, we may see some changes.

We should acknowledge that fact that racism still lives in America. The fact that so many social welfare programs are perceived as "black" programs made them easy targets. No one mentioned race in the debates on those programs, but it was there all along—in the stereotypes of the poor, in the supposed abuses in some programs, and in middle America's indifference to the plight of the poor.

There is a feeling among many white Americans that they have "done enough" for the black and the brown poor. There is a widespread belief that federal programs have eliminated poverty for the worthy poor, or the "truly needy." Now, it is thought, the remaining poor have only themselves to blame. "Let them get a job and work for it like we do," is the response.

As I have said, that form of racism flourished throughout the late 1970s and into the 1980s. It helped smooth the path for those who wanted to shrink federal social spending. But I believe that will soon change; for many white people who talked about lazy blacks who don't want to work are now out of work themselves. Many white people who labeled recipients of welfare and food stamps as cheaters are now hungry themselves. Many formerly middle-class people are now finding that they can't get a job, can't pay the mortgage, and can't afford to send their kids to college. They are beginning to learn the truth: that more whites than blacks are on welfare, are on food stamps, are in other vital programs they labeled "black."

And many millions more are looking over their shoulders and are beginning to see that while they never needed those programs themselves, federal social welfare programs were a safety net that would sustain them in bad times. Now that safety net is cruelly being ripped away, and the insecurity is increasing. People now know that all it takes to drop out of the middle class is a factory closing or a spell of sickness. All that separates many millions of stable, secure families from the instability and insecurity of poverty is luck.

If the breaks go the wrong way, they will need food stamps, they will need welfare, they will need job training. What we call social welfare programs are really a form of social insurance, a compact among all Americans to protect everyone from dropping below some minimum level of sustenance. Those many millions are the real silent majority in America, and as they begin to understand that their hopes and dreams are being placed in peril, I believe they will no longer remain silent.

I was struck by an article written by an Indiana factory worker. She wrote about the belief that working people are fed up with paying high taxes to help support federal social programs. Not true, she says:

> So far I have never had to rely on welfare, free lunches or Medicaid,
> but I very well might someday. . . . People like me who live only a

hairbreadth from economic disaster, are glad those programs are out there, though we pray we'll never have to use them.

The polls show it too. In poll after poll, responses indicate that while they may back parts of the President's program, Americans are disturbed by its effects on the poor. Yes, they want their tax burden eased, but not on the backs of the poor. Slowly but surely the message is coming across that driving the poor to desperation will not solve our nation's problems—it will just make them worse.

It is significant that welfare, the program everybody loves to hate, is coming to be seen as an important safety net that must not be abandoned. In April of 1982 the National Urban League held a day of hearings in sixteen cities across the nation on the impact of the cuts in welfare. A dozen other national organizations joined with us, and many social workers took part in hearings in their communities.

That experience documented the hardships and misery imposed on the poorest and weakest among us. Over three hundred people—a cross section of recipients, experts, and service providers—gave testimony on the negative impact of those cuts.

The result will reach far beyond those hearing rooms to reach the public with the message that the cuts have hurt the helpless—women and children most of all. The report of those hearings will be presented to Congress. It will provide all of us in the social work profession with information and ammunition to fight for the poor.

It is ironic that a conservative administration has chosen not to take a fundamentally conservative solution to the welfare mess. Just cutting survival programs is not conservatism. Shirking responsibility by trying to turn welfare over to the states is not conservatism.

True conservatives have favored a solution that puts cash directly into the hands of the poor, reduces the red tape and regulations that have such arbitrary power over poor people, and gives to the poor the same freedom of choice and the same responsibilities enjoyed by others. So a truly conservative solution to welfare points to the plan the National Urban League has advanced: an income maintenance system based on the refundable income tax. Our plan would ensure that all people have minimum income levels and maximum freedom. It is a realistic alternative to the monster system that serves both the nation and poor people badly.

The basic components would include:

1. A basic annual grant, or tax credit, would be given to all.
2. The grant would be taxed away from the affluent, while those below a certain income level would keep all or part of the grant. So working people with modest incomes would get the income assistance they need but for which they do not qualify under the present system.
3. Automatic payments would be made through the tax system as a matter

of right. The elimination of means tests and coercive regulations would
do away with stigma.
4. Almost everyone would pay taxes at a flat rate. But because everyone
would get a tax credit and because all loopholes would be closed, the
tax system would be far more fair than the present system.

The essential point is that the universal, refundable tax credit offers a way
to rationalize an irrational tax system that favors the rich at the expense of
working people. It offers a means of reducing the numbers of the poor. While
the cost of such a program depends upon the amount of the tax credit and
the level of the primary tax rate, it would amount to not much more than the
cost of the present system that leaves poverty intact and is expensive and
inefficient.

Putting a floor under a family income for all, combined with a full-employ-
ment policy that provides decent jobs for all workers, is a double thrust at
the roots of poverty and the social ills that arise from it. This plan is a
pro-work, pro-family, pro-dignity proposal for a humane, responsive society.
Such a universal system that benefits all poor people and all working people
would go a long way toward healing the scars caused by competition for
scarce jobs in a society that refuses to ensure decent minimum standards for
everyone.

I have a strong enough grip on reality to understand that such a plan is not
likely to be passed soon. I am also optimistic enough to believe that today's
war on the poor will grind to a halt and a new phase of social justice will be
inaugurated.

It is social workers and those of us in the helping professions who must
be in the forefront of the effort to turn our society around. We cannot simply
minister to the victims of budget slashes. If we have any sense of professional
mission and personal responsibility, we must fight for change. Our profession
has been in the forefront of every major social movement to better our society.
We cannot be silent today. We know, better than most, the truth of Whitney
Young's statement:

> No one is meant to live in poverty—and no one is meant to tolerate the
> wrongs of oppression. Where poverty exists, all are poorer; where hate
> flourishes, all are corrupted; where injustice reigns, all are unequal. Our
> society is as strong as its weakest link—thus the links that bind black
> and white, poor and rich must be strengthened or we all will perish.
> Every man is our brother, and every man's burden our own.

Whitney's words span the years with their truth and their direct statement
of the essence of our profession's social mission.

These are hard times for our constituents. There are hard times for our
agencies. We have to do more with less. We have to kindle hope as the flames
of opportunity die out. We have to care when caring is out of fashion.

But the social work profession has never seen good times. Hard times are not new to us. We have always dealt with society's walking wounded, with the victims of neglect and indifference, with the people thrust to the margins of our society. So we cannot despair now. We cannot escape our responsibilities to those who need us, to the principles of our profession, and to the dictates of conscience.

As we labor in the desert an uncaring society has created, as we strive to bring our society back to the ideals of decency and justice that inspired it, let us keep our faith in our mission and in ourselves. And let us keep our faith in the basic goodness of our people, for we have seen America change before; we have seen Americans tap the deep vein of fairness and decency within our traditions, and we have seen right triumph over wrong.

Let me leave with you an expression of that faith by Whitney Young, an expression of faith that I share, an expression of faith that should inspire us in the difficult days ahead:

> I do have faith in America—not so much in a sudden upsurge of morality nor in a new surge toward a greater patriotism—but I believe in the intrinsic intelligence of Americans and of the business community. I do not believe that we forever need to be confronted by tragedy or crises in order to act. I believe that the evidence is clear. I believe that we as a people will not wait to be embarrassed or pushed by events into a posture of decency. I believe that America has the strength to do what is right because it is right. I am convinced that given a kind of collective wisdom and sensitivity, Americans today can be persuaded to act creatively and imaginatively to make democracy work. This is my hope, this is my dream, this is my faith.

Public Charity Versus Private Entitlement: or, Who is Holding the Safety Net?

ELLIOT L. RICHARDSON

PERHAPS THE single most interesting question confronting a group with such a long history of concern with problems of social welfare, is the question: Why are the forces arrayed against human suffering, deprivation, and disadvantage now in retreat?

Only a decade ago, or a little more, this nation launched a war on poverty. I remember making speeches in those days, and for some years after that, in which I again and again referred to the fact that now, for the first time in the history of humanity, we actually foresaw the realistic possibility of an end to the age-old scourges of mankind.

Sources of suffering and deprivation that earlier generations could only endure were within reach of eradication. And certainly that was an era in which, if anything went wrong, it was that this heady prospect generated excessive expectations. We were guilty, perhaps, of not stressing often enough the need for better answers, the need for more adequate resources, and the need, most especially, for larger numbers of qualified people. At any rate, as we look at the question today, why are we on the defensive? Why are the resources dedicated to these purposes being contracted? It may be useful to look at some of the most obvious answers.

One answer that we hear over and over again is that it is because the programs did not work. We hear that today from people who, if we pressed them one more step, could not even tell us what programs that don't work they are talking about.

It was one thing in the days when I was at the Department of Health, Education and Welfare (HEW) to warn that we were generating excessive expectations; it is quite another now to cite these as a justification for doing even less than we were doing then. I produced a pamphlet in late 1971 that I used to call my "Castro Speech" because it said everything I would have liked to say in a four-hour harangue to all the people in HEW gathered together in a huge square, like Castro in Havana addressing the docile citizens of Cuba.

ELLIOT L. RICHARDSON is the senior Washington partner in Milbank, Tweed, Hadley and McCloy.
This article is an edited transcript of the author's extemporaneous speech at the Annual Forum.

In that brainwashing exercise I pointed out that our expectations were like a runaway balloon soaring out of sight. I warned that in too many cases we were yielding to the "don't-just-stand-there-do-something" syndrome. We were attempting to respond to various social ills that we did not really know how to treat, and it was all too likely that the shortfall would lead to a negative reaction. I also warned that we were not doing enough to try to evaluate the effectiveness of what we were doing. We were not doing enough to find objective criteria for allocating the available resources among competing claims, so as to assure that these resources were being allocated in the ways most likely to produce positive results. But it is one thing to be concerned about what does not work in a situation where the basic social commitment of the day is supportive of increased resources. It is quite another to use this concern, not as the basis for reallocating a given level of resources among various new and expanding undertakings, but as an excuse for cutting back on things whose effectiveness is not even in issue.

Who is to say, in the case of the mother of three dependent children who is forced—indeed, feels that it is her duty—to stay home and take care of those children, that the assistance which makes possible the survival of her children and herself "doesn't work"? Besides, attacks predicated on the proposition that programs don't work, really, when you examine them, often turn out to mean something quite different. The failure of expectations, which was very real and foreseeable more than a decade ago, was traceable only in part to the failure of the know-how needed to deliver services that could achieve their promised results. For example, in the case of such intractable difficulties as the rehabilitation of criminal offenders, or of drug abusers, or of alcoholics, the problem was even more visibly the failure of expectations resulting from the promises held out by programs whose authorization levels were never met. They were failures, moreover, of the expectations generated by authorization levels that were never high enough in the first place. In the case, for example, of the program of hot meals for the elderly, so loudly proclaimed by the Democrats in Congress in 1970, its authorization level, even if fully funded, would never have reached more than 5 percent of the eligible elderly. There were, in addition, the demonstration projects put forward for the ostensible purpose of testing proposals that had been tested over and over again; the demonstration project approach was rationalized on the sole basis that no one was willing to put an authorization number on the program that anywhere near corresponded to the visible demand.

I calculated in those days that there were $11 billion in unfunded authorizations which would be at least twice that in today's dollars. These were promissory notes that were not being honored—notes issued by the Congress of the United States to various groups from the elderly to the parents of retarded children. Beyond that, we calculated that if one were to take the percentile of support for various programs at the level two thirds of the way up the scale, on the theory that the nationally prescribed minimum could not be expected to be at the highest percentile but certainly ought to be above the median, it would cost an additional $250 billion to provide that level of services or benefits to all those who were, theoretically, eligible. And I mean by theoretically eligible the entire group of those who could qualify for a service already being provided with federal assistance or funding to some members of the group.

An additional $250 billion, on top of what we were already spending in those days, would have meant doubling the entire federal budget, which, including Social Security and so on as well as defense, was then only $250 billion. Much of the disappointment, therefore, that is now attributed to the inability to respond to visible needs can be accounted for by the frustrations generated by expectations that we were never prepared to fulfill.

A third point needs to be made in answer to the "it doesn't work" proposition. It is that even when we find programs that do not work very well, or maybe not much at all, the answer, given these accumulated needs, is not that the money should be turned over to some nonhuman resource-related purpose. The alternative is to make the liberated funds available to some needed but still underfunded service that can work. And, God knows, the figures I have just cited would, updated, overwhelmingly demonstrate that there are, in fact, plenty of those.

There is, secondly, apart from the "it doesn't work" rationale for retreat, the contention that human service programs, without regard to their workability, are wasteful and inefficient. Human beings in their ordinary activities are to a significant extent wasteful and inefficient. Wasteful and inefficient things happen all the time in every program, even the Pentagon's. The answer, once again, is not to lop off an arbitrary amount, even assuming that we can get at the inefficiency, but to reallocate the money to those programs that can deliver services or benefits more efficiently.

It is also true that apart from these attacks, there is the concern that programs have become too centralized and too fragmented. In my view that charge was, and to a degree still is, valid. There has until recently been a persistent trend toward narrow and categorical programs. A significant part of the impetus for this trend derives from the simple fact that for the proponent of a given program or activity it is a lot easier to deal with a particular entity at the federal level, particularly with allies in that entity concerned with the same set of social needs or problems, than to have to deal with fifty state legislatures and a multitude of localities.

The concern, on the other hand, that seemed to me most troublesome was not so much that there were thereby generated the pressures inherent in what has since been called the Iron Triangle but rather that the process was spinning out of democratic control—that it was beyond the effective reach of any process which the ordinary citizen could hope to grasp and to follow. There were so many programs, so many different pockets into which federal funds were being put, that no one but a specialist could hope to keep track of them. When I was at HEW I estimated that no more than forty-six people ever looked at the HEW budget as a whole, and that was giving the benefit of the doubt to the full membership of each of the House and Senate appropriations subcommittees.

The fact remains, nonetheless, despite what I believe to be the continuing justification for simplification of this structure and for greater reliance on the initiative of localities and voluntary agencies, that none of the above addresses the question of what level of resources should be available.

It seemed to me in the days when I was pushing hardest for simplification that this could only be achieved, as a practical matter, at a time of rising commitment of resources, for only then would it be feasible to overcome the difficulties that we inevitably run into when we try to reallocate levels of responsibility and hold benefits level or cut them back. These difficulties will, as John Hansan has pointed out in a thoughtful op-ed piece in the New York Times (February 24, 1982), become dramatically apparent if and when a serious effort is made to turn Medicaid over to the federal government. The federal government can hardly expect to get away with establishing minimum standards of eligibility and minimum benefit levels no higher than the state average. Acceptable minimums will inevitably have to approach those of the generous states, and these are relatively few in number. Applying a higher-than-average standard nationwide would, of course, greatly increase the aggregate cost.

Given, then, the nature of a combined challenge which seems to doubt the validity of much of what you and I have worked for for so long, while at the same time seeking to reduce the resources available for generally accepted purposes, what kind of an answer can we make? I would urge you and all those like you who are committed to the proposition that ours is a compassionate nation with a basic level of responsibility toward those in need, to march forth confidently under a banner proclaiming the words "Cooperate, Plan, Share."

Your starting point is with people in need. This, of course, is a commonplace, but like a great many truisms, it is one that people brush over and give lip service to without ever fully grasping with their whole imagination. It is also a truism that you are all here as representatives of some form of service to whole individuals and families. And yet the various traditional forms of responsiveness to human needs, down through the evolutionary lines of social work, public health, and vocational rehabilitation, have maintained separate compartments, notwithstanding that each has evolved its own form of training for people whose fundamental role is the provision of first-line counseling to those in need.

This is a service that is going to be required at the neighborhood level, whatever the structure of the system. The more complex the development of the capacity to serve and, therefore, of the subspecialties that are required in order to provide the appropriate levels of professional skill, the more need there is for someone to serve as an understanding point of contact. And understanding in this context means understanding in a dual sense: understanding the individual and the family, and understanding the array of resources available to serve. Creating that match-up, or the beginning of it, is certainly the most fundamental first step. And yet you would not guess from the manner in which people are trained to help, nor from the way in which services are organized for delivery, that these simple propositions are even dimly perceived.

Next to the need for the creation of a point of contact in the community that can represent the entire array of available resources, there is the need for awareness that the subdivisions among professional skills are fundamentally arbitrary. They tend to be treated by their practitioners, nevertheless, as sacrosanct in much the manner that votaries of the so-called academic disciplines have come to regard economics or political science as a "real thing."

The craft unionism of the helping professions is no credit to them. They need, you need, constantly to reemphasize the fact that the only justification for subdividing human services rests on the need to make possible the attainment of levels of professional skill that could not otherwise be acquired within a reasonable period of academic training. Given that necessity, the remaining need must be to cooperate.

As for planning—I am, I suppose, once again playing what for me is an old record—I am pleased to have noted in your agenda for this meeting that it is a record that is going to be played by others. Its theme is the recognition that because resources of money and manpower, or "personpower," are limited, the provision of services to people, whether by voluntary or governmental agencies, must be fitted into a coherent plan at the point of delivery, or within the area in which the services are provided.

Each service provider ought to be part of a total combination, a "network" as Martha Eliot called it, or, as your program refers to it, a coalition. But a coalition which consists merely in the coming together of people to exchange ideas and problems and compare notes is not enough. A plan, a real plan as distinguished from the compilation of boilerplate mandated by categorical programs, is a blueprint which sets forth identifiable goals, spells out how it is proposed to get there from here, and holds each component of the team working toward those ends accountable for its contribution to the success of the total effort. Just such an allocation of function and accountability is vital to the existence of anything that deserves to be called a plan. And yet it is that precise ingredient that has been resisted over and over again by entities jealous of their own autonomy and insistent on going their own way.

Autonomy has its uses, of course, particularly in a pluralistic society which values the independence of voluntary organizations and relies on the role of localities as essential parts of the federal structure. Indeed, individual freedom implies autonomy. Every individual is, in a sense, as separate as it is possible to be. We stand on a unique piece of ground and look at the rest of the world only with our own two eyes. But we do not forfeit our individuality when we work together with others toward a common end.

An entity that forms part of a coalition directed toward the fulfillment of a coherent plan need not sacrifice its autonomy or individuality or purpose. The plan calls upon it for its unique contribution to the whole effort. And once it has undertaken that function, it must be held accountable for performing it. It follows that there must be some means whereby it can be disciplined if it does not fulfill its assignment.

Without that kind of planning, the whole array of resources, individuals, and organizations directed to helping people will always be vulnerable to the charge that they are doing less well than they should. So, I submit that in the concept of a combination of resources under the banner of cooperating, planning, and sharing, there is strength; there is thereby gained the ability to say to the appropriations authorities and the political leaders, "When you cut, you are cutting service."

We say it anyway, of course, but we have not quite convinced them. I remember a time in the Eisenhower administration during the winter of 1957 when the so-called Economy Block, whose formation had been triggered by a statement by then-Secretary of the Treasury, George Humphrey, to the effect that Eisenhower's $60 billion budget, barely enough now to pay the service on the national debt, would touch off "a depression that would curl your hair." The Economy Block made a major effort on the House floor to make deep cuts in the HEW budget. As Acting Secretary of HEW, I got all the agencies in the department to produce a one-page response to each proposed cut. These papers said, if you make this cut, these will be the consequences in terms of services to people.

It worked at the time. In five days of debate, which was then a record for the debate on any single appropriations bill, we lost about $300,000. The trouble is that during the intervening twenty-five years it has too often been impossible to demonstrate the linkage between money and service. There have been too many examples like the survey of youth-serving organizations in a series of typical Massachusetts communities conducted when I was lieutenant governor of the state. Not only did these organizations not cooperate, but they could not even be regarded as competing because they were scarcely aware of what each other was doing.

The public reaction that has been manifested in the massive endorsement of protests like California's Proposition 13 and Proposition 2½ was only partly accounted for, I believe, by resentment against high levels of taxation. It was also to a large extent actuated by the perception that there has been a failure effectively to achieve the synergism that ought to be possible among the organizations and professions whose basic function is to respond to the needs of people. These were warnings, not yet adequately heeded, that it was high time for the service-providing agencies to cooperate, to plan, and to share.

Finally, I think it is important and useful to focus consecutive attention on the question: What does it mean when we say that we cannot "afford" funds for research into the problems of dependency, or better ways of organizing and delivering services? Or that we cannot afford the appropriations that can return disabled people to productive roles in society? Or that we cannot afford decent benefit levels for families and children who would otherwise be destitute?

What is the competition? An obvious answer would be defense, but the defense share of total GNP is well below what it was in the days of the War Against Poverty and at the beginning of the Nixon administration. Is it personal consumption? Certainly personal consumption is higher than it ever was. Flying over the country and looking down at the swimming pools and the marinas, one cannot escape the impression that, despite the recession, ours is a lush standard of living. The fact is, however, that levels of consumption do not seem to account for the squeeze on spending for social programs; total taxation, as a fraction of GNP, is or was until the Reagan tax cuts at a new high.

Part of the answer, I think, is that we feel poorer because our standards of living are no longer rising; part is a consequence of the growth of other government claims that did not used to exist at all, such as combating environmental pollution. The most important factor, however, may derive from the manner in which the increase in resources available for response to human needs has been allocated among the competing claims for those resources. And, of course, by far the greatest share of this increase has gone to the Social Security programs for income benefits and Medicare.

While I cease at this point to be dogmatic, I urge that the issue be addressed. Given our responsibilities for meeting basic human needs, are we making the right choices of ways to apportion the present level of resources? Suppose that level could be increased, rather than cut, by some defined proportion, like 5 percent? How should that additional 5 percent be allocated?

This, of course, raises the question of whether or not we have allowed the upward adjustment of Social Security benefits to move too fast in relation to the wage base, the standard of living, and the growth of GNP. That question should not be taboo, particularly among people whose responsibilities are to all those in need.

Since 1873 the National Conference on Social Welfare has addressed many challenges. You have survived during all those years with the recognition that your efforts have always been poised between the competing claims of an action-oriented body working to reform society and an organization whose mission is to perform a programmatic function including the exchange of information and education. I urge a synthesis of these roles. Such a synthesis would embrace, first, the generation of ideas; second, better ways of responding to human needs more efficiently, more effectively, and with a higher degree of sharing, planning, and cooperating; third, the supplementation of these ideas by the definition of concrete goals; and, finally, the setting of priorities among these goals and the formulation of strategies and tactics for meeting them.

This is a role in which thought serves as the bridge leading to action. It is a role distinguishable both from direct involvement in the execution of strategies and from tactics, but it demands much more than serving simply in the capacity of a clearinghouse and center for informational exchange.

The NCSW can be the national headquarters, the creative source, where the thinking and planning necessary to effective action are developed and whence they are disseminated. The need for such a contribution has never been more critical, nor has there ever been a more rewarding opportunity for the fulfillment of so great a challenge. In the hope that you will perceive the task ahead in these terms, let me wish Godspeed to your efforts.

The Canadian Health Care System

I. MAUREEN LAW

IN DISCUSSING Canada's health care system, I shall concentrate on our national health insurance programs since it is that feature of our system which is most distinct from any part of the United States system. On superficial examination it may seem surprising to some Americans, as it often does to Canadians, that our countries, which are so similar in so many ways, have adopted such very different approaches to the financing of our health systems. Consider for a moment some of our similarities. We share the same strong commitment to democratic processes; both countries are federal systems in which health matters are primarily the responsibility of states or provinces. In both cases we rely on voluntary, religious, and municipally owned hospitals, although Canada has never had separate hospitals for the indigent, nor do we have "for profit" hospitals. Our health professions are similarly organized, with our doctors being mostly in private, independent, fee-for-service practice. Our professionals are trained to the same standards as those in the U.S., and we have the same programs of accreditation. Finally, we share many of the same problems of inflation, unemployment, and government deficits.

On the other hand, while we may be twins, we are not identical twins. Some fundamental points of difference may help to explain why we have so far followed different paths with respect to health care financing. An obvious and important difference is that we have a population of only 23 million and only 10 provinces. Perhaps it is simply easier to plan, administer, and monitor programs which depend upon federal and state or provincial cooperation when the numbers are so much smaller. Perhaps, too, when a society is faced with providing services to a relatively small population spread over a country as vast as Canada, it is understandable that public enterprises of various kinds are more likely to be the preferred option. While most of our political parties would quickly reject the label of "socialist," and certainly we do retain a strong commitment to free enterprise, I think that we have to view Canada realistically as a social democratic country. Even "conservative" governments, both federally and provincially, have launched major public enterprises. Consider the fact that we have publicly owned and operated hydroelectric power systems, a national railway system, Air Canada, the Canadian Broadcasting

MAUREEN LAW, M.D., is Assistant Deputy Minister, Health Services and Promotion Branch, Canadian Department of National Health and Welfare, Ottawa.

Corporation, several provincially owned telephone systems, and, more recently, Petrocan—a publicly owned oil company. Furthermore, we have a long history of cooperatives and marketing boards.

It is really not so surprising, then, that Canadians have developed a series of universal social security measures which include:

a universal, noncontributory old age pension

a contributory pension plan, mandatory for all employed persons

a universal family allowance program

a universal contributory unemployment insurance program

a range of financial assistance and social services provided to persons in need, administered by provinces and cost-shared on a 50-50 basis by the federal government through the Canada Assistance Plan

and, last, but certainly not least—from my biased viewpoint—a national health insurance program.

CANADA'S NATIONAL HEALTH INSURANCE PROGRAMS

A few important factors facilitated the development of our programs. In our parliamentary system we do not have separation of legislative and executive powers, and we have more cohesive and disciplined political parties. These factors may make possible earlier action on contentious issues. Furthermore, we have an elaborate system of federal-provincial conferences which can be utilized to foster cooperation between the two orders of government to initiate joint programs. In addition, the concept that federal taxation powers should be used to ensure relatively equal standards of public services across the country through equalization arrangements (or block funds to provinces) is firmly entrenched in our political system. More specifically, with respect to the development of health insurance programs, we were fortunate in having the support of the major hospital and medical associations for the concept. Finally, on a more mundane level, but nevertheless important to the early success of the programs, we had a standard national hospital accounting manual, and all provincial medical associations had fee schedules.

The development of the programs, in typical Canadian style, has been pragmatic, incremental, evolutionary, but they have become part of the basic fabric of Canadian society. It would be far more revolutionary to remove any aspects of the program than it was to introduce them.

HEALTH INSURANCE PLANS

The programs were implemented in three stages. We introduced hospital insurance in 1958 and medical care insurance in 1968 and revised the arrangements in 1977, adding federal support for extended health care services. By virtue of our Constitution, the federal government is not involved in day-to-day administration of these programs, but the provinces administer the programs for their residents, and the federal government pays roughly half the cost.

To receive federal financial support each provincial scheme must meet certain basic national standards, which are based on five common points. The first point provides that coverage must be comprehensive with respect to the medically required insured services of the national programs, that is, hospital and physicians' care. Coverage is not limited to areas traditionally covered by the private insurance sector, such as treatment, but also includes a wide range of preventive services, much as, checkups, immunization, well-baby care, family planning, and so on, and there are no disease exclusions. Patients have complete freedom of choice of physicians.

The second condition, that provincial plans must be universal, means that they must cover a minimum of 95 percent of the population on uniform terms and conditions. There can be no experience rating on account of age, sex, previous health, occupation, ethnic background, and so on, and there can be no distinction in the premium charge for nongroup coverage compared with group coverage.

When we introduced this program we eliminated all previous categorical programs for indigents, Indians, fishermen, and a number of other special groups. All these were absorbed into the basic program and now have benefits identical to those for the general population. In actual practice, over 99 percent of Canadians are fully covered by the programs.

The third condition is that patients must have reasonable access to services without financial barriers. There are no deductibles and no upper dollar limits. Only a few provinces have user charges. When these do exist they are for hospital care and are mainly for chronic—essentially permanent—hospitalization where a small "room and board" charge is considered to be justified. In some provinces extra-billing by physicians is permitted.

The fourth requirement is that benefits must be portable, extending to cover individuals when they change residence within Canada, or when they are temporarily anywhere in the world. Coverage is not related to jobs, and therefore a person who is changing occupation or retiring is not affected.

Finally, the fifth requrement is that the plan must be administered on a nonprofit basis and must be publicly accountable. In every province those who administer the plan are responsible to a cabinet minister who, in turn, has to report to the provincial legislature.

Most of the provinces operate their plans from general tax revenues, but Ontario, Alberta, and British Columbia rely partly on the collection of premiums. Usually these premiums are paid, at least in part, by employers.

For the sake of simplicity, I have used the term "national" health insurance plans. It would really be more accurate to say that Canada has a national program which is dependent upon interlocking provincial and territorial plans. This is important to note because there are quite substantial differences in the benefits provided by each provincial plan. The national program ensures that all medically necessary hospital and physician's services are covered. However, coverage for additional services, such as home care, nursing home care, dental services, eyeglasses, and prescription drugs, varies from province to province. For example, seven provinces now have insurance programs to cover dental services for children, and some cover dental services and prescription drugs for all senior citizens. Of course, all these services are covered by provinces for persons in need, and for such persons they are cost-shared by the federal government though the Canada Assistance Plan.

In 1977 the federal arrangements for contributing to the hospital and medical care insurance programs were changed from a cost-shared to a block-funded basis. During the 1970s the provinces had complained that the programs were too restrictive, since federal funds were available only for the most expensive forms of care, hospital, and physicians' services. They were seeking more flexibility. At the same time, the federal government was concerned that the arrangements were completely open-ended since only the provinces could take measures to control costs. As a result, the 1977 Established Programs Financing and Fiscal Arrangements Act provided that the federal contributions would be partly a transfer of tax room to the provinces and partly a formula-based cash contribution. At the same time, a new federal program of per-capita grants was instituted for the development of extended health services such as home care, nursing home care, ambulatory care, and adult residential services. Those contributions escalate according to the same formula as the rest of the cash contributions but are not subject to the program conditions just described.

COSTS

Naturally, any government which is considering the implementation of such a major public program will be concerned with the cost implications. It is self-evident that for the most part there is simply a transfer of spending from the private to the public sector in order that the cost may be borne by society as a whole on a prepaid basis rather than at the time of need, since that may well be the very time when people are least able to pay. The fear then seems to be largely related to the question of whether the demands of consumers and/or providers will increase significantly. I would argue that the Canadian experience demonstrates clearly that such factors, at least in our context, are unjustified. Our cost experience has been extremely favorable. During the 1970s our health care costs as a percentage of the gross national product (GNP) were virtually stable at about 7 percent.

Of course, I would like to argue that this favorable outcome results solely from the efficiencies involved in a publicly administered system, and indeed I believe that efficiency is part of the answer. For instance, our administrative costs are less than 3 percent, whereas the figures I have seen for the United States have been at least 10 percent. Furthermore, we have probably been able to achieve greater rationalization in terms of the sharing of services and the appropriate use of new technology, the expanded use of generic drugs, and the like because of government financial involvement, combined with the retention of some of the best aspects of an entirely private system.

In fairness, I must acknowledge that there were some other factors in our favor during the 1970s, and I do not know whether they were equally important in the United States. In the first place, we had a favorable demographic situation since the birth rate was low and the percentage of the population in the 0–4-years age group was, therefore, low. At the same time, we had not yet experienced a significant increase in the percentage of the population over age 65. During that decade we also had two years of wage and price controls which certainly helped to contain costs. Finally, we continued to have a shift of people from rural to urban areas, which has decreased the use of expensive hospital services, although urban dwellers do use more physicians' services.

Unfortunately, many of these favorable factors will not persist into the 1980s. Certainly we are not experiencing the same rapid growth in GNP as we did in the early 1970s; and we do have an aging population, although the major shift there will not occur for about fifteen to twenty years. On top of that, we are now witnessing a growing militancy among all types of health workers. I am pleased to report, though, that despite our current economic difficulties, the federal government has just completed a new five-year agreement which guarantees the provinces increases in federal contributions which will be somewhat above the projected rates of inflation. In other words, there will be some real growth, at least in respect to the federal contributions.

Canadians are justifiably proud of their insurance programs. But there are always problems with any program, and in recent years there has been growing concern over some aspects of the programs. In particular, there is public concern over extra-billing by physicians and concern on the part of providers over the level of funding of the system. We are also concerned about the growing oversupply of physicians.

In over 90 percent of cases, doctors are members of the provincial medical care plans, and they bill the plans directly so that the patient receives no bill from the doctor. Doctors who opt out of the plans in all provinces except Quebec can bill their patients directly, and the plan will then pay the *patient* the amount allowed for the service in the provincial schedule of benefits. In Quebec the patient cannot receive any payment from the plan for services provided by opted-out physicians. As a result, there are only two or three opted-out doctors in the whole province. In other provinces, opted-out doctors can extra-bill the patient. This practice is quite limited at present, and the amount of the extra-bill is usually not very large. In a few provinces the doctor is allowed to bill the plan directly (that is, to remain opted-in) and to extra-bill the patient as well. That arrangement we call "balance billing." The total amoung of extra-billing amounts to only about 3 percent of the total plan payments. Nevertheless, there is concern that unless steps are taken to restrict the ability of doctors to extra-bill, there may be a gradual erosion of the program and real financial barriers may develop in the future.

The various proposals to deal with this issue have created considerable controversy between the doctors and the governments, and between the federal and provincial governments. In the past three years we have had two major inquiries into the programs to consider extra-billing and other issues. One was conducted by Mr. Justice Hall who chaired the Royal Commission on Health Services in 1963 which set the stage for the introduction of the medical care program, and the other was a federal Parliamentary task force. The reports of both recommended that the practice of extra-billing be eliminated but that the right of physicians to reasonable compensation be protected by a mechanism such as binding arbitration.

With respect to the concern of providers about the adequacy of funding, both reports concluded that the current level of funding of the system is adequate to maintain the existing range of services, although it would not allow for the development of new programs. Given the current economic climate, it seems unlikely, therefore, that we will see much expansion during the next few years.

As it happens, we are just about to launch the next phase in the evolution of the national health insurance programs. Unfortunately, as I have noted, this will be aimed not at the extension of the programs which we would all like to see, but rather at the consolidation and protection of the gains we have made. Both Mr. Justice Hall and the Parliamentary Task Force have called upon the federal government and the provinces to renew their commitments to the program, and specifically for the federal government to clarify and strengthen the program conditions for its cash contributions. In June of 1982 the Minister of National Health and Welfare met with her provincial colleagues to set forth federal proposals for a new piece of federal health legislation to replace the existing acts.

One may well say that all of this sounds great, but the proof of the pudding is in the eating. It is extremely difficult to correlate the supply of health services or expenditures on health to meaures of health status. I do not suggest that the health status improvements which we have achieved in Canada can all be attributed to a national health insurance plan, but they do suggest—at least to me—that there is no reason to conclude that it has been detrimental either. To quote some specific examples—again from the 1970s—our supply of hospital beds remained stable at about 7 per 1000 population, our population-to-physician ratio improved from 659:1 to 551:1, our infant mortality rate declined from 16.8 per 1000 live births to 10.9, and life expectancy has continued to improved, being about two years longer for all ages, for both males and females, than is the case in the United States.

The programs were designed primarily to relieve personal and family financial problems associated with illness, and I find it interesting that a major national health survey of Canadians conducted in 1979 found no reports of individuals failing to seek or receive care for insured services because of economic barriers—although there were reports of lack of access, for financial reasons, to services, such as dental services, which are not universally insured.

Numerous opinion polls, including some conducted in 1982, have consistently found a very high level of public satisfaction with the program. Indeed, it is clearly the most popular government program. As one might expect, the providers of care are sometimes less enthusiastic, for there are occasional skirmishes over money or policies.

There was no attempt to tie the implementation of our insurance programs to any other major changes in the delivery system. Some would argue that this was a mistake. Our delivery system tends to be very difficult to change now since there is little motivation on the part of either consumers or providers to make significant changes. I would personally argue that it was better to do what was feasible at the time than to wait in hope for the opportunity to go all the way. A quotation from Mr. Justice Hall's 1980 report may perhaps suggest that most Canadians would agree: "I found no one, not any government or individual, not the medical profession nor any organization, not in favor of Medicare. There were differences of opinion, it is true, on how it should be organized and provided, but no one wanted it terminated."

The United States in 1982

II. MELVIN A. GLASSER

THE PAST sixteen months have witnessed a cataclysmic upheaval in health programs in the United States. A new national administration, determined to halt the increases in costs of social programs, has slashed expenditures, reduced eligibility and benefits in publicly supported personal health services, and increasingly makes clear its intention to shift payment responsibilities to private sector health insurance and to consumers.

These new emphases are based on a series of assumptions about the operations of a health care system and the behavior of consumers and providers in that system that require careful examination. If there is substantial evidence to support the basis for the new program approaches, there is reasonable hope that the administration's goals of improved health at lower costs will be achieved. If the evidence disproves the assumptions, one must assume that the massive changes made and proposed have as their basis ideological and political objectives unsupported by the facts.

We are today afforded a unique opportunity to look at the experience and results of a 21 billion a year research and demonstration program, involving some twenty-three million people, in a research sample called "Canada." Comparisons with other nations are always fraught with difficulties because of differences in culture, history, population mix, and economic conditions. But Canada is more comparable to the United States than any other nation. Its economy is closely intertwined with ours. It has a federal-provincial system of government. It has voluntary hospitals, solo practice fee for service physician providers, vigorous unions of health care employees; and before national health insurance protection became a reality, Canada had a partial and spotty health insurance protection from a voluntary health insurance industry.

Among the principal concerns in Canada have been three issues similar to our own: the costs of health care, the quality of the services, and how to improve access to health services. In this connection there are five major assumptions and hypotheses of the administration and its supporters about health care:

1. Making comprehensive health services available to all the people is far too costly. The United States cannot afford it. We must make do with less.

But Canada is providing more health care and spending less than the United States. In 1966, the year the second part of their national health insurance,

MELVIN GLASSER is Director, Committee for National Health Insurance, Washington, D.C., and Past President, National Conference on Social Welfare.

Medicare, was passed, Canada and the United States were spending 6.6 percent of gross national product (GNP) on health care. They then expanded the program to provide full protection to all Canadians. Today we still have more than 45 million Americans who either have no private health insurance or have such inadequate coverage that it is of little value.

Between 1966 and 1980 Canada's total health costs rose from 6.6 percent to 7.3 percent of GNP. In the same period U.S. costs rose to 9.4 percent of GNP.[1] While our costs continue to escalate, Canada's health costs as a percentage of GNP have actually gone down in the last decade. They were 7.7 percent in 1971, 7.5 percent in 1975, and 7.3 percent in 1980.

Canada has demonstrated that they are able to provide full health care protection at substantially less proportionate cost than the United States is paying for inadequate protection.

2. More and more health care protection should be turned over to the private sector and the individual. Government administration and regulation are inefficient and costly.

In Canada administrative costs of the wholly publicly run national health insurance plan are 2.3 percent.[2] This compares with administrative costs more than three times higher for U.S. private group health insurance, and fifteen times higher for individual insurance.

Less than a year ago Canadian economists told a federal parliamentary task force that U.S. spending may be higher because no one is responsible for holding it down. Insurance plans pass on higher medical and hospital charges to consumers. In Canada, each provincial government has a substantial stake in holding down expenditures; and as the single payer it has the clout to enforce expenditure limits.

3. Costs will be restrained by making the consumer cost conscious. Requiring economic deterrents to care, like deductibles and coinsurance, is essential, even for the very poor.

Cost sharing has been permitted in Canada. The province of Saskatchewan had it from 1968 to 1971. Prior to 1968 Saskatchewan had the lowest rate of cost and utilization increase in the country. After cost sharing was instituted there was a drop in utilization in the first year, following which utilization began to increase again, but at a higher rate than ever before. There was a rebound phenomenon. Unfortunately, the decrease in utilization fell disproportionately on the aged, large families, and the poor.

Study of the experience failed to demonstrate that so-called unnecessary medical services were eliminated. On the contrary, physicians generated an increased demand to offset their income losses from seeing fewer patients.

As noted Canadian medical economist Robert Evans has stated, "if physician behavior is the key to utilization and expenditure, as our experience suggests,

---

[1] *Ministry of Health and Welfare, Canada, Division of Health Insurance, Internal Report, 1981.*
[2] *Emmett M. Hall, C.C., Q.C., Special Commissioner, Canada's National-Provincial Health Program for the 1980's, Report of the Royal Commission, August 29, 1980, p. 44.*

it follows that efforts to modify patterns of expenditures by incentives directed at the consumer of care cannot hope to influence cost trends." "Co-payment," says Evans,"is pretty much a dead issue in Canada because it cannot come to grips with the real problems" of the health care system.[3]

4. "Free care" or first-dollar coverage is a major cause of frivolous use of health services. It creates needless demands which will swamp the health care system and bring about rationing of health services.

There is nothing in the Canadian experience to support this oft-repeated assertion. As a matter of fact, when public hospital insurance was first instituted there was no grand rush to hospitals. The annual rates of increase in days per 1,000 population *declined* in the years after the program began.[4]

There was initially a very modest increase in physicians' visits.[5] This was attributable primarily to contacts with doctors by a previously uninsured population. One study, in the province of Alberta, found that the number of such visits per patient for the previously uninsured *urban* population dropped slightly, from 3.42 to 3.08, per year while in the previously uninsured *rural* population it increased from 2.22 to 4.11.[6]

Studies of physicians' visits before comprehensive first-dollar insurance in the province of Quebec, compared with utilization after insurance began, revealed a net decline of 7.5 percent in home, office, and hospital outpatient visits.[7]

U.S. policy-makers should be interested in a major conclusion of this same research team: "Of particular significance is the increased frequency with which patients were seen for a series of common and important medical symptoms."[8]

Another study of the Quebec experience reported to the Canadian Medical Association supported the conclusion that increased utilization, when it occurred, combined with removal of economic barriers to care, may actually improve the general level of health of the population. First prenatal visits during the second trimester of pregnancy dropped by 15 percent. Earlier visits during pregnancy are, of course, a desirable consequence of "free" or first-dollar coverage.[9]

Knowledgeable health care specialists in the United States and Canada have

---

[3] *Robert G. Evans, "Beyond the Medical Marketplace," in* National Health Insurance, Can We Learn From Canada? *Spyros Andreopoulos, ed. (New York: Wiley, 1975), p. 163.*

[4] *Malcolm G. Taylor,* Health Insurance and Canadian Public Policy *(Montreal: McGill Queens University Press, 1978), p. 234.*

[5] *Maurice LeClair, M.D. "The Canadian Health Care System," in Andreopoulous, ed.,* National Health Insurance, *p. 49.*

[6] *Personal letter to author from Maurice LeClair, M.D., Deputy Minister of Health and Welfare, Canada, July 21, 1973.*

[7] *Philip E. Enterline et al., "The Distribution of Medical Services Before and After 'Free' Medical Care,"* Medical Care, *July-August 1973, pp. 60—86.*

[8] *Philip E. Enterline et al., "Effects of 'Free' Medical Care on Medical Practice—the Quebec Experience,"* New England Journal of Medicine, *May 31, 1973, pp. 1153–55.*

[9] *Personal letter to author from Maurice LeClair, M.D., footnote 6.*

long since agreed that so-called overutilization of health services is much more likely to result from an oversupply of hospitals and physicians rather than from increased demand. And the new health policy-makers in Washington are proposing further restrictions on demand, combined with removal of constraints on hospital expansion. They are also opposing efforts to slow the expansion in numbers of physicians in overcrowded medical specialties like general surgery.

5. Government's role in medical care must be reduced, not only because it is too costly, but because it makes for bureaucratic, lower-quality medical services. Long delays in obtaining services and deterioration of the doctor-patient relationship result from government programs.

The Canadian experience appears wholly contrary to this view. A 1978 Gallup poll revealed that 84 percent of Canadians rate health care as good value for their tax dollars—a higher rating than for any other public service.[10]

An American medical economist investigated the hypothesis that government medical insurance leads to these alleged undesirable consequences. He studied a matched sample of U.S. citizens living in Colorado and a similar group of Americans then resident in British Columbia. He found that most respondents living in British Columbia reported that their experiences with the health system in Canada were the same or better than they had in the United States. However, in finding a doctor in an emergency, obtaining appointments to see a physician in a nonemergency, and seeing a physician of choice, the British Columbia experience was more favorable than that in the United States.[11]

The evidence from Canada is perhaps best summed up by Justice Emmett M. Hall who, as a special commissioner conducted a year-long study of the entire health system in 1980. "I found no one," Justice Hall reported, "not any government or individual, not any medical profession or any organization, not in favor of Medicare."[12]

While much of what I have reported of the Canadian experience is highly favorable, it would be misleading to leave the impression that the Canadian health care system is without problems. As with any major program, government or private, continuing adjustments to changing conditions are essential. Canadians are today grappling with the question of appropriate allocation of funds between the federal and the provincial governments. Along with this is the familiar issue of whether more decision-making authority should reside in the provinces and less at the national level. In constructing its health insurance plans the Canadian government chose not to deal with questions of reorganization of the delivery system, the promotion of preventive services,

[10]*Business Insurance, December 11, 1978, p. 11.*

[11]*R. D. Peterson, "Patients' Experiences with Government Medical Insurance in British Columbia,"* Inquiry, *Spring 1980, pp. 72–84.*

[12]*Special Commissioner Emmett M. Hall's comment on his Royal Commission Report; see footnote 2, quoted by Gordon George and Michael Storgre, "National Health Care in Canada,"* America, *January 31, 1981, p. 80.*

or participation by consumers in policy decisions. These questions, along with those relating to augmented financing sources, are the subjects of heated and continuing public policy debates.

I have chosen not to go into these, for my focus has been on the United States. It appears from the evidence cited, and from a great deal more as well, that the principal assumptions on which health policy is being advanced by the administration in Washington have been proved to be wrong. Our 21 billion research-demonstration project, "Canada," provides the needed time-tested proof.

Since the hypotheses on which the new U.S. programs are based have been demonstrated to be invalid, the programs will not work. Slashing benefits and programs, abdicating public responsibility, disregarding the health needs of the working poor and the needy, and mandating increased costs and new deterrents to care for those who work must therefore be seen as ideological and political objectives, but not as sound or effective health programs.

Where does that leave us?

First, there is the recognition that the Canadian experience demonstrates that comprehensive universal national health insurance, properly structured, is indeed a practical, sound goal for the United States. We will eventually achieve it because it makes good sense, and because it is the only effective way over the long run to solve America's health care problems. It is not likely, however, that we can achieve this objective in the current political climate.

This leads to a second course. The tested evidence from our Canadian research-demonstration project provides the data necessary to challenge the administration's health initiatives. Their assumptions are wrong. The proposals built on these assumptions are not likely to succeed.

Third, looking only at the short run, an alternative health care cost-containment plan developed by the health Security Action Council reduces the escalation of health care costs without the carnage of denied benefits and likely increases in morbidity and mortality, which are part of the costs of the administration's retreat from responsibility.[13]

This alternative program is built on the best of U.S. and Canadian experience. It is both sound and controversial—the latter because it is aimed principally at protecting consumers and more effectively governing providers.

But even here is hope. For the Canadian experience demonstrates that it is possible to achieve equity in health programs to such an extent that over time both consumers and providers will support the programs.

---

[13]*Health Security Action Council,* Health Care Cost Containment; a Constructive Approach, *Washington, D.C.: Health Security Action Council, 1982.*

President Reagan's Economic Policies and Their Social Cost

JAMES M. HOWELL

I am not a social programmer; I am chief economist of a Boston bank with assets of nearly $20 billion and roughly 15,000 employees scattered in 36 countries around the world. Nonetheless, as an economist, the social cost of President Reagan's policies is as much a matter of concern to me as it is to social workers.

On March 4, 1933, in President Franklin D. Roosevelt's inaugural address, he spoke of the Northeast "moneychangers," which are banks like ours. He said: "Those bankers know only the roles of a generation of self-seekers. They have no vision, and where there is no vision, the people will perish." It soon became abundantly clear that FDR, as Walter Lippmann so often said, "took the power of the White House from Wall Street to Washington, and introduced a social revolution to deal with America's problems." On so many counts most of us would judge the social programming efforts to be of positive benefit to our country at large.

Today, we are looking at President Reagan's economic program and its social consequences. But, before assessing the social costs of this administration's policies, we need to look more closely at the impact of the President's recovery program on the economy.

THE ECONOMIC OUTLOOK: POSITIVE BUT UNCERTAIN

The best single statement that describes my view of the economy over the next twelve to eighteen months is that there will be a significant recovery in consumer demand—but without the necessary follow-on business investment.

In many respects the Reagan administration's position on the economy has been difficult to follow. In the fall of 1981, President Reagan himself announced that the economy was in a recession. I cannot remember any time in the post-World War II period when an incumbent President has acknowledged that the economy was in a recession. This is a statement that is usually left to the party out of the White House. About six months later, Secretary of the Treasury Regan announced that the economy was "dead in the water." More recently, a White House aide was reported as saying: "The recovery is going to take place, but at a lower level than anyone had hoped, and it may

JAMES M. HOWELL is Senior Vice-President, First National Bank of Boston.

be that the only people who are aware of the recovery are the economists who track the figures."

I find all this discussion very confusing because our analysis supports the view that the economy will turn up in the summer of 1982. The June-July turnabout will be attributable largely, if not solely, to the $33 billion tax cut on individual income and the $12 billion cost-of-living adjustment to Social Security recipients.

Bear in mind that at no period in our economic experience have we had such a significant injection of income thrust into the economy. And this $45 billion increase is coming at a most propituous time—the trough in a business cycle recession. That infusion of funds will most likely lead to noticeable economic recovery in the consumption sector. Thus, the recovery from the 1981–82 recession is at hand and reasonably secure. The economic statistics that we will read in the fall and early winter of 1982 will generally be encouraging as the economic recovery becomes a well-established reality.

This positive near-term outlook notwithstanding, I continue to be deeply concerned that there will not be the subsequent business capital formation to sustain the growth of the economy in 1983–84. This concern is valid even though business is going to receive roughly $151 billion worth of tax cuts over the next five years. As I travel around the country, businessmen tell me: "We really want to invest in this country. We want to create jobs, but it is exceedingly difficult to do so at this time within the environment and the context of high and far too unstable interest rates."

So, to be candid, we have to conclude that the economic situation over the short-term is going to be positively dominated by strong consumption expenditures, but in the intermediate term it will be dominated by a lack of strong business capital formation. To put this generalization into its business cycle perspective, we conclude that there will be initial cyclical recover in the fall of 1982 that will not likely give way to widespread economic growth in 1983–1984.

BUSINESS INVESTMENT AND CENTRAL-CITY POVERTY

To an economist, poverty has two dimensions—rural poverty and central-city poverty. Rural poverty in the South is perhaps the most noticeable problem in that region. Central-city poverty, however, is not exclusively found in the North. It is a problem for inner cities all over the country.

Significant national population and economic forces are moving in the direction of leading to some improvement. During the decade of the 1970s, nonmetropolitan county population growth began to accelerate. Indeed, the 1980 census shows that the population in nonmetropolitan counties grew 50 percent faster than the population at large. And for the first time, more Americans migrated out of urban areas than into urban areas. That leaves central cities even in growing regions with a heavy concentration of those who stay behind—most notably, the poor.

Although some would argue that it is a "chicken-and-egg" issue, it is safe to say that an increasing share of business investment will continue to take place in nonmetropolitan counties. To the extent that this has raised the demand for entry-level labor, there is a positive dimension in the social outlook for these areas for real economic reasons.

To repeat, we are not going to have much new business investment during 1983–84. Within this context, there are strong and well-established factors that support the view that weak national investment will translate into stagnant business investment in our nation's cities. It would be tempting to make a "just-share" argument that cities ought to have a larger part of any increase in investment, but with weak national investment this argument is simply not credible. At the same time, it is clear that we are not going to have much of a grant-in-aid program to deliver services to those who need them and to provide private investment leverage in cities.

We may summarize that the economic outlook for America's older cities is not encouraging. Weak national investment coupled with a reduction in federal assistance simply does not bode well for the future. We must seek out new issues and define alternative strategies.

THE CAUSES OF CENTRAL-CITY POVERTY

In April of 1982, the U.S. Bureau of the Census released new and alternative definitions of poverty. According to one of these definitions, the number of persons living below the poverty line could be reduced by as much as 42 percent if the most liberal method of counting noncash benefits were adopted. I do not think social workers embrace that view, but it is a viewpoint that has been articulated.

In the language of a bank economist, the central cities of America face a severe balance-of-payments problem with the more affluent suburban areas. First, by and large, most of the residents of a central city live on low incomes and work in service sector jobs. In far too many instances, the wage level is scarcely above the minimum wage. Second, the central-city balance-of-payments problem results because there has been a shift in the production of goods and services out of the city and into the suburbs. Today, those individuals who live in the central city on low incomes must buy many of their necessary goods and services from suburban production sites. As a result, there is an adverse trade balance—an outflow of limited neighborhood resources to purchase goods and services from the suburbs.

Finally, in almost all of America's cities, those who control the city's economic resources are people who work in the city but live in the suburbs. And all too often the good intentions of these individuals are channeled into the places where they live, not where they work. They defend their quiet suburban existence by simply saying they prefer multiacre zoning. Yet, they leave behind an inadequate tax base because the city is economically stagnant.

No small wonder, then, that the result is central-city poverty and municipal fiscal strain.

How can we attack the causes of central-city poverty in an environment of sluggish national growth with only modest increases in investment and with major cuts in federal grants?

NEW PARTNERSHIPS FOR CENTRAL-CITY ECONOMIC DEVELOPMENT

NCSW, whose members have to deal with central-city poverty on a day-to-day basis, must decide what role it is to play in answering this question. The reason is straightforward: President Reagan has taken away much of the capacity to finance service delivery programs to the poor in central cities. NCSW can become either a strenuous critic of this administration, or it can become a constructive partner with banks to create central-city jobs. I certainly hope that you will choose the latter role.

This new partnership must revolve around community ownership of viable business enterprises in the central city—the only appropriate response to the poverty problems in central cities. But new techniques are needed if this partnership is to be transformed from rhetoric to reality.

The Council for Northeast Economic Action and the U.S. Conference of Mayors have been working on a project called Triangular Partnership Program. The partners are city hall, community development corporations (CDCs), and bankers. The goal of the Triangular Partnership Program is to achieve business equity for neighborhood residents though the active integration of CDC aspirations into bank financing to produce new businesses and to expand existing ones where there is a latent growth potential.

Initially, one of the obstacles to achieving any such partnership has been the way in which bankers, mayors, and CDC representatives talk to each other. Our experience has demonstrated that this is basically the same in Boston, Cleveland, and Tucson. In cities like these all over the country there are individuals trying to do something about poverty, but, neighborhood groups, and bankers especially, are having a tough time communicating their common needs and developmental aspirations.

When these groups get together, the community development people invariably ask the bankers to allocate substantial sums of capital in a development pool from which they can borrow as they see fit. That, as one can imagine, is disquieting to the bankers. The bankers ask to be shown how the CDCs are going to lend this money and, more particularly, how it will be repaid. As a result, matters get stuck, and very little happens.

The Council for Northeat Economic Action is attempting to find a way out of this impasse. The Council has developed a practical technique through which we can identify precisely for any targeted urban area businesses with a high probability of start-up and expansion success. The technique is called the Urban Business Identification System (UBI). In Boston, Hartford, Connecticut, and Flint, Michigan—our three test site cities—we now have a list of the best business opportunities which bankers and CDCs can use as a guide to start new businesses with an equity ownership on the part of the CDC. Once the UBI concept is understood and accepted, the targeted businesses become far more attractive to bank lending officers.

We want to share this work with the social work profession. I would welcome the opportunity to sit down with representatives of the profession to talk about UBI as a means of starting businesses in other cities.

I quoted President Roosevelt's remark that "the Northeast moneychangers . . . have no vision, and where there is no vision, the people will perish." I believe that we do have vision. Together we can figure out the nature of the problems confronting us and we can conceptualize solutions to them. Through the UBI we are now able to target business enterprises with a high probability of start-up success in cities.

Again, Walter Lippmann said, "President Roosevelt took the power of the White House from Wall Street to Washington." What President Reagan has done, it seems to me, is to bring the power of the White House back to us. Whether banking and social action organizations are able to translate this fundamental shift into new job opportunities for the poor in our cities is up to ourselves. No longer can we fail and blame Washington.

We may not like some of the forms in which we are getting this power right now, but we are going to get it one way or another. In whatever form, we can use this power positively to deal with urban poverty. This will require, perhaps more than anything else, new partnership building between banks and community groups. The National Conference on Social Welfare can play a vital role in this partnership-building process.

Rationale for Social Programs of the 1980s

ROBERT MORRIS

FOR SEVERAL decades American citizens have believed that government should act to remove the causes of human suffering when possible; or, if not possible, to relieve them. This simple belief is no longer sufficient to confront the most serious challenge to such humanitarian views in at least fifty years. The Reagan social program for the 1980s is comparable, in its punitive character, to the English Poor Law Reform of 1834 which, for its first time, was the most punishing for poor people in 300 years of English history. That backward step came fifty years after a time when 25 percent to 30 percent of residents received some relief from local taxes. Our step back comes fifty years after the great depression.[1]

The one-time wide consensus about how to relieve human suffering, about the "natural rights" of poor minorities, has been broken. Some of us seek more social help or action by government than others—a majority?—are prepared to support. On what principles can we rely to bridge this gap? It is necessary but not sufficient to be against this new trend or to reiterate our past programs; the times call for an affirmation about what we are for. Reaganomic budget cuts are, thus far, less damaging than the basic philosophies which underly them—and these challenge us to reexamine our own concepts.

PREMISES ON WHICH WE HAVE BEEN FUNCTIONING

Since the sixteenth century, one principle has governed the evolution of national states and the industrial and postindustrial era: that government has a direct interest in assuring the welfare of all its citizens. This does not mean that government does all things directly; rather, the interest of government is to assure that the combined efforts of all components in society—associations, corporations, and so forth—add up to the welfare of all. If these fail, the health of the nation requires that government act. This premise prevailed in

[1]C.F. Bahmueller, The National Charity Company *(Berkeley: University of California Press, 1981)*.

ROBERT MORRIS is Professor Emeritus, Florence Heller Graduate School for Advanced Studies in Social Welfare, Brandeis University, Waltham, Mass.

mercantilist thinking in 1600 and in welfare state thought in 1980. Even laissez-faire freebooting capitalist thought provided for government action when the free marketplace failed.

Our assumptions have been based upon a balance between two conceptions:

— *Humanity:* that every man, poor or rich, is entitled to life and to independence in a free and healthy society even if he cannot support himself through his own efforts because the economy does not provide the means.

— *Justice:* that individuals should not be deprived of the fruits of their labor to benefit others unless necessary for the wider welfare of the nation. This is the ancient conflict between those who pay taxes reluctantly and those who are helped for humanitarian reasons. In planned economies the conflict is between those who make large national plans and ordinary citizens.

THE CURRENT CHALLENGE TO THESE ASSUMPTIONS

The major changes which have occurred over the last 400 years in the balancing act between these demands have been the replacement of personal charity by concepts of equity and right and the great increase in what some want to treat as natural rights. Social policy in the United States in the last fifty years has seen the evolution of the idea, incorporated in legislation, that whatever the society decides to do about human needs, it makes available not as a matter of grudging charity but as a matter of human right.

This is a recent development and the one least deeply rooted in the American consensus. There are signs that some—perhaps many—citizens have had their attitudes about community responsibility and about the disadvantaged changed by the rhetoric of the new government. The consensus of the past about the nature of a decent social order is being dislodged, giving way to a citizenry fragmented into self-centered private estates in which each small group comes to believe that it only has to look after itself; that those who are well-off are entitled to government policies which directly benefit them, through tax breaks, through loopholes and industrial incentives; while others, less fortunate, are not entitled to the same even-handed attention of their government. Even worse, they may come to believe that the less well-off are in that state through some personal flaw in character, but never because the economy is twisted against them.[2]

The central challenge, mounted by the present administration, is that the national government has *no* significant responsibility for the well-being of its citizens except through military defense and the stimulation of industry through the tax provision of subsidies to encourage industrial activity. If the industrial decisions are insufficient to meet human needs, this is no responsibility of the national government. And if the decisions made by the economic sector

---

[2]*S. Middleton and P. Goldring,* Images of Welfare; *quoted in* New Society, *April 1, 1982, pp. 12–13.*

are not in the interest of all citizens, this still is none of the business of the national government. It is this central challenge that confronts us: that the national government will use taxes, raised from all, to help the economically secure who control economic enterprises, but has no obligation for the consequences of insufficient or erroneous judgments taken by that sector. It is this which needs to be met even though we are daily exercised by evidences of mean-minded attitudes about the poor and the working poor.

It is too early in the career of a radical new administration to draw final conclusions about what its history will be, but it would be wise to view with caution the claims that the poor and the needy—truly needy—will never be neglected and that the "safety net" will be maintained, given this viewpoint. In such a period, it may be useful to look first at the foundations for a humanitarian view about a better, but not utopian, world.

THE HISTORIC BASES OF RATIONALES FOR SOCIAL PROGRAMS

The moral underpinnings for social programs in general, whether or not they are provided through government, have emerged from 3,000 years of painful human experience. The first ethical rationales for helping others were also quite practical. There was always a clear and evident exchange between giver and receiver; obedience to a supreme deity to ward off disaster or to secure personal salvation; or friends and members of a small clan who saw the value of helping each other since anyone might need help sometime. As the clan or tribe grew larger, there came the need to build a sense of wider community loyalty with rules which would promote the welfare of the larger group, or city state, as in Rome and Greece. Such views were developed by Plato, Aristotle, Cicero.

At a still later stage, there evolved the conviction that people have a few rights which are prior to government and that true morality consists in upholding rights as ends in themselves and not instrumental to the needs of the state or for self-protection. Such higher morality has roots in the Old Testament and in early Christian thought.[3] In the religious ethical view it is more important to make sure that no one who might be in need is overlooked than to base one's giving on careful inquiry. But even in religion, such justice was tempered by the caution of early church fathers who wrote: "We ought not only lend our ears to voices of those who plead, but also our eyes to look into their needs."[4]

Yet, for the most of this 3,000-year history, only the most obvious forms of distress were given public or private attention: orphans, widows, hunger, natural disasters, safety of person. Only in periods of special economic distress

---

[3]*Lawrence Kohlberg,* Essays in Moral Development, *Vol. 1 (New York: Harper and Row, 1982).*

[4]*Karl DeSchweinitz,* Who Speaks for the Poor? The Dilemma of Need; *fragments of uncompleted manuscript in the Social Welfare Archives, University of Minnesota, Minneapolis.*

were the able-bodied poor given much attention: in ancient Rome where 90 percent of the Roman residents were poor; in early industrial Europe, when 50 percent of the citizens were poor or starving; in 1930 in the United States when 33 percent of the public were ill-fed or ill-clothed. For the rest of the time, the able-bodied poor were treated badly.[5]

Only in the present century, and in the United States only since 1935, has there evolved a belief that more subtle forms of disadvantage required and justified government attention. Ideas of fair treatment of all, of more equalization among classes, of rights not charity, began to take root. But compared to the millennial evolution of charitable thought and belief, these roots have not gone deep, and it is this fact which is now being attacked.

When we turn from ethical appeals to acts of government, other rationales begin to emerge, which decision-makers and citizens have used in deciding what to do for or about the poor:

1. Perhaps the most prevalent rationale treats the state as a vastly enlarged tribe: a large, undifferentiated collectivity of individuals which has only loose ties that bind. The well-being of such a collectivity requires that there be productive workers, that they be healthy, and that they be educated in order to produce the goods. This ensures the well-being of all. The Poor Laws grew up as an early way for governments to carry out this limited obligation. The provisions were harsh and class differences dominant, but some responsibility was never denied. Individuals as well as businesses were the concern of government, even if treated unequally.

2. Another rationale is that of fear. Frequently, governments make provisions for the poor, not because they are generous but because of fear of the consequences of not being generous. Disorder is avoided.

3. Less clearly articulated, but nonetheless powerful, is the rationale of reciprocity which takes its modern form in the concept of fairness. Through a tortuous history, concepts have evolved which force individuals to jduge what behavior is considered fair to others and to themselves. In the days of Greece, philanthropy was seen as a gift between peers who expected to be repaid by equivalent treatment in the future. Later, generosity expected repayment though devoted labor in a commonwealth. Today the beneficiary still owes something in return: once it was gratitude; now it is readiness to work or to share in a consensus about the social order and observance of accepted legal or moral standards.

The current debate over fairness is reduced to material terms: how much of the national product should be given to the poor in the interests of fairness and how much should be retained by those who, through one means or another, produce the goods? This simplified approach to fairness is much obscured because so much production of goods is determined by inherited wealth whose owners did little to create the wealth, whereas many of those who are not

[5]*A. R. Hand*, Charities and Local Aid in Greece and Rome *(London: Thames and Hudson, 1968)*.

wealth-creating are not simply reluctant but have not been given the opportunity, due to flaws in our economic structure.

Philosophers such as Rawls[6] and others have tried to develop philosophical methods for determining fairness, but for a very long time we resolved this question of fairness by an essentially utilitarian concept: that act which produces the greatest good for the greatest number is probably as fair as we can be.

THE SIGNIFICANCE FOR THE 1980s

This history represents the most deeply rooted beliefs about welfare. To conserve the foundation for a more decent society, we need to consider not only what we "ought to do," but what most of us can be persuaded to agree to do.

The American electorate, for reasons of history, geography, and education (or brainwashing, if you will) may still be generous to some clearly handicapped persons such as the very sick, the handicapped, the aged, and perhaps children. At the same time, we are doubtful, as people have been throughout history, about able-bodied adults who are not working (unless they have property). We treat the unpropertied less generously. The growth in social programs, and especially of social work, in many new areas in the last few decades should not mislead us into believing that such recent growth has very deep roots.

So what are the foundations on which we can build in the immediate period ahead? I suggest that social welfare and its social work allies confront a resumption of the long uphill struggle, the end of which is greater equity and equality in human conditions. In order to resume that fight with a fair chance of success, we will have to build our strategies on a few basic considerations. The period may not be too different from that in the early nineteenth century in England when the relatively benign aspects of the Poor Laws came under attack by very conservative governments , which led to the Poor Law reforms of 1834 which were punitive and hostile to the poor. It took the rest of the nineteenth century for liberal forces to rebuild on a much better basis the concept of public responsibility for the whole people. I would consider the following considerations basic to our future:

1. The infinite variety of individualized services for all kinds of human need will have to be given second place (for a time) to the overwhelming need to ensure that opportunities for employment or, lacking that, a basic income are made available. For social workers, this is not easy, for ever since the late 1930s or 1940s, most social workers have withdrawn from the income or work programs (except for giving lip service). Most have concentrated upon professional activities concerned with treating individuals, forgetting that the strength of clinical and therapeutic and caring programs depends upon the strength of the economy; and that human dignity without history (and in

[6]*John Rawls*, A Theory of Justice *(Cambridge, Mass.: Harvard University Press, 1971)*.

the view of the American public) depends upon the self-supporting individual as the first objective. We should join forces with allies concerned primarily with employment and income as the bedrock of planning for the future. This assumes strength rather than weakness in most clients.

2. The second part of our platform has to be an unremitting and determined insistence upon fairness and equity. This will force us to consider many kinds of conflicting rights. I doubt if we can argue that the immediate condition of all disadvantaged persons should be made as good as that of people who are not disadvantaged. We *can* insist that each major activity be tested by the extent to which the gap between those who have and those who have not is lessened rather than widened.

The spread in income between the top and bottom 10 percent or 20 percent of the population is 1-9 in the United States; in other industrial countries it is 1-3 or 1-7. In the United States this spread was slightly reduced between 1950 and 1978. Since then the percent of aggregate income received by the bottom 20 percent of the population has dropped, and the percent received by the top 20 percent has risen.[7]

Between 1965 and 1978, the proportion of Americans living below the official poverty line dropped from 16 percent to 11 percent. Only one percent of this decline was produced by the private economy; for 40 percent of families, the market share of income actually dropped from 11.0 percent to 8.5 percent.[8]

Even in relatively good times, private enterprise has not dealt with poverty at all. The reduction in federal income transfers can have only the result of increasing the proportion of people, especially of children, who live in poverty for reasons of economy, not of psychology. Even in 1600 it was recognized by governments that a poor and sick and ill-educated population could not produce wealth for the state.

There is no doubt that the strategy of the present administration is to widen the gap between those who have and those who have not. The only counterstrategy is to define ways in which we can appeal to the underlying sense of fairness against such an approach. Life in the jungle may not be fair, but as human beings we have constituted governments to increase the likelihood of fairness in treatment so that the social fabric of society remains strong, not torn apart.

3. While we resume the long struggle for work and fairness, we can also appeal strongly to the thousand-year-old concern for protection of the helpless. In a modern society, this includes not only maintenance of the well-being of the elderly who have played their part in society, but also attention to the protection of vulnerable children and youth, who constitute the future. The power of appeal for the elderly has recently been demonstrated in Congress.

---

[7]*John B. Oakes, "Tragicomedy Act II," New York* Times, *February 4, 1982, p. A-23.*

[8]*Sheldon Danziger and Robert Haveman, "The Reagan Budget: A Sharp Break with the Past,"* Challenge, *May/June, 1981, pp. 5–13.*

It has not yet been made so clear in relation to children, mainly because we are no longer dealing with orphans. Modern life places many parented children in the kind of jeopardy only orphans once confronted. But this is only dimly perceived by most citizens. These are old ideas, but concentration upon them might find a citizen response.

4. The age-old doctrine of reciprocity in welfare philosophy also has a contemporary value. Whereas reciprocity once meant salvation for the giver in giving, or peace against rebellion, today it means mutual aid and cooperative action at the grass roots and at the national level. Giver and receiver have newly defined obligations as well as rights.

Such foundations for the 1980s do not rely exclusively upon the appeal to do something for other people simply because it is "the decent thing to do." That will satisfy us, but not others. Instead, the importance of *fairness*, of *work opportunity*, of *protection* of children and the eldelry, and of *mutual aid* can be clearly demonstrated as essential to the economic health of the nation and the social stability of the nation.

But such a platform alone is not sufficient. We need to repeat and repeat and repeat a few elementary truths overlooked by the current White House rhetoric:

1. The federal budget is *not* being reduced, nor is the scope of government, despite the assertions of this administration. What has occurred is a shift of money for life to money for war. We do not object to a fair defense posture, but we can insist that it be paid for fairly and not mainly by the poor. The federal budget is increasing military allocations faster than the social budget is being pared, while tax concessions and give-backs go mainly to the well-to-do.

2. Evidence about state and voluntary ability to replace the federal government must be accurately displayed. The recent plan to transfer programs and taxes to the states was less than candid. In 1982, many states appeared to be in deficit. The states can do more only if they tax more, which means raising net tax levels while the federal "generous uncle" can claim to be cutting taxes.

3. Current policies increase unfairness, but our economic ability to reverse this is not zero, despite a depression. Our taxes as a percent of gross domestic product (GDP) are still among the lowest in the industrial world (sixteenth of eighteen), and our social expenditures as a percent of GDP are also lowest (thirteenth of eighteen). We need not demand equality, but we can call a halt to increasing inequality. We do not have to make households earning under $23,000 poorer by $30 billion while making households above that level $230 billion richer.[9]

4. We should yield to none our pride of country and history. But we can be clear-minded about what we are in danger of: dividing the population, one group from another; demeaning the poor and disadvantaged by insisting that their poverty is always their own fault; treating some classes so much better

[9]Oakes, "Tragicomedy Act II."

than the worst-off. The latter leads to: a breakdown in our nation's cohesiveness; a drop in our mutual confidence as well as in ourselves; a growing underclass, completely outside what was once a mainstream and which may now become one of several competing underground streams.

5. Finally, we should confront the current mythology that individuals are always to blame for their troubles but never community, government, business, or industry. It is an illusion that, left alone, these factors will assure both a vibrant economy and human well-being for all needs.

Social work has a long welfare tradition to draw on in facing this illusion. As far back as 1906, Edward Devine, president of the National Conference on Social Welfare, identified certain corporate behaviors as essentially exploitative both of individuals and of the national well-being: "Is it not time to recognize that practically all forms of . . . dependence require . . . some weakness in the individual *and* an overt temptation or an *unfavorable* condition external to him which would not be present at all if it were not to the advantage of another party to the transaction?[10] Note the emphasis upon the external social economic condition. The two Roosevelts, Eisenhower, and many presidents between them, have documented the case that reliance upon the abstract beneficiary of industry may result in greedy behavior and a reduction in national as well as individual well-being.

This is not so much a matter of accusing businessmen and large corporations of being evil (although some of them may be), but rather that our present narrow views about the sanctity of economic enterprise and of bottom-line profit force us to ignore the long-term consequences of some decisions taken by business.[11]

In this country, a concentration upon short-term gain rather than long-term economic thinking by both business and government may prove to be the flaw which needs to be directly confronted by social workers as well as by economists, for the social consequences of private decisions are more important than ever. Where the social consequences are destructive of the national well-being, those who make such damaging decisions need to be held accountable in one fashion or another in the same way that an entrepreneur who fails is held accountable through bankruptcy. We may be able to develop the concrete form of something we could call social bankruptcy to match that of economic bankruptcy so that the decisions made by industry and business on the one hand and by government and by individuals on the other can be treated equally.

Perhaps what we are facing is a transformation of our concept of equality: the search for equality of condition for everyone has a reciprocal: equality of responsibility by corporations and government plus obligation of beneficiaries to strengthen the national economy and cohesion.

---

[10]*Edward Devine, Conference on Charities and Corrections, Proceedings, Philadelphia (Press of Fred J. Heer, 1906), p. 9.*

[11]*Robert Hayes and William Abernathy, "Managing Our Economic Decline," Harvard Business Review, July-August 1980.*

We can accept the necessity for government to use tax dollars to bail out large corporations on the brink of failing because of their past policies or because of uncontrollable international events; but that kind of treatment also demands that individuals who suffer from those bad decisions or disasters— those who are unemployed or cannot find employment—may be treated by government with at least the same regard it treats managers and stockholders.

In sum, the period ahead calls for a reconsideration of the things which the supporters of social welfare hold dear, and a return to the basic core for human decency in behavior, which will also secure the widest support.

The Reagan administration seeks to divest the national government of as much responsibility for human well-being as it can get away with. Those of us who believe otherwise can only offer a counterprogram which requires accountability on the part of government and industry as well as of citizens: accountability for work or income, for fairness, for mutual aid and cooperation.

If there is not enough money to go around, then the wealthy as well as the poor, the military as well as civilian industry, are going to have to share the burden in ways which are appropriate to the strength and means of each.

The administration supports the strong with weak claims, as David Stockman acknowledged.[12] It is for us to support the weak who have strong claims.

---

[12]William Greider, *"Education of David Stockman,"* Atlantic Monthly, *December, 1981, p. 39.*

Social Security: Toward a More Equitable and Rational System

MARTHA N. OZAWA

SOCIAL SECURITY—the most popular social welfare program ever enacted in the United States since the Great Depression of the 1930s—has, for the first time, become a serious public concern. People of all ages regard Social Security as a necessary federal program for ensuring that the elderly have an income. Political leaders are concerned whether the current level of benefits can be maintained for a growing number of beneficiaries. Because Social Security constitutes a social contract between the young and the old, the successful resolution of the program's financial problems is of the utmost importance in preventing a generational conflict.

Social Security is facing both short-term and long-term financial problems. The short-term problem stems from the imbalance between revenues and outlays caused primarily by the poor performance of the American economy during the recent inflationary period. Inflation results in an automatic increase in benefits, and high unemployment prevents wages from catching up with the cost of living. Thus, the Social Security system has been paying out more in benefits than it has received in contributions.

Faced with financial difficulties in Social Security, the 97th Congress, through the Omnibus Budget Reconciliation Act of 1981, provided various measures to trim the outlay for Social Security. Under the act, the $122 monthly minimum benefit will no longer be provided to workers who retire after January 1, 1982. A father or mother with surviving children will no longer receive benefits when the youngest surviving child reaches age sixteen; the previous age limit was 18. The burial payment of $255 will no longer be provided unless surviving relatives exist. Finally, interfund borrowing among Old Age and Survivors Insurance, disability insurance, and hospital insurance funds wills be allowed.

Other proposals for solving the financial problems of Social Security are currently being discussed. Proposals range from the reallocation of tax rates among three trust funds, to use of a special consumer price index for calculating benefits, and raising the retirement age from sixty-five to sixty-eight.

MARTHA N. OZAWA is Professor, George Warren Brown School of Social Work, Washington University, St. Louis.

This paper was adapted from Martha N. Ozawa, *Income Maintenance and Work Incentives: Toward a Synthesis* (New York: Praeger, 1982).

The provisions already enacted and the proposals now being debated may be adequate for solving Social Security's short-term problems, but not its long-term ones. The long-term problems derive basically from the impending demographic shift. Currently, one Social Security beneficiary is supported by three workers. In 2030, when many from the baby boom generation will have retired, the ratio will decline to one to two. These provisions and proposals for solving Social Security's problems are incremental; predicated on the assumptions that the system is structurally sound in equity of benefits, in its dealing with the changing labor force participation of women, and with the increasingly greater demand of labor from the aged segment of society.

In my opinion, the incremental approach is not adequate to meet Social Security's long-range financial problems, nor is it structurally sound. Social Security benefits, particularly in the subsidy component, are inequitably distributed; the program is not adequately addressing the changing role of women in the labor force or fostering sufficient work incentives for the elderly. If these problems are dealt with effectively, economy of fiscal resources will result in the long run, and the substantial part of the long-range financial problems will be solved. Thus, this discussion of three basic problems in the old-age insurance component of Social Security: (1) subsidies through Social Security, (2) treatment of women under Social Security, and (3) the earnings test and work incentives for the elderly. On the basis of this discussion, recommendations are offered for reforming the Social Security program.

SUBSIDIES THROUGH SOCIAL SECURITY

Although most elderly persons on Social Security believe they have paid for Social Security through their past contributions, a sizable portion of their benefits is intergenerationally subsidized. Social Security is not a fully funded program. It takes the pay-as-you-go approach, using revenues collected from the working people to pay benefits for those who have retired. Taking a chain-letter approach, benefits of each cohort of retired generations are heavily subsidized by those still working.

How are such subsidies distributed? Are they fairly distributed?

Table 1 presents monthly benefits that are then disaggregated into two components of benefits—an annuity based on past contributions and interest, and subsidies—for workers who will retire at age sixty-five in 1982. It highlights the magnitude of intergenerational subsidies depending on level of earnings, sex, and marital status. Table 1 is based on the benefit/contribution ratios calculated by the office of the arctuary of the Social Security Administration. The office used the interest rate of 2.5 percent over the inflation rate to arrive at the current value of past contributions to the old-age insurance (OAI) component of the Old-Age, Survivors, and Disability Insurance (OASDI)

TABLE 1

DISAGGREGATION OF SOCIAL SECURITY BENEFITS INTO ANNUITY BENEFITS AND SUBSIDY
FOR HYPOTHETICAL WORKERS RETIRING AT AGE 65 IN 1982[a]

Type of Worker	Monthly Benefits	Benefit/ Contribution Ratio[b]	Annuity Based on Contribution	Subsidy	Subsidy as Percentage of Monthly Benefits
Single Male					
Maximum Earner	$705	2.485	$284	$421	59.7
Average Earner	555	2.755	201	354	63.8
Minimum Wage Earner	371	3.535	105	266	71.7
Single Female					
Maximum Earner	705	3.105	227	478	67.8
Average Earner	555	3.440	161	394	71.0
Minimum Wage Earner	371	4.410	84	287	77.4
Married Male Worker w/Dependent Spouse					
Maximum Earner	1,058	4.595	230	828	78.3
Average Earner	832	5.090	163	669	80.4
Minimum Wage Earner	557	6.530	85	472	84.7

[a]Figures based on intermediate assumptions (alternative II-B) in 1981 Social Security Trustees Report. Benefits are computed under the wage-indexed system, without regard to the transitional provision.

[b]In calculating the ratio, contributions by employers are credited to employees.

SOURCE: Data provided by the Social Security Administration, and by U.S. Congress, Advisory Council on Social Security, *Social Security Financing and Benefits: Reports of the 1979 Advisory Council on Social Security* (Washington, D.C.: U.S. Government Printing Office, 1979), Table 3, p. 65.

funds, and of future lifetime benefits.[1] To calculate lifetime benefits, the office used current probabilities of survival beyond age sixty-five. The table is also based on the following assumptions: (1) that workers contributed to the system from the time of the program's inception in 1937; and (2) that contributions made by employers belong to employees.

[1]*U.S. Congress, Advisory Council on Social Security,* Social Security Financing and Benefits: Reports of the 1979 Advisory Council on Social Security *(Washington, D.C.: U.S. Government Printing Office, 1979), pp. 58–68.*

In the preparation of Table 1, the ratio of the discounted value of lifetime benefits to the compounded value of lifetime contributions to OAI was superimposed onto the ratio of actual monthly benefits to the monthly benefits that past contributions plus interest might have bought in terms of an annuity. Table 1, then, shows monthly benefits broken down into two additive components: one is directly related to past contributions plus interest; the other is the amount in excess of contribution-based annuity benefits (in other words, the amount of subsidies).[2]

Subsidies in benefits for the elderly are substantial, as evidenced from the table. These subsidies vary, however, depending on level of earnings, sex, and marital status. Other things being equal, low-paid workers receive greater subsidies in proportionate terms. But in absolute terms (that is, in exact dollar amounts), high-paid workers receive more subsidies. Subsidies for married workers with dependent spouses are far greater than those for single workers, both proportionately and absolutely. This is because Social Security provides dependent spouses with 50 percent of the basic worker's benefit, the primary insurance amount (PIA). Thus, the absolute amount of subsidies for high-paid workers with dependent spouses is large indeed. Subsidies for female workers are greater than those for their male counterparts, attributable to their longer life expectancy.

How can one relate the distributive patterns of subsidies to the issue of equity? Put another way, who are subsidized more than others? Most experts in the field believe that Social Security subsidizes low-paid workers more than high-paid workers because low-paid workers receive greater subsidies in relation to their past contributions. Those who believe this tend to argue that benefits for low-paid workers should be reduced over time so that benefits for all workers will be in straight proportion to past contributions.[3] As though agreeing to this view, Congress, through the 1977 amendments to the Social Security Act, froze the minimum benefit at $122. In 1981 it eliminated the minimum benefit for workers who retire after January 1, 1982. This change reflects the policy direction to move Social Security closer to the image of private insurance. The problem with this view, however, is that Social Security provides much greater benefits than private annuity programs.

---

[2]*This breakdown is done by first dividing the benefit/contribution ratio into two parts. One part of the ratio represents the contributions plus interest; the other part represents the remainder or subsidies. By definition of the ratio, the segment representing contributions plus interest is always 1.0. Taking the ratio 2.485 (applicable to single, male, maximum earners) as an example, the portion in excess of 1.0—that is, 1.485—is attributable to subsidies. One can then break down the monthly benefits of $705 into two parts so that their ratio will stay the same: 1:1.485. When this is done, one arrives at $284 for contributions plus interest, and $421 attributable to subsidies.*

[3]*See, for example, Alicia H. Munnell,* The Future of Social Security *(Washington, D.C.: Brookings Institution, 1977); Joseph A. Pechman, Henry J. Aaron, and Michael K. Taussig,* Social Security: Perspectives for Reform *(Washington, D.C.: Brookings Institution, 1968).*

In my opinion, subsidies should be assessed on their own, independent of past contributions. After all, the government is not obligated to subsidize retirement benefits in proportion to the worker's past productivity. Furthermore, if subsidies reflect the social adequacy principle (or the welfare objective), one could question the wisdom of providing greater dollar amounts of subsidies to high-paid workers than to low-paid workers.[4]

This discussion suggests that a sizable portion of the Social Security outlay to the elderly could be redistributed in meeting their needs. For example, by distributing subsidies equally across all earnings levels, low-paid workers could receive more adequate payments. If, on the other hand, the legislative intent is to reduce Social Security expenditures, the benefits of high-paid workers could be justifiably lowered. Or, the legislature could consider changing the way in which benefits for dependent spouses are calculated. Lawmakers might move toward providing the dependent spouse with either a smaller percentage of the PIA (it is now 50 percent), or with flat-amount dependent benefits across all earnings levels.

TREATMENT OF WOMEN UNDER SOCIAL SECURITY

When the Social Security Act was passed in 1935, most females were homemakers. The condition of women is now quite different. More than one half of women aged sixteen and over work, compared with a little over a third in 1960.[5] Because more women work, the number of two-worker families has increased also. In 1940, for instance, in only three out of twenty households were both the husband and the wife working at the same time. But in 1980, in one half of all households both the husband and wife were working concurrently.[6] As a result, inequity in Social Security for single-working, married-working, and married-nonworking women is becoming more visible. To compound the situation, the increasing divorce rate is leaving many women without Social Security protection in old age unless they have been married ten years or more, or have worked long enough to be eligible for benefits. Thus, women in old age are in a complex financial security situation depending on their work history and marital status.

It is a challenge to reform Social Security so that women of different backgrounds will be considered more equitably. The changing role of women

---

[4]*For a detailed discussion on the issue of individual equity versus social adequacy, see Martha N. Ozawa, "Individual Equity versus Social Adequacy in Federal Old-Age Insurance," Social Service Review, March 1974, pp. 24–38.*

[5]Economic Report of the President, 1981 *(Washington, D.C.: U.S. Government Printing Office, 1981), p. 268.*

[6]*Richard V. Burkhauser, "Earnings Sharing: Incremental and Fundamental Reform" (paper presented at Conference on Social Security and the Changing Roles of Women, Cosponsored by the Institute for Research on Poverty and the Women's Studies Research Center, University of Wisconsin, 1980).*

provides an opportunity, moreover, for designing a more equitable and efficient program.

Under the present system, as shown in Table 1, single workers are discriminated against in comparison with married workers. Among married couples, the system favors one-earner couples over two-earner couples. One-earner couples receive larger benefits than two-earner couples even though their household earnings may be the same. Table 2 illustrates the inequity in treatment of couples under the 1982 decoupled benefit formula.

TABLE 2

BENEFITS FOR ONE- AND TWO-EARNER COUPLES
WITH THE SAME TOTAL EARNINGS, 1982

| | Average Indexed Monthly Earnings | Portion of Benefit Payable | | |
		As Worker	As Spouse	Total Payable
One-Earner Couple:				
Husband	$1,200	$517	$ 0	$517
Wife	0	0	259	259
Combined	$1,200			$776
Two-Earner Couple:				
Husband	$ 600	$325	$ 0	$325
Wife	600	325	0	325
Combined	$1,200			$650

The inequity results from the fact that one and one-half times the worker's benefit (PIA) at the $1,200 earnings level is larger than the sum of the two workers' benefits when each is at the $600 earnings level. Indeed, an empirical study by Burkhauser confirms the effect of the benefit formula on the amount of intergenerational subsidies received by different types of families. His findings indicate that, other things being equal, one-earner households receive larger intergenerational subsidies than two-earner households. Furthermore, the disparity becomes greater as the level of earnings increases.[7]

Faced with emerging problems of women, the Department of Health and Human Services (HHS) studied, under the mandate of the 1977 amendments to the Social Security Act, two alternative plans for the future of Social Security: the earnings sharing plan and the double-decker plan.[8] In essence,

[7]*Richard V. Burkhauser, "Are Women Treated Fairly in Today's Social Security System?" Institute for Research on Poverty Discussion Paper No. 530–78 (Madison, Wis.: Institute for Research on Poverty, University of Wisconsin, 1978).*

[8]*U.S. Department of Health, Education, and Welfare,* Social Security and the Changing Roles of Men and Women *(Washington, D.C.: the Department, 1979). An abbreviated version of this report was published in* Social Security Bulletin, *May, 1979, pp. 25–33.*

the earnings sharing plan allows the annual division of combined earnings of the husband and the wife into two equal parts, and lets each spouse establish his or her own account of earnings credits. The sharing of earnings credits would continue until one of the spouses reaches age sixty-two. If the couple were divorced, each spouse would take one-half of the combined earnings credits for each year of the marriage. At the time of retirement, benefits for each spouse would be based on the earnings of each while unmarried, one half of their annual earnings while married, plus the earnings of each after the division of earnings terminated. Thus, benefits for dependent spouses would become unnecessary and therefore are not provided for under the earnings sharing plan.

The earnings sharing plan follows the community property principle, practiced in eight Western states, and is enacted under the federal income tax law which provides joint income tax returns for married couples. This plan explicitly recognizes women's work at home as paid work and lets the husband pay for it by sharing his earnings credits. Under this plan, marriages are considered a partnership between a man and a woman who could claim equal right to, and obligation for, income security in old age.

The double-decker plan is structurally different from the earnings sharing plan. The double-decker plan provides each U.S. resident a flat-amount benefit of $122 a month (in 1979) upon attaining age sixty-five (a reduced amount at age sixty-two). This provision would constitute a universal first-deck flat-amount old-age pension. On top of this first-deck benefit, the beneficiary would receive a second-deck benefit based on the worker's earnings in employment covered by Social Security. The second-deck benefit would be equal to 30 percent of the worker's average indexed monthly earnings. The double-decker plan allows the sharing of earnings credits in a divorce, but not for calculating retirement benefits for each spouse of the married couple. Like the earnings sharing plan, the double-decker plan would not provide benefits for dependent spouses.

Both the earnings sharing plan and the double-decker plan go a long way toward establishing women's economic independence in old age. Under the earnings sharing plan, women are assured of economic independence whether they stay married or get divorced. Under the double-decker plan, divorced women would have this same financial protection. Under this plan, even those women who stayed married would be assured of at least first-deck flat-amount benefits. In either plan, women are considered workers whether they work for pay or work at home. The prototype of women under Social Security changes, then, from dependent spouses to workers. Such a transformation is compatible with the economic role that women now play, and will increasingly assume in the future.

In addition to addressing the changing role of women successfully, both plans would succeed in making the distribution of Social Security benefits more equitable. Under both plans, there no longer would be benefits for dependent spouses. Elimination of benefits for dependent spouses would make the treatment of different categories of women more equitable than at present; that is, these plans would establish a closer relationship between household contributions and eventual household benefits. Thus, other things being equal, greater earnings credits acquired collectively as a couple, or individually as a single worker, would always bring greater benefits. Anomalies in benefit provisions for one-earner and two-earner couples, as illustrated earlier, would no longer occur.

Elimination of benefits for dependent spouses would also economize the Social Security program. Under either plan, society no longer would pay benefits to dependent spouses. Under the earnings sharing plan, benefits would be redistributed from the spouse with greater earnings credits to the spouse with fewer credits when calculating retirement benefits or in a divorce settlement. Under the double-decker plan, a similar redistribution of benefits would occur in the divorce situation; otherwise, each spouse would depend on his/her own earnings credits beyond the protection that first-deck flat-amount benefits provide.

Both the earnings sharing plan and the double-decker plan would go a long way toward distributing benefits equitably among beneficiary households, and in economizing expenditures for Social Security. However, both plans fail to deal with the important issue of intergenerational subsidies. There is no way to determine in either plan what portion of the benefits are a return on past contributions (or an annuity), and what represents subsidies. Although the double-decker plan is conceptually close to the idea of partitioning benefits, it cannot be accomplished because second-deck benefits are earnings-related rather than contribution-based. When benefits are related to past earnings it is difficult to show how much is due to contributions plus interest and how much to subsidies. A further modification of the double-decker plan is necessary if a division in benefits is to be pursued.

Indeed, facing the issue of equity between generations—or, intergenerational subsidies—might be just as important as the issue of equity within the retired generation. How much in the way of subsidies can and should younger generations finance? During this time of financial austerity, expected to be even more severe in the next century, it is particularly important for all generations to come to grips with the problem of financing Social Security through intergenerational subsidies. Unfortunately, neither the earnings sharing plan nor the double-decker plan faciliates public debate on the vital issue of intergenerational subsidies and intergenerational equity.

THE EARNINGS TEST AND WORK INCENTIVES OF THE ELDERLY

Another controversial issue in Social Security is the earnings test (or the retirement test). Currently (in 1982), retirees aged sixty-five and over but younger than seventy-two are allowed to earn up to $6,000 a year without their benefits being reduced. (The exempt amount of $4,440 applies for those under sixty-five.) Earnings in excess of the exempt amount are subject to benefit reduction at the rate of $.50 for each dollar of excess earnings. The earnings test does not apply to those seventy-two or older. This age will be lowered to seventy in 1983. The elderly who are subjected to the test and who wish to earn extra income feel that they are subjected to an unreasonably high implicit tax rate on their earnings. Combined with Social Security taxes and possible income taxes, many elderly persons are implicitly taxed at 70 percent or more. Policymakers, too, might be concerned with work disincentives resulting from this earnings test. If the earnings test is discouraging the elderly from work, this is indeed bad for the elderly and the general economy as well. Also, decisions by the elderly not to work because of the earnings test may be causing larger Social Security outlays than is necessary.

Indeed, several studies indicate that the earnings test is related to retiring early or limiting work once retired. For instance, Boskin's study indicates that the earnings test increases the probability that the elderly will retire. He predicts that the liberalization of the earnings test would result in a significant decrease in this probability.[9] A study by Pellechio indicates that the earnings test reduces work effort among persons between 65 and 70 years, analyzed in the study, by 151 hours (or 8 percent) in a year.[10] Also, a 1969 study by the Social Security Administration shows that about a half of those who worked after retirement held their earnings within the exempt amount.[11]

Notwithstanding research findings on the effects of the earnings test, opinions are divided on the issue of the earnings test. Proponents of the earnings test argue that those affected by the test are high-paid professionals, as shown in a study by the Social Security Administration.[12] It seems to be unwise public policy to provide windfall benefits to such high-paid professionals by abolishing the earnings test. Abolishment of the test for those 65–71 would cost an additional $2 billion. The repeal of the test altogether would increase program costs by $6 to $7 billion.[13]

Probably a more compelling argument is that the Social Security program, as it is now constituted, is not an annuity fully paid by the retired population, but rather an earnings-replacement program through which a sizable intergenerational redistribution of income takes place. Thus the abolition of the earnings

---

[9]Michael J. Boskin, "Social Security and Retirement Decisions," Economic Inquiry, *January 1977, pp. 1–25; also see Michael J. Boskin and Michael D. Hurd, "The Effect of Social Security on Early Retirement,"* Journal of Public Economics, *December 1978, pp. 361–78.*

[10]*Anthony Pellechio, "The Social Security Earnings Test, Labor Supply Distortions and Foregone Payroll Tax Revenue," National Bureau of Economic Research Working Paper 272, 1978.*

[11]*Virginia Reno "Retirement Patterns of men," in* Reaching Retirement Age: Findings from a Survey of Newly Entitled Workers, 1968–70, *Research Report No. 47, U.S. Department of Health, Education, and Welfare, Social Security Administration (Washington, D.C.: Social Security Administration, Office of Research and Statistics, 1976), p. 32.*

[12]Ibid., *p. 35.*

[13]*U.S. Congress, National Commission on Social Security, Social Security in America's Future: Final Report of the National Commission on Social Security (Washington, D.C.: U.S. Government Printing Office, 1981), p. 146.*

test would result in even greater income redistribution from the working to the retired population, with most benefits going to the high-income elderly. It would be unfair to ask the working population to bear the burden of higher payroll taxes, a regressive form of tax.

The opponents of the earnings test have compelling arguments too. They argue that the earnings test is forcing many elderly persons to retire or curtail their work effort against their will.[14] Typically they are low-paid workers who need to supplement their small Social Security benefits with income through work.[15] Furthermore, if they did not work, the probability of their being in poverty would be decisively higher.[16]

Some may also argue that it is not fair for earned income to be subjected to the reduction in Social Security benefits, whereas unearned income, such as rent, interest, and dividends, is not. But again, the issue comes right back to the basic nature of Social Security. The program is not an annuity fully paid for by retired people. Thus, they cannot receive benefits unless they substantially withdraw from the labor force.

The dilemma is clear. The earnings test is detested by the elderly, considered an undesirable public policy by many policy-makers, and proven a deterrent to work by researchers. And yet, because Social Security is in part an insurance program against loss of earnings due to retirement, and is in part an instrument for redistributing income from the young to the old, policy-makers cannot simply repeal the earnings test. Faced with this dilemma, policy-makers have only two options: to liberalize further the earnings test, or provide a partial refundable income tax credit for people sixty-five and over who forego Social Security benefits under the earnings test. Such a tax credit measure was recommended by the National Commission on Social Security. Under the recommendation, workers sixty-five and older would be allowed to claim a fraction of foregone benefits (benefits multiplied by a specified multiple and by the lowest federal income tax rate) as a credit against federal income taxes.[17] If total elimination of the earnings test is desired, a drastic structural reform in Social Security is required.

---

[14]*Richard J. Zeckhauser and W. Kip Viscusi, "The Role of Social Security in the Income Security of the Elderly," in Michael J. Boskin, ed.,* The Crisis in Social Security: Problems and Prospects *(San Francisco: Institute for Contemporary Studies, 1977), p. 59.*

[15]*Virginia Reno and Carol Zuckert, "Income of New Beneficiaries by Size of Social Security Benefit," in* Reaching Retirement Age: Findings from a Survey of Newly Entitled Workers, 1968–70, Research Report No. 47, *U.S. Department of Health, Education, and Welfare, Social Security Administration (Washington, D.C.: Social Security Administration, Office of Research and Statistics, 1976), Table 9.7, p. 131.*

[16]*For example, for the couples newly entitled to Social Security benefits during January–June 1970, only 8 percent of those who reported earnings had income below the poverty line, compared with 41 percent of the couples without earnings. See Alan Fox, "Income of New Beneficiaries by Age at Entitlement to Benefits," in* Reaching Retirement Age, Table 8.7, p. 105.

[17]*U.S. Congress, National Commission on Social Security,* Social Security in America's Future, p. 139.

TOWARD A MORE EQUITABLE AND RATIONAL SYSTEM

So where do we go from here? How can policy-makers reform Social Security so that these three vital policy issues can be simultaneously resolved? How can Social Security be reformed so that: (1) subsidies are more equitably distributed across earnings levels; (2) women of different backgrounds are treated more equitably; and (3) the earnings test can be repealed? Policy-makers must deal with these problems simultaneously if they are intent on economizing social security outlays now and into the next century.

It is my opinion that these multiple goals can be achieved simultaneously if the double-decker plan developed by HHS is further modified. First, second-deck benefits should be directly tied to past contributions and interest instead of to the average indexed monthly earnings. In other words, they should amount to a lifetime annuity on the basis of past contributions and compounded interest. Second, the sharing of contribution credits between spouses should be allowed for calculating retirement benefits as well as for getting a divorce. In addition to these structural changes in the original double-decker plan, first-deck flat-amount benefits should be increased to the level of poverty-line income for a one-person family. First-deck flat-amount benefits would be financed by general revenue.

To summarize, the modified double-decker plan, all individuals aged sixty-five and over would receive noncontributory universal pensions (first-deck, flat-amount benefits), financed by general revenue, at the level of poverty-line income. On top of such benefits, the elderly would receive an annuity on the basis of their past contributions plus interest (second-deck benefits). The sharing of contribution credits between spouses would be allowed.

If such a modified double-decker plan were adopted, one could expect the following results with respect to the three policy goals. First, as second-deck benefits are an annuity—or the precise return on the past contributions plus interest—first-deck, flat-amount benefits would represent subsidies from the working population. All elderly individuals in the United States would then receive the same amount of subsidies from society. Absolute equality in subsidy payments is more equitable than unequal subsidy payments that depend on level of earnings.

Second, since the modified double-decker plan allows the sharing of contribution credits between spouses, economic independence of women would be ensured. Moreover, equity in treatment of single, married-working, and married-nonworking women would be greatly enhanced. Second-deck benefits for homemakers would be financed internally by the working spouse. That is, second deck benefits would be entirely by the beneficiaries themselves, directly or indirectly, regardless of work history or marital status. Thus, all women of different marital status and work history would be treated equally.

Third, because second-deck benefits are an annuity, at last the much detested earnings test could be repealed for second deck-benefits. An income test of any kind does not seem necessary for first-deck flat-amount benefits either since these benefits are universal pensions for all elderly persons. Work incentives among the elderly would improve if the first- and second-deck benefits were not subjected to an income test and to an earnings test respectively.

In addition to accomplishing these three policy goals, the modified double-decker plan would have several secondary positive effects. Making second-deck benefits an annuity would provide a conceptual and political breakthrough in Social Security. This double-decker model would clearly show both the retired population and the rest of society exactly how much past contributions of retired persons are worth in terms of benefits. The two populations would no longer suspect that either group was unduly taking advantage of the other. When all generations know exactly how much retired persons have saved for themselves through Social Security, then society as a whole can determine how much it wants to support the retired population over and above what the retirees have done for themselves. Such societal support would be expressed in first-deck, flat-amount benefits financed by general revenues. Also, the public would better understand the principles of social adequacy and individual equity as applied to Social Security if social adequacy were tied to intergenerational subsidies (first-deck flat-amount benefits), and individual equity tied to an annuity based on past contributions and interest (second-deck benefits). Under today's system, or under the original double decker plan studied by HHS, it is difficult to put these concepts into operation because benefits that reflect these concepts are commingled.

Further, if the level of first-deck, flat-amount benefits is pegged to the poverty-line income, the Supplemental Security Income program could potentially be eliminated. Such a move would remove social stigma from public income support for the elderly. All elderly persons—rich or poor—would be supported and cared for under one system of Social Security with a single ideological overtone. Indeed, the basic floor of income for the elderly, with no stigma attached, would be finally established in the United States.

Another secondary effect of the modified double-decker plan would be the establishment of intertemporal equity. Retired workers would then receive the same benefits regardless of when they worked as long as their contributions were the same. Second-deck benefits based on the average indexed monthly earnings, as presented by HHS, could not establish this type of intertemporal equity. For example, two retirees having the same average indexed monthly earnings, and thus the same Social Security benefits, may have paid different amounts of Social Security taxes depending on when they worked. This is attributable to increasing tax rates over the years. This situation would not occur if second-deck benefits amounted to an annuity.

Finally, the modified double-decker plan would create a built-in fiscal restraint. Each retiree's benefits would be equivalent to the investment value of that retiree's past contributions. Beyond that, benefits would depend on the judgment of Congress to finance first-deck, flat-amount benefits through general revenue. This way, the views of working people who foot the bill for the first-deck benefits would be incorporated in the decision-making. In addition to fiscal restraint, this model also provides flexibility in the use of financial resources since the level of first-deck, flat-amount benefits could be adjusted as Congress saw fit. For example, different levels of first-deck benefits might be provided depending on the age of the elderly. Or, as second-deck benefits become extensive, Congress could decide to reduce first-deck, flat-amount benefits. On the other hand, if Congress wished to maintain the range of combined benefits within a certain limit, it could keep the ratio of second-deck benefits to the first-deck, flat-amount benefits intact over time. At any rate, if a sizable portion of Social Security benefits were maneuverable—and indeed it would be under the modified double-decker plan—Social Security expenditures would be more in line with the value and resources of society at a given time in history. This would lead to economy in the Social Security program.

Social Security is indeed a "hot" political issue. Few politicians venture to speak out on the subject. Meantime, financial problems of the program are mounting. It is not too early for Congress to explore the facts pertaining to the distribution of benefits, the financing of the program, and plans for the future of Social Security. As elderly persons increase in number, the development of a just and fair Social Security system which cares for both the elderly and the nonelderly should be an exciting part of building our nation.

Workfare and Work Requirement Alternatives for AFDC Recipients

DEMETRA SMITH NIGHTINGALE

Major legislative and policy actions in 1981 and 1982 have potentially far-reaching implications for the national employment and training system, with particularly significant impact on recipients of public assistance. The Omnibus Budget Reconciliation Act of 1981 included workfare and training components for Aid to Families with Dependent Children (AFDC), thus amending provisions of the Social Security Act. Past programs, focusing on the financial incentive to work and on the provision of employment and training opportunities, have been criticized for not serving enough individuals and for not significantly reducing welfare costs. The recent legislative changes have increased the flexibility of state welfare-employment programs. However, the simultaneous reductions in budgets and work incentives in AFDC have reduced the resources available to program administrators. Several years of federal and state program experience, experimentation, and research in the welfare-employment areas provide insight into how these new changes might be implemented.

OVERVIEW OF WELFARE-EMPLOYMENT EFFORTS

Current Programs

The 1961 amendments to the Social Security Act allowed states to expand their AFDC programs to families with an unemployed father. Since that time there has been considerable public and political pressure to formulate policies aimed at getting able-bodied adults, especially males, off welfare and back to work. The community work and training projects, created in 1962 and expanded by Title V of the Economic Opportunity Act of 1964, were forerunners of the current Work Incentive (WIN) Program, established in 1967.

DEMETRA SMITH NIGHTINGALE is Research Associate, The Urban Institute, Washington, D.C. Opinions and conclusions are those of the author and do not necessarily reflect the position of the Institute or its sponsors. Gordon Berlin's contributions to this article are gratefully acknowledged.

WIN serves as the work registration program for AFDC. That is, certain AFDC recipients are required to register with the WIN program as a condition of continued eligibility to receive a grant. Individuals who are exempt from WIN registration include the aged, disabled, medically incapacitated, youth, mothers or caretakers of children under six or of a medically dependent relative, and students. Recipients who live unreasonable distances from a WIN office are also exempt, but may volunteer to register with WIN to receive employment and supportive services.

Since 1967 WIN has been jointly administered by the U.S. Department of Labor (DOL) and the Department of Health and Human Services (HHS). At the state level, employment security agencies and welfare agencies jointly run WIN. Until recently the DOL side has been the dominant partner in WIN. The Omnibus Budget Reconciliation Act of 1981, however, allows state welfare agencies to administer WIN alone on a three-year demonstration basis. Approximately twenty states are in the process of planning for the WIN demonstrations.

Services provided by WIN include: job counseling, job placement, work experience, on-the-job training, institutional training, employability planning, job-search instruction (particularly job-finding clubs), allowance payments during training, transportation to job interviews, and child care. WIN has experienced a 30 percent reduction in funds ($365 million reduced to $254 million) for the 1982 fiscal year, and the administration has proposed to eliminate the program entirely in the next fiscal year.

The Comprehensive Employment and Training Act (CETA) of 1973 is administered through DOL and has provided classroom training, public service employment, work experience, and on-the-job training with private sector employees. Economically disadvantaged persons are eligible for CETA services. This group includes those on the welfare rolls. Until 1978, however, little emphasis was placed on serving welfare recipients, and few CETA slots went to that population. The 1978 CETA amendments lowered eligibility requirements for participants and increased targeting toward welfare clients, thus encouraging somewhat improved coordination at the local level between welfare agencies and local prime sponsors under CETA.

The CETA program gradually increased its efforts to enhance the employability of welfare recipients. In fiscal year 1980, 22 percent of CETA participants were on welfare. CETA, however, has also taken drastic budget cuts in the past eighteen months. The elimination of public service employment (PSE) alone reduced funds by over 40 percent. Various legislative proposals have been presented for replacing CETA, which expires at the end of fiscal year 1982. All proposals provide for a significantly smaller training program (about half the funds that were formerly available), focusing on training in the private employment sector and targeting on youth and low-income individuals. Past experience of CETA indicates, however, that without strict targeting, welfare recipients are not likely to be given high priority.

Most state welfare laws require that recipients of general assistance also register for work and be actively searching for a job and/or "working off" their grants in a form of public service. These welfare programs are administered either locally or by the state and include individuals ineligible for federal funds. For example, New Jersey's general assistance employment program requires able-bodied welfare recipients to show up at sites either to work or to look for work. In Milwaukee County (Wisconsin), participants are paid subminimum wages for public work, mainly custodial and clerical jobs. In New York, state law requires employable recipients of home relief to register with the local job service and pick up their checks there. In addition, local social services departments in New York are required to establish public work projects and assign employable recipients to "work off" their grants.

Past Experiments in Reform

Over the past decade, several demonstration programs have been initiated to test various work and training alternatives for reforming the AFDC system, either by emphasizing extensive services or by focusing on the work requirement aspect of the program. At least three states have also experimented with workfare for AFDC recipients. The design and experience of these programs have been important in the various debates on national welfare reform.

The Carter administration's proposed program for better jobs and income (PBJI) included: (1) providing cash assistance to all low-income persons, (2) sanctions on those who refused to work, and (3) providing jobs to those unable to find employment. PBJI was not enacted, but the Employment Opportunities Pilot Projects (EOPP) were established by DOL in fifteen sites nationwide to test local CETA prime sponsors as administrators of this welfare reform concept. The main services to be provided under EOPP were job-search assistance (JSA), placement of clients immediately into regular private sector jobs, and a guaranteed public service employment (PSE) job if an unsubsidized job was not available.

The earliest emphasis in the EOPP demonstrations was the creation of enough PSE jobs to guarantee employment to clients who could not be placed in the private sector. Soon after planning for the program began, however, the main service priority shifted to intensive job-search assistance to train clients how to look for jobs themselves. The PSE portion of the program received less priority. In time, DOL turned its attention to the WIN mandatory work registration regulation of AFDC that was meant to assure that employable welfare recipients enrolled in JSA and accepted employment. The PSE portion of EOPP (and of CETA as a whole) was eliminated shortly after the Reagan administration took office and the main program emphasis became JSA. Most of the JSA efforts in EOPP were modeled on group job-search programs pioneered and tested in the WIN program.

The Minnesota Work Equity Project (WEP) was designed to reduce welfare costs, to develop uniform administration of work and training requirements, and to provide work experience to welfare recipients. When WEP began in

1976, the intent was to serve AFDC, general assistance, and unemployment insurance recipients in St. Paul and in forty-six rural counties. Gradually, however, WEP was limited to AFDC/WIN registrants in St. Paul, and to AFDC, general assistance and food stamps clients in seven other counties.[1]

The main emphasis of WEP was on placing participants in unsubsidized jobs. It also provided on-the-job training, institutional training, job-search skills, and social services. Major objectives of the demonstration were to test the ability of the CETA system to create meaningful public service jobs for large numbers of welfare recipients and to consolidate WIN and CETA into a one-stop service delivery system. The key aspect of the public service job creation in WEP was the use of community work projects, in which clients were placed for short-term work experience and employability development.

In contrast to the employability development and paid work and training for AFDC, EOPP, and WEP, California, Utah, and Massachusetts have attempted workfare, that is, unpaid work as a condition for benefits received.

California's Employment Development Department (EDD) ran an AFDC workfare demonstration, the Community Work Experience Project (CWEP), from fiscal year 1974 through fiscal year 1976. Employable AFDC clients were to be referred to nonpaying public service work. The major objective was to help the participants to become self-sufficient by obtaining regular unsubsidized employment. Equally important objectives included reducing overall welfare costs and decreasing the number of new AFDC applicants by providing recipients with more of an incentive to work.[2]

California's CWEP was to be mandatory for employable AFDC recipients in thirty-five counties. Local EDD staff first attempted to place individuals in regular jobs. If no jobs were available, clients were referred to a CWEP work assignment (also developed by EDD). While on a work assignment (up to eighty hours per month), clients continued to receive job-placement and employability services. The program faced serious resistance from county welfare administrators, and was never fully implemented. Therefore, it was not shown to be effective in reducing welfare costs or dependency. California's program has served as a model for the current national CWEP programs authorized in the Omnibus Budget Reconciliation Act.

Utah's Work Experience and Training Program (WEAT) has included a workfare component for AFDC recipients for the past three years. Unlike California's experience with CWEP, there has been little resistance to WEAT from legal groups and welfare rights organizations. Public and political support has been strong, and coordination with other programs has been smooth. WEAT is closely tied to the WIN program, has an employability development

[1]*Charles S. Rodgers and E.W. Stromsdorfer,* The First Interim Report for the Minnesota Work Equity Project *(Cambridge, Mass.: Abt Associates, 1979); M. G. Trend et al.,* The Minnesota Work Equity Project: Putting It Together *(Cambridge, Mass.: Abt Associates, 1979).*

[2]*California Employment Development Department,* Third Year and Final Report on the Community Work Experience Program *(Sacramento, Calif. 1976).*

emphasis, and serves WIN unassigned recipients (those who are not receiving other services) by placing them in a work component. This program has, as many others have, focused on working with men, mainly because of the high cost of providing day care if more women were included. No data are yet available on the long-term impact of WEAT on AFDC costs or caseloads.

Utah is currently expanding WEAT by linking vocational rehabilitation, WIN, food stamps, and general assistance in a coordinated effort to develop a range of alternatives for clients, including front-end job search training sessions, individual counseling, and development of subsidized career opportunities development slots in cooperating public agencies.

Massachusetts operated a highly publicized fifteen-month experiment called the Massachusetts Work Experience Program. The project was initiated because of growing concern over rising costs and long-term dependency. Originally, the intent was to require participants to work off their grants in workfare projects. Ultimately, however, the program was run as a work experience program, where screened recipients of AFDC under the unemployed parent component were required to work without pay for thirteen weeks, three days a week, and to participate in assisted job search the other two days.

As in California's CWEP, the Massachusetts program met serious opposition from staff who felt the rules were too punitive, and the program was delayed by court injunctions. The demonstration had difficulty recruiting participants, finding and setting up work sites, assuring attendance, and supervising the work.[3] In addition, since the program was being touted as a model for national welfare reform, it received attention from various advocacy groups. Their opposition, plus resistance from local staff, made it impossible to enroll enough participants to test validly whether or not the model could be effective in reducing the length of time AFDC-U cases remained open.

All of these programs have had to face difficult political, administrative, and implementation issues. All have been criticized for not serving enough individuals and for not significantly reducing welfare costs. WIN, CETA, general assistance work programs, and most of the recent AFDC work experiments have included some combination of: (1) enforcement of work requirement provisions; (2) reliance on the financial incentives in the AFDC regulations (income disregards, allowances); and (3) provision of attractive subsidized employment and training opportunities. Even with these programmatic assets it has been extremely difficult to reduce the welfare rolls and costs substantially.

While recent legislative changes have greatly increased the flexibility to serve welfare clients, the simultaneous reductions in budgets and income disregard incentives in AFDC have dramatically reduced the resources that program operators have with which to serve welfare clients effectively.

[3]*Barry Friedman et al.*, An Evaluation of the Massachusetts Work Experience Program *(Waltham, Mass.: Brandeis University, 1980).*

LEGISLATIVE CHANGES IN WORKFARE AND TRAINING IN 1981

The Reagan administration's response to the high cost of welfare is, in part, to strengthen the enforcement of the work requirement. The 1981 Omnibus Budget Reconciliation Act includes three major work and training components which would allow state welfare agencies broad flexibility in administering work programs and experiments while maintaining a strong work focus. The components are: (1) community work experience programs (CWEP); (2) WIN demonstrations where the state welfare agency can administer the WIN program through a single agency structure for three years; and (3) work supplementation programs.

Under CWEP state welfare departments will have nearly total discretion to set up mandatory workfare programs that include training, supportive service, job development, job clubs, and unpaid work assignments in public employment projects. This is the workfare component of the administration, designed after California CWEP run during the governorship of Ronald Reagan. An objective of CWEP is to provide work experience and training to AFDC recipients in order to move them into regular employment. AFDC recipients can be required to participate in CWEP if they do not have children under three years of age, and if child care is available.

New York, North Carolina, Ohio, and Michigan have been selected by the HHS to run CWEP demonstrations for up to three years. Other states may be added in the future. The legislation allows any state to implement CWEP programs by requesting waivers from HHS. Another six or seven states are likely to design workfare components under this act.

The legislation allows states the option of running the WIN program through a single agency for three years. The AFDC agency would be responsible for the entire program. Twenty-six states submitted plans for the WIN demonstrations. Six have since dropped their plan, and there are indications that three more may drop out. Several states may postpone implementation of the demonstration until after a decision on the continuation of WIN funding is made by Congress.

Over the years, WIN's dual-agency structure has been both praised and criticized. On the one hand, the structure has provided the opportunity to maximize the expertise and services available in each agency by removing clients' barriers to employment. On the other hand, the dual-agency system is more difficult and complex to administer. The WIN demonstration option is in response to claims by some welfare administrators that their departments are in the best position to enforce the AFDC work requirement and to serve clients' needs efficiently.

The third work component in the welfare legislation would allow state welfare agencies to establish an optional work supplementation program in portions of the state. This would allow states to subsidize employment of AFDC recipients in public and nonprofit agencies. Welfare grants can be reduced by allowing application of different needs standards for different categories of AFDC recipients. This employment subsidy would be financed by diverting funds saved from the reduced welfare grants.

These three provisions alone very clearly move welfare agencies into the work and training arena. The great discretion and flexibility are especially important, given that CETA is likely to be replaced by a much smaller, privately focused training program. Furthermore, there is a strong possibility that the WIN program will either be transferred totally to HHS or eliminated altogether. If WIN is terminated, it is possible that state welfare agencies may be required to establish work requirement programs to serve all AFDC recipients. Thus, the employment security agencies' role in welfare employment is gradually decreasing, and welfare agencies' role is increasing.

WORKFARE AND WELFARE ISSUES

The various welfare-employment programs have been enacted to reduce welfare dependency and program costs, to provide services that will benefit participants, and to respond to community, political, and public opinion toward welfare at any given time. Three issues important in implementing policy with these objectives are: (1) understanding the characteristics of poverty, (2) deciding on program focus and emphasis, and (3) managing the program and providing the necessary services.

CHARACTERISTICS OF POVERTY

In implementing and evaluating welfare-employment programs it is essential to consider the dynamics of the poverty population. First, the number of recipients on public rolls is not static. Studies have shown that more than 60 percent of welfare recipients move on and off welfare as their employment and family status changes.[4] This means that it is very difficult to measure, particularly in a short time, whether people are leaving the rolls due to a program's services or whether this would occur naturally without major services. Furthermore, it is not valid to assume that a person who leaves the rolls and remains self-sufficient for a short period will in fact remain off welfare for an extended period. Thus, it is extremely difficult to reduce the rolls significantly at any given time.

Second, there are clear differences among types of recipients of public assistance. For example, AFDC mothers typically have low educational levels, and little previous work experience. One study of WIN mothers estimated that 47 percent had not worked at all over a five-year period and 56 percent

---

[4]*Frank Levy, Michael Wiseman, and Frederick Doolittle,* Income Dynamics of the Poor *(Washington, D.C.: U.S. Department of Labor, 1976).*

had less than a high school education.[5] General assistance recipients are more likely to be single males between twenty and forty years of age. Fewer support services, particularly child care, are required to enable men to work. Not surprisingly, studies have shown that work programs with proportionately more males than females have higher job placement rates.[6]

Third, public opinion traditionally has been more insistent on men being removed from welfare and more sympathetic to mothers with children. This opinion has transferred also to welfare caseworkers and administrators. State and local practices have been more likely, therefore, to focus employment programs on men, either those on general assistance or on AFDC-U. Men are easier to place, more acceptable to employers, more likely to have previous work experience, and have few if any social service needs.

This philosophy has been used in some sectors to define the employable welfare population. AFDC mothers with children under six years of age have been exempt from registering with WIN. There is some indication that individual local welfare workers have declared persons in need of day care and those with less than adequate literacy skills as "unemployable."

Thus, even in a voluntary program, the determination of employability is critical, either before an individual is referred for registration or at the point of determining continuation in the program. The definition and application of employability criteria will strongly determine the number of clients who enter a program.

PROGRAM FOCUS AND EMPHASIS

Different attitudes and beliefs about the characteristics and dynamics of the poor have led to various philosophic emphases and objectives in welfare-employment programs. At one extreme are the coercive approaches. These include stringent work requirements for recipients of public aid, and adherence to sanctioning laws for those recipients who do not comply with the requirements. Workfare, or work-for-benefit programs, fall into this category. The assumption is that all persons who are able to work, should work, either in a self-supporting paid job or in a public work setting. This approach has been most common in state and local general assistance programs where men without children are the majority of recipients. Many states require local welfare departments to place employable general assistance recipients in public works projects where they must work enough hours to work off their grants.

Until recently, however, only a few states have experimented with workfare for AFDC recipients. Several reasons are obvious. First, since AFDC has

[5]*Leonard Goodwin,* The Impact of Federal Income Security Programs on Work Incentives and Marital Stability *(Worcester, Mass.: Worcester Polytechnic Institute, 1981).*

[6]*John J. Mitchell, Mark L. Chadwin, and Demetra S. Nightingale,* Implementing Welfare-Employment Programs: An Institutional Analysis of the Work Incentive (WIN) Program *(Washington, D.C.: U.S. Department of Labor, Employment and Training Administration, Research and Development Monograph No. 78, 1980).*

been mainly a federal program, states would have had to request federal waivers to set up workfare programs. The CWEP regulations now encourage states to experiment with the concept. Second, before requiring workfare programs for AFDC, costly supportive services, such as child care, must be guaranteed. This remains a critical issue in designing workfare. Third, there has historically been, and continues to be, less public and political pressure for forcing women with children to work than there has been for assuring that ablebodied men do not receive public assistance. Finally, state legislatures and county boards are more sensitive to costs of general assistance programs than of AFDC since general assistance is funded totally from state and local revenues.

At the other end of the spectrum are the assistant approaches to welfare-employment. These programs tend to focus on recruiting volunteers to receive intensive services. In EOPP, for example, there was initially a guarantee of a PSE job if a participant could not find unsubsidized employment. Similarly, CETA has always been a voluntary program attracting participants through outreach efforts and referral from other agencies.

Once again, research has shown that the critical part of a voluntary program is recruitment, screening, and outreach to draw the number of clients planned. EOPP, for example, eventually evolved into a mandatory program, integrated with WIN because of the difficulty of attracting eligible clients. This was particularly so when PSE was cut from EOPP and from CETA as a whole. The critical part of the program then became administering the work test, following up on no-shows, and instituting sanctioning if necessary.[7]

The WIN program and most state plans now being developed for employment and training policy in 1983 have a combination of coercive and assistant approaches. The work requirement attached to AFDC means that a portion of the recipients are mandatorily required to register and cooperate with WIN. Some states have placed very high priority on the work requirement and application of sanctions for those clients who do not cooperate. Imposing sanctions, the actual reduction of a grant, is very difficult and time-consuming, however, because of complex adjudication procedures backed by federal and Supreme Court rulings. Very few grants are cut and most grants are reinstated after the brief sanction period. In short, the adjudication process imposes more of a burden on staff than on clients. The existence of a sanctioning rule, however, satisfies political and community demands that welfare recipients be required to register for work.

Many states, on the other hand, have designed WIN programs that provide a wide scope of services, including individual counseling for clients with multiple barriers to employment. Noncooperative clients are counseled by employment and social services staff, and few clients are entered into adjudication. High-performing state and local programs were found to have this

---

[7]*Tracey Feild, Sabrina Deitrick, and Brenda Chapman-Barnes,* The Work Requirement and the Welfare Reform Demonstrations *(Washington, D.C.: MPR, Inc. and the urban Institute, 1981).*

approach toward dealing with noncooperation.[8] Thus a broad range of services, rather than any one component, was the most effective way to help individuals enter employment and reduce their welfare dependency and also to reduce overall welfare costs.

PROGRAM MANAGEMENT AND PROVISION OF SERVICES

Research studies of most recent welfare-employment programs indicate that there are extensive problems in implementation and management. The management problems in EOPP, WIN, CWEP, Massachusetts Work Experience, and Minnesota WEP have included delays in planning, insufficient resources to accomplish all plans, little staff training or technical assistance, inaccuracies in management information and reporting data, and lack of consensus on program objectives. In addition, programs have suffered when there is a lack of coordination with other agencies and programs. Services have often been duplicated by different programs, and agencies compete for the same clients.

When programs, especially demonstrations, encounter implementation delays and management problems, it makes client impact evaluation of the impact on clients very difficult. Evaluation results may show no effect of the program on clients simply because the treatments or services were never provided as planned. Thus, the failure of a design or a model should not be confused with failure of implementation. Ideally, a program should be allowed to stabilize, to reach "steady state," before evaluating its effect. This is usually not possible in the real world of social programs.

Many studies have found that the success of welfare-employment programs is affected by interagency communication and cooperation, local economic conditions, receptivity of employers, and the availability of complementary employment services, supportive services, and delivery methods. It has been shown that the availability of a wide variety of services and approaches is necessary to allow client needs and backgrounds to be dealt with during the transition from welfare to employment. An interagency approach, drawing on staff expertise in various aspects of the services, is one solution. Other problems, however, arise in coordination and cooperation across agencies and potential tension between different philosophies, as between social worker versus job developer. If those problems can be overcome, however, the services available to clients are enhanced and overall effectiveness increased.

Findings from a previous study that identified characteristics of high- and low-performing WIN programs suggest that certain types of service delivery components may work best for AFDC recipients.[9] First, high-performing programs provided clients with job-seeking skills, either in a formal model like job clubs, through individual counseling, or through a combination of the two. Second, job development efforts in the private sector were client-

---

[8]*Mitchell, Chapwin, and Nightingale,* Implementing Welfare-Employment Programs.
[9]Ibid.

oriented. That is, jobs were sought for specific individuals rather than collecting a list of job openings to which several participants might be referred. This individual approach seems particularly important in dealing with individuals with multiple problems. High-performing programs also were more likely to have a broad spectrum of supportive services available. Even if day care availability and funding were limited, social workers in WIN separate administrative units emphasized individual counseling, assisted clients in providing their own child care, offered counseling on home financial management, and assisted clients or referred them to other agencies where services could be obtained.

The group approach to job search has gained excessive exposure over the past several years. Job finding clubs, job factories, and self-directed placement are three of the major models used and adapted by local employment and training programs. The objectives of group job-search sessions are to: (1) cost-effectively provide needed skills and knowledge to job seekers; (2) use peer group interaction and support, instill motivation and self-confidence in participants; (3) intensively pursue job interviews through structured telephone contacts, sharing of leads, screening job openings in available sources; and (4) move a client immediately into a job.

Experiences with group job-search methods show that participants find jobs faster than through other methods.[10] Some of the EOPP job-search programs reported placement rates above 60 percent. Some program operators and staff, however, warn that emphasis on group job search may encourage some participants to accept too quickly jobs that are not suitable for them, and a number of individuals may not remain on the job, thus returning to public assistance. No studies yet have addressed the long-term status of welfare recipients exposed to job-search clubs, but the approach has clearly been an effective service option in the short run.

Finally, a major part of managing an employment and welfare program concerns maintaining the involvement of the business sector and representatives of other community and citizen groups. Federal and state policy-makers have responded to the importance of these sectors by making advisory groups an integral part of program administration. Public and community support in EOPP was shown to be a major asset, and lack of support or hostility can permanently cripple the operations.[11]

[10]*Robert Wegmann, "Job Search Assistance: A Review,"* Journal of Employment Counseling, *December 1979; Andrew Hahn and Barry Friedman,* The Effectiveness of Two Job Search Assistance Programs for Disadvantaged Youth *(Waltham, Mass.: Brandeis University, Center for Employment and Income Studies, 1981).*

[11]*Veronica Nieva et al.,* The Planning and Start-up of EOPP *(Washington, D.C.: MPR, Inc. and The Urban Institute, 1981).*

RECOMMENDATIONS

The three components of the Omnibus Budget Reconciliation Act and the forthcoming replacement of CETA are providing governors, legislatures, and state welfare departments a new opportunity to be innovative in designing comprehensive policies on work programs for welfare recipients. Unfortunately, the same policy-makers and planners are severely restricted by the extensive budget cuts in social programs, and a deep economic recession. Nonetheless, the foregoing discussions offer some guidance in designing state work requirement programs for welfare recipients.

Most important, the objectives of a policy or program, particularly a workfare component, should be clear. If reducing welfare costs is a primary objective, expectations must be modest. High turnover on welfare, short-term sanctions, and high numbers of clients with multiple barriers to employment (medical problems, low education levels, child care, lack of work experience, continuing race and sex discrimination) suggest that any employment program will have a difficult time to decrease overall welfare costs substantially.

If the primary objective is to move as many individuals as possible into unsubsidized jobs, then the program should emphasize job-finding clubs and other job-search and placement techniques which place responsibility for seeking work on the clients. It has been estimated that 60 percent of WIN registrants are able to participate in job-search sessions. The expected placement rate from a well-run six-week job-search program approaches 60 percent, at an average cost per client of $500.

If, however, the program is interested in reducing long-term welfare dependency, then employability development services, career planning, and extensive individual supportive services must be made available. The group job-search approach is likely to focus on quickly obtaining a job, often not at high wages nor with clear advancement possibilities. In order to increase individual wage rates, career development, and long-term employment, more costly services are necessary: institutional training, job development, individual counseling, remedial education, medical services, supported work experience, on-the-job training, and so on.

Part of the cost of intensive services, however, could be defrayed by considering innovative financing mechanisms. Legislation now allows grant diversions. Converting a welfare grant into wages, for example, with a cash or in-kind contribution from public or private employers, could be used to fund supported work experience and training. Coordination among agencies should also be encouraged to allow maximum flexibility in combining different funding sources. For example, CETA (or its successor program), WIN, AFDC, social services, economic development, and community development funds can all be used to support some form of employment initiative.

The determination of employability has been a most difficult aspect of work programs. Individual staff often make decisions on employability. Concerns about equity across clients and "creaming" the most employable for the best opportunities have been serious issues in all past programs. However, overstandardization of criteria for determination of employability has also been criticized, particularly by local staff who feel they are best equipped to decide on a case-by-case basis whether clients are employable and whether they should be required to cooperate with a work program.

The determination of employability and the application of sanctions are particularly important if a workfare component is included. The program must communicate to the public and to clients that receipt of welfare requires certain responsibilities and obligations to participate in a program of employment and training. To be fair and effective, that program must be able to provide real service and assistance to all employable, or potentially employable, recipients as well as actually to reduce grants of seriously noncooperative recipients.

If workfare, where recipients are required to work off their grants, is included there must also be clear and equitable criteria for determining which individuals go into a workfare position and which ones are given other options. The main goal should be to transfer individuals out of workfare, off the rolls, and into permanent unsubsidized jobs that will allow them to become self-supporting. Workfare assignments should be the last option, used only when other types of activities, such as intensive job search, job development, and remedial services, have not resulted in employment. While individuals are in workfare positions, they should continue to receive employability development services.

Finally, it is critical to develop cooperative relationships between the welfare and social services network and the employment security and training network. Dealing with the employment problems of the welfare population requires the expertise, knowledge, and services available from both professional systems. Receptivity of employers to hiring welfare recipients must be cultivated by professionals who are intimate with the operation and needs of the private sector. Supportive services, counseling, services for children and families can only be provided by social welfare professionals. Bureaucratic and interagency hostility and competition can seriously obstruct the development of an effective welfare-employment program.

The challenge of reducing welfare cost and dependency is enormous. Budget reductions, program uncertainty, and regulatory changes compound the problem. There are opportunities to design programs that are flexible enough to adapt to the different types of clients, innovative enough to provide a broad scope of service delivery options, and fair enough to balance enforcement of the work requirement with provision of employability development services to clients.

National Youth Service and the Black Community

FREDRICK E. SMITH and MICHAEL W. SHERRADEN

NATIONAL YOUTH service, or simply national service, refers to a program of nonmilitary national or community service. Generally, national service discussions focus on teenagers and young adults, and this is our primary interest here, although national service could include the elderly and other age groups as well. National youth service was first proposed by the social philosopher and psychologist William James. James' seminal essay, "The Moral Equivalent of War," was originally presented in 1906 as a major address at Stanford University. James viewed national service as a means by which a nation could maintain social cohesiveness in the absence of the external threat of war. He proposed a conscription of the youth population to provide a new sense of "civic discipline." In James' colorful language, young people would be sent off "to coal and iron mines, to freight trains, to fishing fleets in December, to dishwashing, clothes washing, and window washing, to road building and tunnel making, to foundries and stokeholes, and to the frames of skyscrapers." Childishness would be "knocked out of them." The moral equivalent of war would promote "toughness without callousness, healthier sympathies and soberer ideas."[1] Although James' words have an antique ring today, he did introduce the idea of national service in a memorable and lasting way.

Since James raised the issue, national service proposals have resurfaced on many occasions. Over the years such prominent individuals as John Conyers, Erik Erikson, Theodore Hesburgh, Hubert Humphrey, Morris Janowitz, Vernon Jordan, Margaret Mead, Willard Wirtz, and many others have called for national service programs. In the White House, both Franklin D. Roosevelt and Lyndon Johnson gave serious consideration to a permanent national service before World War II and the Vietnam War absorbed the nation's attention and resources. Today national service is supported by a bipartisan group in the Congress, and by a growing number of educators and others outside government. Due to pressing unemployment problems among young people

FREDRICK E. SMITH and MICHAEL W. SHERRADEN are Assistant Professors, George Warren Brown School of Social Work, Washington University, St. Louis

[1] *William James, "The Moral Equivalent of War,"* International Conciliation, *February 1910, p. 17.*

and the possibility of renewed debate on a military draft, there is a strong likelihood that national service will appear on the public policy docket some time during the 1980s.

Vernon Jordan, in writing about an "endangered generation" of black youth, has argued for structural changes that "go beyond inadequate piecemeal programs." Jordan has suggested "a National Youth Service, open to all, but with emphasis on aggressively recruiting young people from economically disadvantaged backgrounds." A major commitment to youth development, according to Jordan, "would enable Black youth to break the chains of poverty and discrimination that imprison so many millions of minority Americans."[2] To combat youth unemployment, which is officially reported at more than 40 percent for blacks, Franklin Thomas, President of the Ford Foundation, endorses compulsory national service of some kind for every young person, male or female.[3] Black leaders have viewed national service as a pathway out of poverty for unemployed black young people, hundreds of thousands of whom are looking for work and unable to find it.

THE UNEQUAL ECONOMIC AND SOCIAL BURDEN ON BLACK YOUTH

Although the nation has witnessed high rates of unemployment and other economic and social problems among young people of all races, a disproportionate share of the burden has fallen on blacks. The unemployment rate for young blacks is much higher than for young whites. This holds true in suburbs and nonmetropolitan areas as well as central cities. Moreover, the long-term trend is toward increasing disparity. As the labor market has become less hospitable to young workers, blacks have been squeezed out of employment at a much higher rate than whites. At the end of 1981, black teen-age unemployment had reached a staggering 44.5 percent. In Detroit, unemployment among black teens had risen to 68 percent.[4]

For those inclined toward a victim-blaming analysis of these unemployment statistics—that is, that blacks lack motivation, are inherently less intelligent, do not dress or talk appropriately, or any of a thousand other variations on this theme—it is illuminating to look at some inequalities in the way black and white children grow up in America. Marian Wright Edelman and Paul V. Smith of the Children's Defense Fund are the authors of a work that clearly and succinctly details differences in the social and economic conditions faced by blacks and whites when they are children.[5] A few examples of the relevant

---

[2]*Vernon E. Jordan, Jr., "Black Youth: The Endangered Generation,"* Ebony, *August 1978, p. 88.*

[3]*Cited in Ken Auletta, "The Underclass," Part III, New Yorker, November 30, 1981, p. 139.*

[4]*"Black Teenagers Without Jobs: Time Bomb for U.S.,"* U.S. News and World Report, *January 18, 1982, pp. 52–54, citing statistics from the U.S. Department of Labor.*

[5]*Marian W. Edelman and Paul V. Smith,* Portrait of Inequality: Black and White Children in America *(Washington, D.C.: Children's Defense Fund, 1980).*

data begin to describe the problem: Less than half of all the black children live in a two-parent household, while more than four fifths of all white children live with two parents. The per capita family income for blacks is 55 percent that of whites. One in four black children has no parent in the labor force, while the ratio is one in sixteen for white children. Almost half of all black families are headed by a person who has not graduated from high school, while only one quarter of all white families are headed by nonhigh-school graduates. The infant death rate for blacks is twice as high as for whites. Teen-age childbearing rates are much higher for blacks than for whies, and larger percentages of blacks have out-of-wedlock births. As a percentage of population, more black children than white children are not immunized against major preventable diseases. More black children than white children have nutritional intake below established standards. More than twice as many black children as white children live in inadequate housing. Twice as many black children as white children live in some kind of institutional setting away from home.

This is a portrait of racism. With disadvantages so deep and passed along from generation to generation, it is not surprising that black youth have not competed successfully in the labor market. Blacks contend not only with outright discrimination, but also with backgrounds of poverty, inadequate housing, poor health care, inadequate schools, and all the other negative effects of institutionalized bigotry. These effects will not easily disappear, especially in the political and economic climate ushered in by the 1980 elections. Black youth will face the same disadvantages as in the past and quite possibly worse. Bernard Anderson has recently assessed future employment prospects for black youth:

> Projections for the years ahead promise continued labor market difficulties for black youth. Although their numbers will begin to decline in the late 1980s, the rate of decline will be significantly less than that among white youth. For example, the annual rate of change in the labor force among black men age 16–24 will be about 1 percent while that among white men of the same age will decline by 2.4 percent. As a result, black youth will comprise an increasing proportion of the youth population, and probably will continue to be concentrated in areas with limited job opportunities.
>
> The challenge of reducing black youth unemployment will also be more difficult because of increased competition for jobs. According to the U.S. Bureau of Labor Statistics, black workers must obtain at least one of every five new jobs created during the 1980s, if the black-white unemployment gap is to be closed. This goal will be hard to reach at a time when many well-prepared youths will be looking for good job opportunities. For example, BLS predicts that nearly one college graduate in four will probably have to enter an occupation not previously requiring a college degree during the 1980s, because the pace of job creation will not keep up with the flow of graduates leaving college. Black youth have

narrowed, but not eliminated the differential between their college enrollment and that of white youth. Also there are still broad differences between the two youth groups in college completion, and large numbers of economically disadvantaged black youth still drop out of high school and never get to college. For such youth, labor market opportunities will be bleak.[6]

Crime is another area in which black youth bear a disproportionate burden, both as perpetrators and as victims. With such severely restricted employment opportunities, anger and economic necessity are evidenced in crime statistics at very young ages. Among eleven- to seventeen-year-olds, the major property crime arrest rate for blacks is more than twice as high as that of whites; and the violent crime arrest rate for young blacks is seven times greater than that of young whites.[7]

It is startling that youths under seventeen already exhibit marked statistical differences in arrests for serious crime by race. Part of the difference is probably due to preferential treatment of whites by police and juvenile authorities; that is, white youths are reprimanded and released to parents without criminal charges more frequently than black youths. But greater leniency for whites does not explain all the differences. Many blacks react at young ages, through crime, to the dismal future which lies ahead of them. The message is delivered very early in life to many black children that society does not have a place for them.

The violence which results also disproportionately affects black young people as victims of crime, especially in number of homicides. Black young people ages one through nineteen are killed by homicide at five times the rate of whites in the same age group.[8]

Would a program of national service begin to deal with the unemployment, crime, and other problems which literally destroy the futures of so many black young people? As a starting place in discussing this question, it is instructive to look at some past experience with national service programs in the United States.

PRECEDENTS: NATIONAL SERVICE EXPERIENCE IN THE UNITED STATES

By far the largest and most prominent category of service opportunities has been not civilian service, but military service. In general, the military has

[6]Bernard E. Anderson, "Economic Patterns in Black America," in James D. Williams, ed., The State of Black America 1982 (Washington, D.C.: National Urban League, Inc., 1982), pp. 1–32.

[7]Calculated from U.S. Department of Justice, Sourcebook of Criminal Statistics, 1977 (Washington, D.C.: U.S. Government Printing Office, 1978), table 4.7.

[8]Calculated from U.S. Department of Health, Education, and Welfare, Health, United States, 1976–1977 (Washington, D.C.: U.S. Government Printing Office, 1977), Tables 26, 27, and 28.

provided many blacks with a pathway toward economic security that otherwise would not have been open. In a labor market that has discriminated so heavily against blacks, the military has been a major employment alternative. This alternative, however, has been controversial in the black community from the Revolutionary War through the Vietnam War to the present all-volunteer army concept. Elsewhere, Smith emphasizes that this controversy tends to subside "with the rattle of sabers or the sound of gunfire."[9] Blacks have paid disproportionately with their blood and their lives during times of war. The military, for the rewards it has offered blacks, has in turn exacted a high price.

The Freedmen's Bureau

Nonmilitary service programs have been far less prominent in the United States than in other countries, but there have been a few major experiments from which lessons can be drawn. Some of these have had great economic and political impacts on the black community. One of the first was the Port Royal Experiment in the South Carolina Sea Islands during the early 1860s. The Port Royal Experiment was created by charity organizations and Freedman Aid Societies to demonstrate that blacks, especially freedmen, could be self-sufficient. This venture and similar activities were the basis for the most comprehensive service program in the United States prior to Roosevelt's New Deal—the Freedmen's Bureau. This program, enacted by Congress in 1865, was under military auspices and officially called the Bureau of Refugees, Freedmen, and Abandoned Lands. Refugees, mostly whites, numbered more than four million. Freedmen, in the main freed slaves, also numbered about four million. The program soon came to be known simply as the Freedmen's Bureau. It was designed to provide economic, social, and educational rehabilitation for the newly freed slaves and refugees.[10] The Freedmen's Bureau promoted self-reliant agricultural communities, established Freedmen's Banks and Freedmen's Hospitals, and emphasized higher education—all with the purpose of enabling freed blacks and refugees to work and serve together and become productive U.S. citizens. Many of the projects of the Freedmen's Bureau can be interpreted as precursors to the idea of national service.

Civilian Conservation Corps

In the twentieth century, the first major national service experiment, and among the largest, was the Civilian Conservation Corps (CCC) of the 1930s. The CCC was, in Franklin D. Roosevelt's own word, his "baby." It was a conservation-oriented work program for unemployed young men during the

---

[9]*Fredrick E. Smith, "The Military and Military-like Institutions as Social Welfare Resources in Stabilizing the Black Community,"* in Proceedings of the Tenth Annual Conference of the National Association of Black Social Workers, *(Detroit: National Association of Black Social Workers, 1978), p. 297.*

[10]Ibid.

depression era. Altogther, the CCC enrolled some three million young men over a nine-year period (1933–42). The CCC was productive and popular, with a broad base of political and public support.

How did blacks fare in the CCC? By any objective standard, black enrollees were discriminated against. They were segregated into black camps, and most of the officers in these camps were white. Accounts of red-neck white officers causing disruptions in black camps were fairly common. Racist statements by the CCC officials were the rule rather than the exception, such as a reference to "darkies" by the CCC director.[11]

Such discrimination, however, was no worse than blacks encountered in most job situations at the time. And, as marginal workers in a depressed economy, blacks desperately needed jobs. Virtually any employment opportunity was welcome, and economic considerations far outweighed the familiar insults of bigotry. Black enrollees in the CCC were, above all else, glad to be working.

Evidence supporting this conclusion is abundant. Blacks struggled against discriminatory selection practices to get into the CCC. Selecting agencies in some states systematically attempted to keep blacks out of the program. Nonetheless, blacks persisted; and with the aid of official policy in Washington, blacks gained access to the program. Official CCC statistics reported that, overall, about 10 percent of enrollees were black. (At the time, 12.8 percent of the total youth population was black, and black youth represented 15.3 percent of the "relief" youth.[12]) Once enrolled, black CCCers stayed in the program an average of 50 percent longer than whites—fifteen months for black and ten months for whites. In other words, blacks were much more likely than whites to enroll for second and third six-month terms.[13] In effect, blacks "voted with their feet" in favor of the CCC.

Were black enrollees satisfied with the CCC experience? A random sample of CCC camp inspection reports has indicated that there was virtually no difference in either camp morale or nonhonorable discharges between black and white camps. Black camps and white camps were rated about the same on morale by CCC inspectors, and enrollees in black and white camps tended to desert or receive dishonorable discharges in about the same numbers. On a five-point morale-rating scale, where 5.0 was the most positive, the mean rating for black camps was 3.57; for white camps the mean rating was 3.54. Regarding nonhonorable discharges in a twelve-month period, the mean for black camps was 35; the mean for white camps was 34. These small differences

---

[11]*Michael W. Sherraden, "The Civilian Conservation Corps: Effectiveness of the Camps," (doctoral dissertation, University of Michigan, 1979), p. 136, citing CCC records in the U.S. National Archives.*

[12]*O. L. Harvey and Mapheus Smith,* Statistics of Youth on Relief, *Research Bulletin, Series I, No. 16 (Washington, D.C.: Works Progress Administration, 1936), pp. 1–3.*

[13]*John A. Salmond,* The Civilian Conservation Corps, 1933, 1942: a New Deal Case Study *(Durham, N.C.: Duke University Press, 1967), pp. 88–101.*

do not come close to statistical significance.[14] Overall, the data indicate that blacks were about as satisfied with the CCC experience as whites.

National Youth Adminstration

A second major youth program of the New Deal was the National Youth Administration (NYA). The NYA was a more diversified program, aiding students as well as nonstudents, and undertaking many projects in urban areas. Like the CCC, the NYA was a definite benefit to black youth, although the same problems of discrimination in selection and less than equal treatment in the program are well documented.[15]

Young Adult Conservation Corps

A modern equivalent of the old Civilian Conservation Corps has been the Young Adult Conservation Corps (YACC). YACC began in 1978 as a conservation-oriented employment program for unemployed sixteen- to twenty-three-year-olds, both male and female. In fiscal 1980, YACC served 66,500 young people; 27 percent were nonwhite.[16] The YACC, like the old CCC, has provided economic benefits equal to or exceeding its costs.[17] New York's mayor, Edward Koch, recently reported that YACC crews of primarily black and Hispanic high school dropouts had completed work at a cost of $2.9 million in seventy New York City parks that would cost an estimated $8.8 million in the open market. The mayor called YACC "critical for urban areas."[18] Thus, the CCC idea has been applied to urban as well as rural areas and has proved its worth. Unfortunately, the Reagan administration has cut funding for YACC. The program is scheduled for elimination after 1982.

ACTION Programs

Two other experiments in urban areas are instructive in considering national service and its impact on black communities. ACTION, a federal agency created in 1971 to house the Peace Corps, VISTA, and other volunteer programs, became the sponsor of a national service experiment in Seattle in

[14]Sherraden, "The Civilian Conservation Corps," p. 129.

[15]Walter G. Daniel and Carroll L. Miller, "The Participation of the Negro in the National Youth Administration Program," Journal of Negro Education, 7 (1938) 357–74.

[16]Employment and Training Report of the President, 1981 (Washington, D.C.: U.S. Government Printing Office, 1981), pp. 37–38.

[17]John L. Fulbright, Jr., Director, Office of Youth Programs, Department of the Interior, testifying before the U.S. Senate, in Hearings: Presidential Commission on National Service and National Commission on Volunteerism, March 13, 1980 (Washington, D.C.: U.S. Government Printing Office, 1980), p. 141.

[18]Edward Koch, Mayor, New York City, testifying before U.S. House, Hearings: Youth Conservation Corps and Youth Adult Conservation Corps, June 25 and July 17, 1981 (Washington, D.C.: U.S. Government Printing Office, 1981), p. 160.

1973–74 and a second national service experiment in Syracuse between 1978 and 1980.

The 1973–74 Program for Local Service (PLS) in Seattle, destroyed several myths about national service and yielded valuable lessons for the future. PLS volunteers covered the socioeconomic spectrum. One in ten came from households with incomes below $1,000 per year, and a similar proportion of volunteers had personal incomes greater than the amount they would receive in PLS. A few were mentally retarded; some had college degrees. One was a veteran of military service. A few had criminal records. Of every ten PLS volunteers, two were members of minority groups, six were women, and seven were unemployed and looking for work.

Two of the most dramatic findings relate to the two major reasons given by young people for joining PLS, namely, contributing to the community and gaining work experience. The sponsoring agencies estimated the work done by PLS volunteers to be worth $2,150,000 almost double the $1,086,000 federal grant which funded the program.[19] And the unemployment rate among persons in PLS fell from 70 percent at time of application to 18 percent six months after their leaving PLS.[20]

A second ACTION national service experiment, Youth Community Service (YCS) in Syracuse, New York, operated between 1978 and 1980. There were approximately two thousand volunteers between the ages of sixteen and twenty-one. All volunteers were out of school, unemployed, and looking for work. Service projects included social services, recreation, education, and conservation.

IMPACTS: NATIONAL SERVICE AND THE BLACK COMMUNITY

We have noted that national service experiments, in a variety of forms, urban and rural, and at different times in history, have had positive employment impacts for blacks. This point alone, from the standpoint of the black community, is ample justification for implementing national service. Job opportunities are a critical necessity in most black communities. In addition, there are other national service impacts on participants which positively affect the community; these include improved self-confidence, improved social maturity, and avoidance of criminal behavior.[21] But these outcomes, as worthwhile as they are, are secondary reasons for undertaking national service projects in black communities.

---

[19]*Control Systems Research,* The Program for Local Service: Special Report *(Seattle: Control Systems Research, 1973), pp. 4–12.*

[20]*Kappa Systems, Inc.,* The Impact of Participation in the Program for Local Service Upon the Participant *(Arlington, Va.: Kappa Systems, 1975), Sections 2 and 4.*

[21]*Michael W. Sherraden and Donald J. Eberly, "The Impact of National Service on Participants," in Sherraden and Eberly, eds.,* National Service: Social, Economic, and Military Impacts *(New York: Pergamon Press, 1982), pp. 179–87.*

The primary reason to implement national service is that there is much to be done in these communities. Many impoverished urban areas, in particular, have suffered decades of neglect and destruction. In thinking about national service possibilities in black communities, there is no need to be as romantic as William James in proposing that young people be sent off "to coal and iron mines, to freight trains, to fishing fleets in December," and so forth. For most blacks, there is plenty of work to be done right where they live. The possibilities for projects in energy conservation, day care, education, health, housing, services to the elderly and disabled, recreation, public safety, and public works are nearly endless.

Looking at the nationwide picture, various surveys in the past two decades have pointed to a need for some four million unskilled or semiskilled people in public service work. One recent survey, completed by the Urban Institute and American Institutes for Research in 1978, identified 233 areas of activity and then reported on the need for workers in 115 of these areas. Claiming that the estimates were conservative, the survey found a need for 3,000,000 work years in these 115 areas.[22] A study conducted by Donald Eberly in 1970 for the Russell Sage Foundation identified a need for 4,000,000 nonprofessional service years,[23] a figure consistent with studies in other years.[24] Experience with national service test projects—PLS in Seattle and YCS in Syracuse—has confirmed that service opportunities exist in at least these numbers.[25] In impoverished urban communities, due to long-term neglect of public facilities, and a pressing need for social services, the concentration of needed work is much greater.

Occasionally the argument is put forth that there really is not additional work that needs to be done in our society. According to this view, high levels of unemployment are an indication that there is not enough work that genuinely needs to be done to keep everybody employed.[26] This perspective can be used as a smoke screen for repression and racism, and therefore its thin reasoning should be exposed. For one thing, this view is adrift from the moorings of reality; it is a view which is ignorant of the difficult conditions in which many people live their lives. It is ignorant to suggest, for example, that there is no need for energy conservation projects in a community where

[22]*The Urban Institute,* Assessing the Feasibility of Large-Scale Countercyclical Public Job-Creation, *3 vols. (Washington, D.C.: Urban Institute, 1978).*

[23]*Donald J. Eberly,* The Estimated Effect of a National Service Program on Public Service Manpower Needs, Youth Unemployment, College Attendance, and Marriage Rates, *(New York: Russell Sage Foundation, 1970).*

[24]*Donald J. Eberly,* A Plan for National Service, *(New York: National Service Secretariat, 1966), Donald J. Eberly, "A Model for Universal Youth Service" (paper presented at the* Universal Youth Service Conference, *Eleanor Roosevelt Institute, Hyde Park, N.Y., 1976)*

[25]*Control Systems Research,* The Program for Local Service; Youth Community Service, *Report to the Community (Syracuse, N.Y.: Youth Community Service, 1980), p. 2.*

[26]*One of the more informed and sophisticated analyses suggesting that there is not additional work that needs to be done is by David Macarov,* Work and Welfare: The Unholy Alliance, *(Beverly Hills, Calif.: Sage, 1980).*

people are forced to choose between buying food or being warm during the winter months. It is ignorant to suggest that there is no need for services to the elderly in a community where disabled old people live by themselves and have no way to get out of the house for food and medicine. It is ignorant to suggest that there is no need for parks and playgrounds in communities where children play in abandoned buildings. And all of this in neighborhoods where people are looking for work and unable to find it.

The view that there is not work that needs to be done assumes that the market is infallibly the wisest and most efficient mechanism for allocating goods, services, and jobs. This "invisible hand" perspective, however, rests on assumptions which included perfect competition and absence of discrimination—conditions which simply do not exist in the real world. The invisible hand is a myth which the rich find convenient to rationalize greed and exploitation, and it is a slap in the face to the poor.

There is abundant evidence that a planned program of national service can undertake and accomplish needed work, and do so on an economically efficient basis. This case is presented by Sherraden and Eberly, who point out, for example, that the value of the timber in CCC reforestation projects would pay for the original cost of the CCC many times over.[27] For example, note the value of the tree planting that was done in the Capital Forest area near Olympia, Washington:

> During the early 1920s and into the 1930s the Capital Forest area was completely devastated by intensive private logging operations. The land was abandoned as being of no further value to its owners and was taken over by the state. During 1934–1939, 90,000 acres of this land were reforested by the CCC at an approximate cost of $270,000. In 1960 commercial thinning began and the first returns on this investment began to be realized. Today, 1981, the acreage is being harvested with the timber value placed conservatively at $7,000 per acre or $630,000,000 total.[28]

In this example, $270,000 invested in the 1930s is valued at $63 million in 1981. This represents a 2,333-fold increase in value. As a nation we have reaped tremendous economic benefits from the work of the CCC. The positive economic returns of YACC, the PLS, and other national service-like experiments have also been documented.[29] Looking at the productivity record of the California Conservation Corps, a state-run program, the Los Angeles

---

[27]*Michael W. Sherraden and Donald J. Eberly, "The Economic Value of Service Projects,"* in Sherraden and Eberly, eds., National Service *pp. 163–78.*

[28]*Human Environment Center*, Background Information on YACC Activities in Washington and Oregon *(mimeographed; Washington, D.C.: Human Environment Center, 1981), p. 1.*

[29]*Sherraden and Eberly, "The Economic Value of Service Projects," in Sherraden and Eberly,* National Services.

Times commented: "We cannot think of any part of the state budget that gets that kind of return on a very small investment."[30]

National service has established its worth. There is no need to think in terms of "make work" or "keeping young people busy." There is plenty of important work to be done and, when productivity is emphasized, young people have consistently demonstrated that they can undertake projects which yield benefits exceeding costs.

NATIONAL SERVICE: SUPPORT AMONG BLACKS

The black community has recognized the potential of national service for some time. The Gallup Poll has periodically asked about universal national service. The Gallup question is worded as follows: "Would you favor or oppose requiring all young men to give one year of service to the nation—either in the military forces, or in nonmilitary work here or abroad, such as VISTA or the Peace Corps?" In 1971, 68 percent of whites and 69 percent of blacks favored this proposal. In 1976, 62 percent of whites and 64 percent of non-whites favored the proposal.[31] Note that this is the level of support for *compulsory* service. When Gallup has asked about voluntary service, support has been even stronger.

Support for the idea of national service is one thing, but who would actually volunteer for national service? In a 1979 survey of thirteen- to eighteen-year-olds, Gallup asked specifically if respondents were interested in volunteering. Among non-white youth, 37 percent said "Yes, definitely," and an additional 25 percent said "Yes, might be." Among white youth, the response was 19 percent "Yes, definitely" and 31 percent for "Yes, might be." Thus, among non-white youth, a total of 62 percent gave a positive response, compared to a total of 50 percent for white youth.[32] Based on these remarkable levels of support, it seems likely that both non-white and white youth would respond in large numbers to national service opportunities, and non-whites even more so than whites.

NATIONAL SERVICE: A PROPOSAL

With high levels of public support for national service, and also increasing support among the nation's leaders,[33] it is likely that national service, in some form, will be adopted in the 1980s. If national service becomes a reality in

---

[30]*Los Angeles* Times, *February 23, 1981.*

[31]*George Gallup,* The Gallup Poll: Public Opinion 1972–77 *(Wilmington, Del.: Scholarly Resources, Inc., 1978).*

[32]*George Gallup, "Who's for National Service?" in* National Youth Service: What's at Stake? *report of a Conference sponsored by the Committee for the Study of National Service (Washington, D.C.: Potomac Institute, 1980), pp. 15–22.*

[33]*Some of this leadership support is reviewed by Michael W. Sherraden, "National Youth Service,"* Washington University Magazine, *April 1982, pp. 11–14.*

the 1980s, what would such a program look like? To deal with this question, it is useful to identify key dimensions along which national service models might vary. Ten important issues are (1) voluntary vs. compulsory service, (2) universal opportunity, (3) diversity, (4) control, (5) size, (6) unit cost, (7) productivity, (8) employment implications, (9) educational value, and (10) relationship to the military. Taking these considerations one by one, we propose a program along the following lines:[34]

Voluntary vs. Compulsory service. National service would be voluntary. Civilian youth service activities would be restricted to persons entering of their own volition. Black youth have, for economic reasons, had fewer real choices than whites. Blacks have endured "conscription by unemployment"[35] into the military to a much greater extent that whites. What black young people need are more viable choices for shaping and building their futures. Moreover, regardless of one's philosophical view on compulsory service, there would be serious practical problems in attempting to enforce a compulsory civilian service across the whole youth population.

Universal opportunity. Opportunity would be universal, which would require making administrative and financial arrangements so that almost every young person who offered to serve would be able to serve, including the disadvantaged and the disabled. There would be only minimal mental and physical standards, less rigorous than those of the military. Discrimination of any kind would be guarded against. One of the important noneconomic benefits of a national service is the arena it would provide for young people of different colors, from different backgrounds, and with different abilities to learn to appreciate those differences. The *Wall Street Journal* editorialized: "National service could be a means of acculturation, acquainting young people with their fellow Americans of all different races, creeds, and economic backgrounds."[36] In a universal national service program, there would be slightly higher response rate among disadvantaged youth, simply because their choices are more limited. However, the PLS experiment confirms that national service would attract young people from every race, class, and level of educational attainment.

Diversity. The program would offer many diverse service opportunities, including conservation work, construction projects, social services, education, and work in government agencies. Successful programs which currently exist, such as Youth Conservation Corps and Peace Corps, would be placed under the national service umbrella.

Control. Much of the program would be operated at the local level under the control of private not-for-profit and public agencies. A quasi-public foun-

[34]*This proposal follows Donald J. Eberly and Michael W. Sherraden, "A Proposal for National Service for the 1980s," in Sherraden and Eberly, eds.,* National Service, *pp. 99–114.*

[35]*This phrase originated with Roger Landrum, "Serving America: Alternatives to the Draft,"* USA Today, *January 1981, p.9.*

[36]Wall Street Journal, *May 29, 1981.*

dation similar to the Corporation for Public Broadcasting would be established to receive appropriations, approve applications, and maintain standards; for example, standards would include no displacement of regular employees and no political or religious activity. Decision-making would be largely decentralized to the local level and responsive to local needs and conditions. In this way, the program would remain flexible and adaptive, and this decentralized model would allow urban black communities to take advantage of existing organizations and patterns of service, working with rather than against the existing organizational strength within the community.

Size. The program would be allowed to grow naturally in number of participants depending on demand for national service positions and support for programs at the local level. Because sponsoring organizations would bear part of the costs, the program would have to work well or it would not be supported and would not grow. If national service were not meeting genuine needs, it would remain small. There would be no additional attempt to push any project which was not meeting a genuine need. We anticipate, however, that the program would meet genuine needs, would be recognized as successful, and would grow to about one million participants over a three-year period.

Unit cost. Costs per participant would include direct compensation at, or slightly below, the minimum wage, administrative overhead, and postprogram educational benefits. This figure would be about $10,000 per year in 1981 dollars.[37] To place this figure in perspective, two points should be kept in mind. First, this money would not be thrown away; it would be invested. As we have noted, there is reason to believe the national service projects would yield benefits exceeding costs. Second, $10,000 per year should be compared to some alternative costs. For example, this is less than half of the annual cost of supporting a young person in the military or in a correctional facility.[38] Those who speak loudly for "law and order" or see the military as a convenient institution to ameliorate youth unemployment are advised to pay more attention to the excessive costs of these alternatives. National service would be a much better value—and in addition, communities would benefit directly from the projects.

Productivity. There would be a strong emphasis on productive work and service. National service projects would be expected to pay their own way. Participating agencies and individuals would sign service contracts outlining performance expectations. If these were not fulfilled, the agency or the individual would be fired. Only if there were very high expectations of performance and visible benefits would any community support a national service program in the 1980s. As we have noted, there is much important work to be done in black communities as well as elsewhere, and there is no justification for engaging in "make-work" or tolerating poor performance.

[37]*Costs are examined in detail by Donald J. Eberly and Michael W. Sherraden, "Alternative Models of National Service," in Sherraden and Eberly, eds.,* National Service, *pp. 83–98.*

[38]*Alternative costs are documented by William R. Ramsay, "The Impact of National Service on Education," in ibid., pp. 135–149.*

Employment implications. Employment implications would vary depending on the national service project. Job-training experiences, while not the primary goal of national service, could be adapted to individual situations. Successful job-training programs, such as the Job Corps, also could be adapted to national service purposes. Peter Edelman has cautioned that the employment needs for disadvantaged young people in national service would not be the same as for young people who have brighter prospects. Edelman offers several suggestions for combining and meshing job training and service.[39] For many black communities, these considerations would be important and could be addressed at the community level with the built-in flexibility which we propose.

Educational value. Beyond the direct and substantial educational value of the service experience itself, national service participants would earn a period of post-high school education and training. Much of the current federal aid to education would be shifted to support those who had contributed a period of national service, either civilian or military. As with the old GI bill, educational benefits would be proportional to length of service. This provision would open up educational opportunities for disadvantaged blacks who would have no other possibility of attending college or advanced technical school. Very soon this provision for educational benefits would begin to alter the race and class composition on college campuses. If middle- and upper-class young people no longer enjoyed great subsidies for higher education and this pool of money became available to anyone who elected to earn it through national service, there would soon be more blacks and more students from impoverished communities attending college.

Relationship to the military. Civilian youth service would exist independently of the military establishment, because the need for national service transcends military recruitment policies. If there were a need for a military draft, persons choosing to volunteer for civilian service would bear a relationship to the draft comparable to those volunteering for military service. It is also likely that the civilian service alternative would begin to restore appreciation and respect for military service. The word "service" would take on a more positive meaning and military service would again be viewed more as a citizenship responsibility than as a last-resort employment program for the disadvantaged.[40]

These are the rough outlines of a national service program. We believe these are the best choices, but only time and experience will tell. National service is a broad and flexible idea, and there should be, above all, an attitude of experimentation and evaluation to identify which program features work best. The program we propose incorporates this flexibility. In the black community, national service would reduce unemployment among young people,

[39] *Peter B. Edelman, "The Impact of National Service on Youth Employment," in ibid., pp. 131–34.*
[40] *An excellent analysis of military issues is presented by Charles C. Moskos, "National Service and the All-Volunteer Force," in ibid., pp. 150–62.*

and simultaneously would support and strengthen the community through projects such as weatherizing and/or retrofitting houses and other buildings for energy conservation; development and maintenance of community buildings, parks, and other public facilities; and service projects to address human needs overlooked by federal and state government programs. With the dismantling of many essential programs by the Reagan administration, the need for service projects is now greater than ever.

It is possible also that national service projects can be meshed with the enterprise zone concept. As a concerted thrust toward development of impoverished communities, it makes a good deal of sense to create conditions which spark development on a variety of fronts. There are endless possibilities for combining these efforts, and communities should be encouraged to generate creative responses.

Altogether, national service is a broad idea with great potential. It is a constructive and hopeful idea, focusing on what people have to offer rather than on problems and deficiencies. In the black community young people are ready and able to contribute. They do not want to be a burden on their families, community, or country. But in areas where black youth unemployment is 50 percent or 60 percent or higher, there are currently very few options. The challenge for the nation is to find additional means whereby young people can move ahead under their own power and creativity. National service may be part of the solution, and the black community, as the evidence indicates, has much to gain and much to offer in a national service program.

Voting with Their Feet: Secondary Migrations of Indochinese Refugees

JOHN FINCK

Between 1975 and 1981 about 600,000 refugees from Southeast Asia were admitted to the United States.[1] When the Indochinese Refugee assistance program began in 1975, one of its goals was to disperse refugees evenly across the country so that no city or county would be unduly burdened by their numbers.[2] If refugees were spread from coast to coast like a thin layer of butter, it was argued, each sponsor and host community would have more resources to aid the refugees with their new lives.

What happened, of course, was just the opposite. Placement decisions were made according to the location of relatives or friends or the presence of a local church or private resettlement agency, without regard to the availability of jobs and housing. Today, 60 percent of the Southeast Asians who have arrived in the United States since 1975 live in just forty counties.[3]

The dimensions of these numbers will soon be felt by state taxpayers and legislators, neither of whom have been concerned to date with refugees because the federal government has thus far borne 100 percent of their costs. The honeymoon may be over when states are obliged to pick up the tab for refugees they neither created nor invited.

One of the factors that led to these extraordinary concentrations is: secondary migrations, the term used to describe when refugees move by choice from one city—or state, the site of original placement—to another.

In the last seven years a scene has repeated itself in scores of airports across the country. An American sponsor waits anxiously for the plane that brings an unknown family thousands of miles. A reliable church or private sponsor has an apartment waiting for the new arrivals, some clothing, and a cash

JOHN FINCK is Consultant, Rhode Island Office of Refugee Resettlement, Cranston, R.I.

[1]*U.S. Department of Health and Human Services, Office of Refugee Resettlement*, Report to the Congress, *January 31, 1981, p. 23.*

[2]*Christine R. Finnan et al.,* Alternative Approaches to Refugee Resettlement *(Menlo Park, Calif.: Stanford Research Institute International, 1981), p. 11.*

[3]*U.S. Department of Health and Human Services, Office of Refugee Resettlement, Placement Policy Task Force, "Concept Paper: Refugee Placement Policy," 1981, p. 5.*

advance for their first days in America. Exceptional sponsors have job prospects lined up and English classes arranged for the sunmarked refugees who will soon be filing into the noisy airport lounge. If the new family is fortunate, a cousin, an uncle, or perhaps an entire family will be on hand for the long-awaited reunion. In the best of cases, a supportive sponsor and the presence of not only family, but fellow countrymen, cushion the shock of arrival.

The reality of resettlement, however, often falls short of this ideal. Hmong and Cambodians cite a number of motivations for their recent move to Rhode Island. In reviewing these factors, I follow a distinction between migration for reunification and migration for betterment, made by one Hmong writer on the subject.[4]

In nearly all instances, a refugee's first concern after arriving in the United States is to join his or her family. No matter where that family lives, the new arrival will follow. So strong is the centripetal pull of relatives that a refugee will "close his eyes" (as one Hmong leader said) to substandard housing, racial tensions, or the absence of services, for the security of family. Sometimes, plans to reunite were made long ago in the refugee camps. The immigration papers may say Syracuse or Toledo, but a Hmong's true destination may be his family in St. Paul. By taking a bus to the Twin Cities, he is completing the final leg of a journey that was momentarily interrupted by the arbitrary placement arranged by the church or private resettlement agency. Most Southeast Asians, whether Hmong, Lao, Cambodian, or Vietnamese, prize family unity. A man who lives apart from his family feels at odds with human nature.

In a survey of 51 randomly chosen Cambodian heads of households who moved to Rhode Island from October 1981 to April 1982, 24 families (47 percent) reported they had immediate family members living in the state. On the other hand, 27 families (53 percent) had no immediate family in the state; they came in hopes of bettering their family's situation.

MIGRATION FOR BETTERMENT

Sometimes refugees will speak of "escaping" from a bad sponsor, in much the same way that they spoke of escaping from their own countries. One example is fairly typical of those refugees who have encountered bad or indifferent sponsorship, regardless of location:

> Neak Simoung, his wife, and two sons arrived in New York on September 9, 1981. His sponsor put Mr. Simoung in an apartment with two other Camodian families, a Vietnamese family, and two single Afghan

---

[4]*Chau Thao, "Hmong Migration and Leadership in Laos and the United States,"* The Journal; a Publication for English as a Second Language and Cultural Orientation Teachers *(published by the Center for Applied Linguistics, Washington, D.C.), March 1982, pp. 24–27.*

refugees. Sixteen people shared a single bathroom, one small refrigerator, and four stoves. Because there were four in his family, Mr. Simoung was given four spoons, four plastic bowls, and one large cooking pot. The first time his wife made soup, it melted their bowls.

The refrigerator was a constant source of trouble. The three families and the Afghans tried dividing the space, but each family suspected the other of stealing their food. Several of the men began carrying knives strapped to their ankles.

Simoung was given a few clothes for his family; the rest he found in other people's garbage. He received two worn blankets for the coming winter that looked as if they too came from the street.

His family received food stamps but no refugee cash assistance. Mr. Simoung applied, but no one could speak his language at the welfare office. Neither the sponsor nor the Cambodian mutual assistance association in New York offered to help.

After three months in New York, Mr. Simoung moved to Rhode Island because he heard that things were better there. He borrowed some money from friends and sold $100 worth of food stamps for $80 to pay the bus fare to Providence.

Even without the draw of relatives, refugees will move if they perceive a better deal in another city. They will leave high-rent cities like Boston, New York, and Houston for small cities with lower rents and strong refugee communities, like Madison, Wisconsin, or Providence, Rhode Island. Friends and relations are constantly comparing notes on food prices, rents, the job market, availabililty of cash and medical assistance, and the attitudes of the host community to their presence.

There is immediate pressure to move when a refugee has difficulty registering for cash assistance because of the absence of translators or because of administrative delay. Likewise, when refugees discover the vast differences in cash assistance rates between states like Texas and Oregon, there is additional incentive to move. Both states have high concentrations of refugees. Texas has low unemployment; Oregon has high unemployment. Conversely, Oregon has high assistance rates while Texas has much lower rates. Ten percent of the refugees in Texas receive cash assistance or AFDC.[5] In Oregon 63 percent of refugees receive public assistance.[6] As long as pronounced differences in benefits continue among the states, refugees will be tempted to seek out the most generous state.

Other factors play into a move. The presence of bilingual staff at clinics and hospitals is a big draw for families with limited English. If the city in question employs Southeast Asians as translators, caseworkers, and nursing

---

[5]*Letter to Ellen McGovern, U.S. Office of Refugee Resettlement, Washington, D.C., from John D. Townsend, State Coordinator of Refugee Affairs, Texas Department of Human Resources, January 8, 1982, p. 1.*

[6]*Letter to Ellen McGovern from Keith Putnam, Administrator of Adult and Family Services, Oregon Department of Human Resources, January 11, 1982, p. 4.*

assistants, the host community must be sympathetic—or so the refugees conclude. Without translators it is impossible for refugees to receive appropriate health care. A city with bilingual staff at its health centers will attract refugees.

Each ethnic group values different aspects of a prospective community. Cambodians highly regard the presence of a Buddhist monk. The Hmong value open land suitable for gardens and large-scale farming. Those Vietnamese who were once fishermen, want to live by the sea. Whenever possible, the refugees wish to avoid racial conflict. Entire communities of Hmong, for example, have moved from areas of community unrest rather than defend their recently won turf. A dramatic example occurred three years ago in Orange County, California. In the late 1970s, hundreds of Hmong families congregated in Santa Ana; most lived in the Voltaire apartment complex. Early one morning an old man of the Xiong clan was murdered in his apartment. After the funeral, the leaders concluded that the murder was racially motivated and tied, perhaps, to the city's housing shortage. Many families subsequently moved to Portland, Oregon. During the following two years, fewer Hmong have moved to Orange County, and movement out of the county has increased.[7]

IMPACT OF SECONDARY MIGRATION

Refugees have voted with their feet, for the reasons mentioned, until forty counties now account for 60 percent of all Southeast Asians. From the refugees' point of view, the secondary migration is a positive action in which a family either joins other family members or leaves an unsatisfactory environment.

From the local point of view, however, the additional refugees are a burden. The social service funding which a state receives from the federal Office of Refugee Resettlement is based on its population of refugees who entered the United States over the past three years. When a refugee moves from another state, he leaves behind his per-capita share of social service dollars. Although refugees may begin to use social services upon arrival, the state must wait until the next year to get additional funding. The state, then, absorbs a year's worth of social services for each refugee it accepts from another state.

A more serious problem lies in the abilities of the church and private agencies who sponsor refugees to support them after the initial weeks of placement. For example, the third largest sponsor of Cambodians in Rhode Island is World Refugee Relief Services (WRRS). In January 1982 this agency had 188 Cambodian families on refugee cash assistance, 83 of whom came from other states. To meet the needs of 188 families, the agency employs one full-time minister and a part-time Hmong aide. Obviously, these families are left to fend for themselves. The only way WRRS can get additional funds for more staff is to sponsor additional refugees—which, of course, only

---

[7]*Cheu Thao, "Hmong Migration and Leadership in Laos and the United States."*

exacerbates the problem. Without benefit of the sponsor's services, a refugee's period of dependency is likely to be longer.

The Office of Refugee Resettlement (ORR) has recently concluded that the "failure to resolve the impact issue could jeopardize the entire U.S. refugee program."[8] ORR has proposed a number of policy changes which would attempt to steer nonimmediate families away from areas with high concentrations of refugees. Impact would be defined, for the first time, as three factors:[9]

> Ratio of the number of refugees and entrants resettled in a country to the county's population:
> *High impact.* One refugee or entrant to 199 or fewer persons in the county
> *Medium impact.* One refugee or entrant to between 200 and and 299 persons in the county
> *Low impact.* One refugee or entrant to 299 or more persons in the county.

> Unemployment rate of the Standard Metropolitan Statistical Area during the period of measurement:
> *High impact.* Rate greater than one percent above national average
> *Medium impact.* Rate one percent above and one percent below national average
> *Low impact.* Rate less than one percent below national average.

> Dependency rate for the state of all refugees residing in that state during the last three years:
> *High impact.* Dependency rate over 60 percent
> *Medium impact.* Dependency rate between 50 and 59 percent
> *Low impact.* Dependency rate less than 50 percent.

The proposed rules stipulate that the American Council of Voluntary Agencies (the umbrella organization for the local affiliates of church and private resettlement agencies) must develop a plan in consultation with the states to deal with the number of new arrivals. For the first time the states will have their rightful say in the number of refugees they will take —and where they will live. Only immediate relatives would be sent to areas of high impact. In this manner ORR hopes to divert additional refugees from cities which already meet its definition of high impact.

This strategy has limitations. In the first instance, as ORR itself acknowledges, only 20 percent of placements are nonimmediate family members. Presumably, family reunification would continue, even in impacted areas. This accounts for 80 percent of new arrivals; the vast majority would not be affected by the placement policy. In the second instance, refugees still have the right of self-determination to move to another city or state for any of the reasons previously stated.

[8]*U.S. Department of Health and Human Services, Office of Refugee Resettlement, Placement Policy Task Force, "Concept Paper," p. 7.*

[9]*U.S. Department of Health and Human Services, Office of Refugee Resettlement, Placement Policy Task Force, "Concept Paper," pp. 1–3.*

At the root of secondary migrations lie objective differences in the quality of resettlement efforts, regardless of initial placement. The most certain way to diminish the incentive for relocation is to improve the ingredients for successful resettlement on the local level: sustained sponsorship; job training, counseling, placement, and follow-up services; rigorous English-language programs; and a strong mutual assistance association. Each of these items carries a price tag.

The states have been put on notice that their refugee budgets have peaked; the future will only mean reductions. No state has funds to increase training or job services. The highwater mark in funding has passed, and whatever improvements can be wrought must be done with reduced resources. A new placement policy will not in itself alter the motivation for secondary migration. It will slow the refugee growth rate for areas already heavily affected. But the condition which gives rise to the desire for secondary migration remains the same. Unfortunately, areas with large numbers of refugees are predestined to attract still more.

The next opportunity to test the elasticity of secondary migration comes in the form of recent policy changes from the Office of Refugee Resettlement. This time the federal government proposes to cut in half the thirty-six month period of funding for cash and medical assistance to refugees as required by the Refugee Act of 1980. Instead, ORR proposes that the federal government pay cash and medical assistance for only eighteen months. The states uniformly oppose this change. They argue that eighteen months of assistance to refugees who are illiterate in their own language, possess no transferable job skills, and have little understanding of American society, violate the Refugee Act of 1980 which says that the states will not be unduly burdened by federal decisions to admit refugees. When the eighteen-month limitation goes into effect, states will be obliged to drop hundreds—if not thousands—from the ranks of those entitled to refugee cash assistance. Those states which support general public assistance (GPA) programs have the option of absorbing the cuts. Some states have no GPA program; in others, the GPA rate is significantly lower than the benefits paid by refugee cash assistance.

Oregon estimates that if the termination had gone into effect on March 1, 1982, as proposed, 6,231 persons would have been denied assistance. Since Oregon has no county or local GPA program, no AFDC-Unemployed Parent program, and a state general assistance program limited to single adults medically unemployable, 36 percent of the state's 17,500 refugees would have had no means of support.[10]

Likewise, Texas does not have a state GPA program. According to the State Refugee Coordinator:

> City and county governments and local charitable institutions will have
> to shoulder the burden of providing emergency cash assistance and med-

---

[10]*Letter to Ellen McGovern from Keith Putnam, p. 4.*

ical services to refugees. These services on a local level are very limited in Texas and are not available in all of the State's 254 counties.[11]

Refugee officials in both Texas and Oregon predict that refugees who are not yet self-supporting and are cut out by the eighteen-month termination of federal support for cash and medical assistance will leave the state. In fact, if the cut-off goes into effect, Oregon will encourage refugees to move by providing information and training to refugee leaders and eligibility workers about the employment rate, welfare programs, and social services available in other states.

One state likely to be included in Oregon's list of recommendations is Rhode Island. Some states either do not have a GPA program or fund it at rates significantly lower than Rhode Island. Even then, many states choose not to offer assistance through the GPA program. By contrast, Rhode Island's GPA rates approximate its AFDC rate. Early indications suggest that Connecticut and Massachusetts may not offer assistance after eighteen months, in which case Rhode Island will become the logical destination for refugees whose aid has been terminated in other states.[12]

Even without high benefits, Providence already attracts secondary migrations.[13] Forty percent of the state's current refugee cash assistance cases are Indochinese from other states, drawn to Rhode Island because of its reputation for service and its well-organized Cambodian and Hmong communities, the second and fourth largest communities of their kind in the country.[14] But when a high benefit level and two thriving Asian communities are taken together, the pair becomes a magnet for their dispossessed countrymen in other states.

The recent changes in federal policy as it affects communities with large numbers of refugees is contradictory. On the one hand, ORR proposes to limit initial placements in order not to add to existing concentrations. At the same time, it encourages secondary migrations to states which have chosen to continue some form of benefits beyond eighteen months.

By voting with their feet, the refugees will have the next word.

---

[11]*Letter to Ellen McGovern from John D. Townsend, p. 3.*

[12]*Letter to Ellen McGovern from Cleo E. Lachapelle, State Coordinator of Refugee Resettlement, Rhode Island Department of Social and Rehabilitative Services, January 8, 1982, p. 2.*

[13]*Letter to Senator John H. Chafee from John Affleck, Director, Rhode Island Department of Social and Rehabilitative Services, January 19, 1982.*

[14]*Rhode Island, Department of Social and Rehabilitative Services, Office of Refugee Resettlement, Annual Report, 1981, p. 11.*

Moving Toward a Tripartite Marketplace in the Human Services

JAMES E. MILLS

THE HUMAN services system has traditionally been viewed as a special field of endeavor with actions dominated by objectives and values somewhat more altruistic than those that govern the profit-making sector. Services were provided through a combination of public and voluntary agencies. Events of the past several years, however, demand a closer review of this somewhat pristine view of the world. Severe limitations on available resources, evolution in the delivery system itself, and a federal administration espousing neoconservative values which seriously challenge the current role and organization of human services demand a closer study of the human services system and suggest what may be a major reformulation in its operation.

The human services system has traditionally been seen as a public-voluntary partnership. The growth of the public sector role and slower growth in voluntary resources have made the partnership less than equal. Only limited attention has been paid to the significant growth of a private sector in the delivery of human services—one whose motive is to deliver human services at a profit. While public and voluntary service providers have ignored the private sector, perhaps in the hopes that it would go away, or attempted to diminish its importance by questioning the motives of anyone who would attempt to profit from human misery, the private sector of the human services system has grown quietly and steadily. A significant private sector role exists in nursing homes, hospitals, the private practice of psychotherapy, alcoholism treatment, day care for children, consultation of all sorts, and residential treatment services. Current and projected changes in attitude, policy, resource allocation, and organization of the human service system suggest a period of future growth in the private sector while the traditional public and voluntary agencies experience a period of serious retrenchment.

ENVIRONMENTAL CONSIDERATIONS

Factors which contrbute to this new environment in private human services sector growth include:

JAMES E. MILLS is Executive Director, Community Planning Council, Sacramento, Calif.

Resource limitations. Limitations on the taxing capability of government at all levels mean fewer resources to spend on human services. With reduced reliance on property taxes as a revenue source, the system becomes increasingly dependent on sources more responsive to the general economic climate—a process which often works in an inverse relationship to need and demand for service.

Neoconservative Agenda. The public sector is being influenced by neoconservative philosophies. Not only is the amount of resources to be allocated to human services questioned, but also what role, if any, the federal government has in human service organization and delivery. These same policy-makers are also committed to the development of private sector responses to meet national needs. Within this context, "cashing out" services with attendant reductions in government regulation and control becomes particularly appealing.

Inflation. Years of successive inflation have reduced the capability of both voluntary and public agencies to maintain service levels.

Overstatement of voluntary sector capabilities. Growth reliance on government funding of voluntary sector agencies has overstated the capabilities of voluntary institutions. There has been a tendency to count the human service dollar twice: once when it was appropriated for the public sector and again when it is spent by the voluntary agency.

Growth of a viable private sector alternative. The wide variety of private sector enterprises with growing capability to provide different services offers a private sector alternative heretofore not a factor in the human services system.

Unemployed professionals. Unemployed professionals from the public and voluntary sectors stand ready to develop and provide services to those willing and capable of paying for them.

Growth in demand for social services. Selected social services are in greater demand as cultural resistance to seeking help with social and interpersonal problems has decreased. Reduction in voluntary and public agency capabilities means that the remaining scarce human services must be rationed. The tendency is to ration tax- and donor-funded services to those least able to pay.

Acceptance of purchasing one's needed services. There is a long-standing acceptance in our culture of purchasing needed goods and services. This value is only beginning to be applied to human services.

Increase in discretionary income. Pressures of inflation have forced many families to turn to two incomes to maintain their desired standard of living. At least initially, the additional employment may well mean extra discretionary income which can be utilized for purchase of needed human services. Ironically, the two-income family may create greater demand for such human services as child day care.

Alternative sources of financing human services. In the final analysis, the most significant factor in the development of this new environment will be the emergence of alternative means of financing—responses to growing unavailability of employer-desired services for employees through public and voluntary agencies. These include:

1. *Employee assistance plans.* Over 5,500 companies have employee assistance plans today, up from less than 300 in 1972. Among Fortune 500 companies, the nation's largest industrial firms, 56 percent now have employee assistance programs, up from 25 percent in 1972.[1] These programs today are heavily concentrated in the area of substance abuse. There is however, a rapid growth in the range of services offered as the relationship of services to improved productivity and profitability is demonstrated.

2. *Third-party payments.* Coverage for a wider range of human services is increasingly being offered through group insurance, group practices, and/or collectively bargained benefit plans. Costs of these programs in whole or in part are borne by employers.

An additional area of concern to this greater corporate role in the direct payment for human services is its possible impact on corporate philanthropy. Will the corporation maintain its current level of philanthropic support of voluntary human service agencies when it is increasing its direct provision of services to meet the needs of its employees? A recent study indicates that direct employee benefit was a major factor in the level of corporate contributions for 88.13 percent of major firms surveyed.[2] Any significant reduction in support or diversion of philanthropy to nonhuman service fields will further reduce the service capabilities of the voluntary sector. A similar erosion might occur in already limited support for tax-supported human services in the public sector.

PUBLIC SECTOR CONSIDERATIONS

Dealing with reduced resources is not a new experience for the public sector. Most appropriation levels have not kept pace with inflation. In those states working under a "cap" in Title XX social services, each succeeding year has seen further erosion from fixed allocations and increased costs of doing business. The public sector will be under pressure to reduce service levels further through a redefinition of their basic responsibilities. Already this redefinition has resulted in a service system that increasingly reflects only protective and enforcement functions. Other services primarily preventive in nature or designed to enhance the quality of life have been steadily reduced or eliminated to preserve protective services for children and adults, necessary out-of-home care programs, services to the courts, and basic health and educational functions. Although the eliminated services often have long-term implications for future service needs, they were often provided to individuals whose incomes exceeded the poverty level. The public sector will experience not only a

[1] *United Way of America briefing memorandum, "Employee Assistance Programs," 1981, p. 1.*

[2] *Dennis J. Murphy,* Corporate Contributions; Understanding the Decisionmaking Process, *Alexandria, Va.: United Way of America, 1982, pp. 22ff.*

narrowed range of services but a clientele limited to individuals with very low incomes.

One method of supplementing the available public service dollar is partial or full fee assessment. One might speculate on the efficacy of charging fees for services which, like child protective services, were never requested in the first place. The economic status of the remaining clientele in the public agency will hardly be characterized by its discretionary income available for human service fees. Likewise, the services most likely to be provided to those with discretionary income are the very services which are being reduced or eliminated due to budgetary constraints. When competing for fee-paying clients, the setting in which services are provided must be considered. How competitive is the public sector in terms of the ambiance of their facilities? The general public's negative perceptions of the "Welfare Department" and its clientele are also well known.

Another problem that the public sector must face in a competitive market is the tremendous organizational and fiscal overhead which makes responsive and economically priced services difficult to achieve. Consider the state of California as a highly diversified conglomerate with $27 billion in annual sales. Compare it to a similar enterprise in the private sector. It is difficult to identify another enterprise so poorly organized to do its business. For example, what private enterprise of that size and scope has:

1. a 120-member board of directors, with its staff independent of management, and an annual budget of $100 million?
2. A single corporation counsel?
3. One personnel director and a single personnel system for all operating entities?
4. One purchasing agent?
5. One space manager?
6. A single set of standards for the purchase of equipment and supplies?
7. One controller for the entire enterprise?
8. No corporate planning and marketing capability?

A large private enterprise, rather than centralizing responsibility and authority, would decentralize to the maximum degree possible. Likewise, it would not hold indefinitely "unprofitable" or "incompatible" subsidiaries, a discretion that the public sector, particularly at the local level, does not have. Any "divestiture" decisions must survive a time-consuming, often convoluted, political decision-making process. Unless there is a significant change in the philosophy and operation of government, the public sector enters the new marketplace hopelessly encumbered with structure and overhead costs, which will make it highly noncompetitive.

VOLUNTARY SECTOR CONSIDERATIONS

The voluntary sector, while perhaps free of some of the encumbrances noted in the public sector, is confronted with its unique set of problems in competing in the new human services marketplace. For example, the traditional client of the voluntary agency has been able to pay little, if any, of the cost of service. Differences were made up through voluntary contributions or development of purchase-of-service agreements with public entities. The latter alternative has been responsible for rapid growth in number and size of voluntary agencies. Reduction of available public dollars and a growing focus upon governmental enforcement and protective functions will further reduce voluntary agency service capabilities.

Heavy involvement of voluntary agencies in governmental funding has had an impact on the management of voluntary agencies:

1. In too many cases, the voluntary agency was created as a legal entity to receive public funds. It was not designed as a community-wide agency with the broad base of support considered an integral part of the traditional voluntary agency. Its energies were concentrated on maintaining the flow of funds from the political entity. Little attention was paid (nor was it necessary) to general community understanding of the program or to the development of alternative revenue sources.

2. In the established voluntary agency, there was less urgency for fund raising, due to the presence of governmental support. Now fund-raising efforts must be undertaken in a highly competitive environment with many competitors for the donor's dollars.

3. Decreased board participation in agencies has been noted as a result of diminished control of policy due to the detailed terms of government grants and contracts.

4. There is growing concern about board members' increased legal responsibility in the context of governmentally imposed accountability requirements.[3]

Many volunteer agencies have not vigorously pursued fee revenues. There was less pressure to do so since government contracts were a guaranteed source of revenue. These agencies will be faced with the need to educate their boards and staff to the necessity of fee revenues in order to maintain desired service levels. This may create public relations problems, staff resistance, and board bewilderment. Clients themselves, however, have often been identified as a reasonable factor in the formula. Not only do clients accept the necessity of fees for the service they receive, but experience shows that the fee-paying client has a greater investment in the helping process and makes more economical and effective use of the service. Another fee-related policy to be faced by voluntary agencies will be whether their fee schedule should be designed so that the maximum fees will subsidize services provided to others less able to pay full costs.

[3]*Nelson Rosenbaum, "The Impact of Government Funding on the Voluntary Sector,"* Community Focus, *December 1980, p. 11.*

Voluntary agencies will also have increasing problems in meeting their subsidy needs from philanthropic sources. They will have to reexamine fund-raising policies and analyze the future of various funding sources. Giving, as a proportion of the gross national product, has steadily declined since 1969.[4] The future of philanthropy is difficult to project with precision due to contradictory incentives and disincentives in the Economic Recovery Tax Act of 1981.[5] Federated fund-raising, long a mainstay for some large agencies, has not grown apace with inflation and faces growing demands to enlarge the number of agencies and services that benefit from the campaign.

The growth of voluntary agencies has been hampered by problems of capital formation. It will be extremely difficult to match the aggressiveness of an adequately capitalized competitor in a market situation. Voluntary agencies have also tended to pride themselves on doing business at the lowest possible cost. This may or may not represent the most efficient means of operation. Voluntary agency board members and managers have often been appointed for reasons other than business or marketing acumen. These talents are going to be as necessary in the future as fund-raising and social capabilities have been in the past.[6] Ideas about optimal size and functioning of the voluntary agency's board of directors may also have to be reexamined. Finally, voluntary agencies often perpetuate traditional values and procedures which may not stand the test of rigorous evaluation. For example, are time-honored service standards truly productive of improved services? Or do they merely represent the way business has been conducted for many years and are they the means by which a quality commitment was identified, delineating voluntary services from those of public agencies? If standards cannot be justified in terms of quality of service, they become a burdensome overhead which makes voluntary agency services more costly but essentially no better or competitive. Similar tests must be applied to sometimes circuitous and time-consuming decision-making processes.

PRIVATE SECTOR CONSIDERATIONS

The private sector enters the new human services marketplace with a variety of advantages. Organized for a single purpose, their governing structure will not be burdened by the complex and political decision-making processes of the public and voluntary sectors. The relative ease with which they can approach capital formation will provide developmental resources unavailable to

---

[4]*Giving USA—1981 Annual Report, American Association of Fund-raising Counsel, 1981, p.25.*

[5]*See Lester Salamon and Alan J. Abramson,* The Federal Government and the Nonprofit Sector: Implications of the Reagan Budget Proposals, Urban Institute *, (Washington, D.C.: 1981), for a detailed discussion of this topic.*

[6]*See Dennis R. Young, "Entrepreneurship and the Behavior of Non-profit Organizations; Elements of a Theory," in Michelle J. White, ed.,* Nonprofit Firms in a Three-Sector Economy *(Washington, D.C.: Urban Institute, 1981), pp. 140–51, for an identification of entrepreneurial roles and their application to human services managers.*

the voluntary and public sectors. Unfettered by tradition, the private sector human service organization will have the potential to move with speed, innovation, and flexibility traditionally associated with the voluntary sector. The private human service provider will be in a primary position to "cream" desirable, paying clients for whom the provision of services will prove most efficient. Corporations with their private enterprise orientation will not automatically turn to the voluntary agency through their new employee assistance programs for services but may have a greater affinity with other profit-making enterprises. Likewise, insurance companies will approach vendorization relatively free of traditional value judgments about service-provider sanction and auspices. Finally, the labor market with its current surplus of professionals will offer wide latitude in the selection and utilization of staff for these new enterprises.

The private sector human service providers will not be free of disadvantages which they too will have to overcome. Most critical will be a generally negative attitude toward profit-making enterprises in human services. One might speculate whether or not such feelings are more predominant among the professional community or the consuming public. The experience with private sector nursing homes suggests, however, that negative public perceptions can be a major marketing obstacle for private sector human service providers. One factor contributing to this issue will be the question of adequate regulation and quality control. In an era of deregulation and antiprofessionalism it may be speculated that there will be little development of new, or rigorous application of existing, licensing, and operational standards to these new and growing activities. The absence of effective, self-policing trade associations and the residue of turf wars among human service professions do not suggest satisfactory resolution to quality-of-care issues. If the private sector agency is operating in an environment of tenuous public relations it will suffer disproportionately from the effects of any scandal.

Another problem with which the private human service provider must deal is the role and contribution of the volunteer. Volunteerism provides a significant cost advantage to the voluntary agency. The public sector will seek to increase the utilization of volunteers, though there tends to be somewhat less receptivity on the part of the public institution as well as less enthusiasm from the volunteer for such placements. In 1973 it was estimated that nearly six billion hours of free time, valued at approximately $19 billion,[7] were donated to charitable and religious organizations. While there have been significant changes in the utilization of volunteers since that time, as more women entered the work force, the influence of free time on the cost of services rendered cannot be ignored. The continued involvement of volunteers in the voluntary agency and the success of the private sector human service organization in

---

[7]Paul Menchik and Burton A. Weisbrod, "Volunteer Labor Supply in the Provision of Collective Goods," in ibid., p. 163.

tapping this resource will affect their relative service costs and competitive positions in the marketplace.

GENERAL CONSIDERATIONS

Accepting these various assumptions, one can speculate that there will, indeed, be a significant shift in the manner in which human services are organized and delivered. Reduction in public sector capabilities and their high cost of doing business will limit their direct delivery of service. In spite of public employee union opposition, there will, under the current resource constraints and philosophical attitudes toward government, be even greater pressure to purchase remaining services from private and voluntary sectors.

The voluntary sector will be confronted with ever larger groups of potential clients unable to pay the full cost of services. They will have to develop new funding capabilities at the same time that governmental support is reduced. Although the voluntary sector will be more competitive with new, private sector providers, it will need to accomplish significant changes in institutional and traditional value structures to do so effectively. For those hoping for a return of the "good old days," it must be recognized that dismantling categorical programs also dismantles the advocacy and professional groups which supported their establishment and growth. Even more significantly, if there is considerable growth in the privatization of human services, a wedge will be driven between those professionals, particularly social workers, who address the human condition as a matter for social welfare policy and those who address it as a matter of service delivery. Privatization would accommodate the employment needs of a significant body of practitioners, which could render them less vocal in public policy debate.

If these projections prove accurate, there will emerge a human service environment which looks much more like a market economy than the interagency coordination debates of the past. There will emerge, for at least a portion of the service-consuming public, a true freedom of choice for both service type and provider. An era of client choice will be achieved that will far exceed anything previously anticipated when that rather abstract, universal value evolved. No longer will clients docilely accept a place on the waiting list; they will simply seek another agency without a waiting list. Similarly, there will be an increased focus on the marketing of human services. Concepts such as market segmentation, creation of demand, product identification, product loyalty, and consumer satisfaction will become increasingly familiar and adapted to human-service usage. Service provision will become increasingly responsive to client expectations. Clients will now be perceived as customers rather than as supplicants for a share of services provided by the agency.

Another function of the new marketplace will be to weed out providers whose services are no longer in demand. The halycon years of growth in public sector programming and voluntary agency contracting resulted in the development of specialized agencies focused on relatively narrow services or clienteles. With the absence of a guaranteed clientele or governmental support and with competition in the open marketplace, many of these agencies will cease to exist. To the extent that the service demands of this clientele were legitimate and these clients lack resources to compete in the human services marketplace, a gap will be created (or recreated) in the human services delivery system.

The human service delivery system faces major realignments in financing, service delivery, and client involvement. This realignment will reflect an environment more like a marketplace economy encompassing public, voluntary, and private service providers than the previous semistructured system. Service providers will have to respond competitively to the new environment or they will cease to exist. Government will continue to play a significant but reduced direct service role which will continue to be reflected through purchase-of-service mechanisms and limited to a permanent welfare class. The voluntary sector will have to strengthen its nonpublic image, assume greater responsibility for the "middle-class poor," and seek not only to increase their service revenues but also to increase their discretionary funding as well. Their focus of competition will shift from the public sector to the private sector provider. The private human-service provider will, at least initially, have the advantage of appealing to the most affluent clients who can pay for the specific services and competition in an environment that will foster their growth and expansion through ready access to a skilled labor force and new capital sources. For the policy specialist, it will become even more difficult to assure some modicum of access to basic, quality services for the total population.

Building Local Coalitions Against the Conservative Tide

MADELINE R. STONER

THE IMPLEMENTATION of President Reagan's policies regarding the delivery and financing of social services has renewed earlier questions about the roles and functions of those social workers who have practiced community organization at local levels and have stressed the importance of locality development—social and political action models of practice. Prior to the Reagan administration, these questions were very much alive, and a substantial response had been that grass roots activist community organizing had ceased to feature prominently in macropractice. Much of the evidence for this position rested in the realities of the job market, which had demonstrated scant interest in employing community organization social workers unless they had also acquired technical skills in planning and administration. Additional evidence suggested that clinical practitioners were being called upon to carry out the community practice component along with their clinical responsibilities. This concern for the declining role of social workers trained in community organization heightened when several policies of the Reagan administration specifically eliminated key legislation which supported community organization and community action.

Coupling the earlier doubts with the clear attacks on community activity by President Reagan and his administration, serious questioning about this type of intervention has increased. What, if any, settings remain for community organization practice? Are the knowledge and skills of community organizers obsolete? More dramatically, is there any potential for community organization as a social work function to continue?

These fears have arisen because, under the block grant system, Community Action Programs (CAP) may be phased out by 1983. Prior to the implementation of the block grants, 900 CAP agencies and 700 "limited program agencies" received federal funds.[1] These former antipoverty programs provided a major direction for community organization practice.

A second source of concern is that federal regulations for citizen participation continue, but on a modest scale allowing wide discretion in their application.

MADELEINE R. STONER is Assistant Dean, University of Southern California School of Social Work, Los Angeles.

[1] *National Association of Social Workers, "Memorandum to Block Grant Project Recipients," 1981, p. 3.*

States have already assumed Title XX social service block grants without having to conduct public hearings or publish their plans for public review. Title XVII of the Omnibus Budget Reconciliation Act of 1981 requires public hearings and pre-expenditure reports specifying objectives, target groups, access, and methods for disbursing funds within the states. However, Title XX and low-income energy assistance did not come under the provision of Title XVII of the Omnibus Budget Reconciliation Act.[2] Beyond this, the Department of Health and Human Services has interpreted the law as not requiring public hearings for the other block grants under its jurisdiction — preventive health, drug abuse and mental health, primary health care, and community services — until the second year of operation, thus giving the states and the federal government ample time to make decisions without regard for citizen oversight. What is most threatening about these limited requirements for public participation is their lack of specificity. Public hearings could literally be held on only one day with little advance notice. Similarly, public reports, although more specific directions exist for them, could be issued at the last minute, rendering intelligent citizen response an impossibility. Finally, threats to citizen awareness and involvement in decision-making, long a focus for community organization activists, have emerged because of the federal government's diminished requirements for audits and the disappearance of reporting standards.[3]

Despite such restrictive policies, renewed opportunities for community organization practice at local levels are emanating from reactions to contemporary conservative policies. Against the backdrop of massive cuts in government spending for services at federal, state, and local levels, a growing interest among neighborhood people and larger local networks has encouraged community organizing and social/political action around issues of pressing common concern.

Prior to the Reagan presidency, the debate about citizen participation and community organization as effective strategies was heated and inflamed by doubts as to whether local organizing even existed anymore. Warren describes citizen involvement as a strategy for accommodating the opinions and wishes of citizen participants in ways that give first priority to the convenience and continued viability of the organization.[4] Gilbert and Specht argue that, as a strategy for the redistribution of power to recipients of services, citizen participation has largely proved to be a failure.[5] Rothman takes the opposite position, arguing that "the legacy of the 1960's has been carried forward, not in a spectacular way; but nevertheless with vitality in many areas of American

[2]*U.S. Senate (P.L. 97-35) Omnibus Budget Reconciliation of 1981, 96th cong. 2d. Sess.*
[3]*National Association of Social Workers, p. 1.*
[4]*Roland L. Warren,* Social Change and Human Purpose: Toward Understanding and Action *(Chicago: Rand McNally, 1977), p. 226.*
[5]*Neil Gilbert and Harry Specht,* Dimensions of Social Welfare Policy *(Englewood Cliffs, N.J.: Prentice-Hall, 1974), pp. 116–17.*

life.'"[6] The debate over the effectiveness of community organization and citizen participation continues. This should not, however, obviate Rothman's observations about the extent of neighborhood activity.

Some of this local action has been spurred by legal requirements for participation, but, more broadly, it is a social force which has come into its own and continues on the power of its own momentum. The number of neighborhood organizations determined to get what they want has proliferated well beyond the ferment of the 1960s. It is this participatory momentum which provides the force for renewed social work practice directed toward citizen participation and empowerment—the essence of community organization social work practice.

A second, and equally strong, impetus for community organization practice comes from state and local politicians who are now burdened with the unpopular responsibility for allocating scarce resources to a large and diverse population. Despite the fact that the states have assumed the block grants, they remain reluctant to assume their allocative functions and are developing mechanisms for citizen participation to share their burden in such difficult decision-making. Sophisticated and politically astute community organizers can take advantage of this political vulnerability by organizing local constituencies to participate in whatever structures are established. They can also use their skills to monitor and analyze local legislative activity carefully and bring such information to their organizations and communities. In this matter, it is important to understand that the language and rhetoric of the block grant system encourage self-help, local action, and local decision-making. This rhetoric provides a strong basis for much community organizing strategy in channeling reactions to present conservative policies.

THE MOMENTUM FOR CITIZEN PARTICIPATION

Observations of contemporary life reveal that a wide variety of local organizations has proliferated outside legal mandates. Prominent among these are: advocacy groups; self-help networks; tenants, neighborhood, and block associations; organizations of ethnic and racial populations, women, homosexuals, children and young people, the elderly, single parents, the disabled, welfare recipients, and various ad hoc groups. Labor unions have been actively organizing domestic workers, office workers, and increasing numbers of farm workers. Finally, environmental, antinuclear, and peace concerns remain powerful organizational issues.

Many of these bodies have arisen out of local initiatives and reflect the interests of many classes, while others have developed as the result of organization at the national level. The left-of-center coalition of labor and community activists and concerned citizens that amassed in cities throughout the United

---

[6]*Jack Rothman, "Macro Social Work in a Tightening Economy,"* Social Work, *July 1979, p. 279.*

States on Solidarity Day in the autumn of 1981 has spawned many local coalitions of similar composition, and more are in the process of formation. This coalition at national and local level is perhaps the most vivid example of community organization and mass participation which has arisen in reaction to conservative policies so far.

All the types of organizations identified have mastered the techniques of organization building and social and political action around five basic clusters of interests: (1) single or multiple issues, (2) electoral politics, (3) locality development, (4) establishment of alternative institutions, and (5) self-help and mutual support. Their commonality rests in their determination to participate in those causes which concern them directly. They have learned well the organizing strategies of the 1960s and derive much of their impetus from the sense of empowerment unleashed during that period. Finally, their determination to act and take risks to attain their goals regardless of repressive circumstances remains strong and important as a basis for understanding the continuing organizational momentum in communities throughout the United States.

Of singular interest is the fact that these grass roots organizations are now calling for the formation of local, state, and national coalitions opposed to the Reagan administration's policies. The words "alliance" and "coalition" feature prominently on the contemporary scene, and there is a sense of urgency that such an agenda must be framed quickly. Groups that have not collaborated extensively, such as labor, minority groups, women, peace/antinuclear, and economic rights groups, are coming together in recognition of their common interests and sense of a common opposition. This is potentially one of the most significant efforts of the decade at the grass roots level.

Rothman claims that, excluding the 1960s, there is probably more "grass roots community organizing with professional involvement going on than at any other time in history."[7] Much of this, however, is taking place without social workers or formal reference to community organization practice. Nevertheless, social workers trained in community organization can still be found working with such groups. They tend to refer to themselves, however, in terms of their functions rather than their professions: community relations specialist, patients' rights advocate, campaign coordinator, welfare rights organizer, consultation and education specialist.

Other major institutions, such as churches, synagogues, and voluntary organizations, have adopted participatory mechanisms in their administrative policies and structures. This remains a clear direction for community organization during the conservative retrenchment.

An encouraging example of the status accorded to participation occurred in the city of Santa Monica, California, in September 1981 when the city council offered the post of city manager to a woman because her doctoral dissertation on the importance of democratic participation in government and

---

[7]Ibid.

industry convinced even her opponents that she was committed to an important principle for this top administrative position. The city council, supported by community activists, selected their new city manager because of her knowledge and dedication to economic and social participatory democracy and because of her effective demonstration of this commitment before many community groups.

With such strong momentum for participation, it appears unlikely that any legislation can repress it. For community organization social workers, this impulse toward social and political action around causes, issues, and the powerful concern for individual and collective rights provides a clear direction for practice.

POLITICAL ENCOURAGEMENT FOR PARTICIPATION

Across the nation both states and local governments are waging fierce battles, each blaming the other for reductions in spending and revenues, and each vying for the right to raise additional revenues. Growing out of this battle have come suggestions for involving citizens in decision-making to take the heat off elected officials who are finding themselves reluctantly forced to make unpopular decisions. Without the support and partnership of the citizenry, they have no one with whom they can share the blame, no one to endorse their credibility, and they run the risk of not being reelected. Hence, governors and state legislators, as well as county and city officials, are creating many different types of advisory structures. Some of these are concerned with specific issues, such as mental health advisory committees. Others are more general review boards designed to participate in decisions about block grant implementation. In addition to the political system, monitoring and review committees are being organized within established private welfare agencies, primarily the United Ways and other local planning councils throughout the country.

The surfacing of the vulnerability of political leaders presents community organizers with an opportunity to take advantage of the block grant system as an arena for social change which captures the momentum of participation that remains vital throughout the nation. A certain amount of political naïvete is apparent in this notion, but this is disspelled by Brager and Specht's emphasis on the fact that all contemporary community organization practice is shaped by forces and trends that are at work in society.[8] Indeed, much of the history of community organization practice has its roots in campaigning for scarce resources during repressive eras. Dorothea Dix's crusades for state mental hospitals, the campaigns of the settlement workers, and the campaign for the establishment of the United States Children's Bureau are striking illustrations

---

[8]*George Brager and Harry Specht,* Community Organizing *(New York: Columbia University Press, 1973), p. 14.*

of community organization during times that were unreceptive to government involvement in social services.

EXAMPLES OF LOCAL COALITIONS

In developing coalitions, organizers have to develop potential leadership and interest groups. Some of these leadership and interest groups are beginning to flex their muscles; others are visible only in outline form as the harsh realities of the Reagan administration force them into political action. Some of the following groups should be considered in organizing.

There are roughly 20 million women office workers in the United States today earning, on the average, 59 cents for every dollar that a man makes doing comparable work. More than 90 percent earn less than $9,000 a year, even though an overwhelming number are the sole support of their families. In an economy moving quickly from traditional industry toward service and information, these women may well be the core of the working class in the 1980s. They are almost totally unorganized.

In San Diego, in the fall of 1981, a new union, the United Domestic Workers of America, signed its first contract, covering 2,000 domestics who provide home care for the elderly and the disabled. Organizers claim that there are 2 million domestic workers in the United States. They have historically received no recognition from either organized labor or traditional political parties.

On the labor scene, President Reagan's policies have begun to cause unions to stiffen their backbones, and they are proving to be a source of ideas and political action in new coalitions.

During the past twenty years, 75 million Americans have come of voting age. Only 20 million of them registered to vote. It will be important to capture the imagination and increase the participation of this age.

The constituencies that were brought into the political system by the Great Society are an obvious source of backlash against President Reagan as he carves up the social programs created during the past twenty years. A striking example is the emergence of the physically disabled in pursuit of equal access of political and economic opportunity. It is the democratization of American culture and the participatory movement of the past decade that have transformed an anonymous mass of isolated shut-ins into a distinct, organizable constituency.

Perhaps the most painful result of the 1980 presidential election is that Ronald Reagan owes nothing to minority communities, and this has resulted in formal neglect and insult to them. Any community pushed to the wall will rebel, and the dismantling of affirmative action programs, the Comprehensive Employment and Training Act, and the income-maintenance programs that tend to serve minority groups and women have definitely pushed minority groups to the wall.

The list goes on, embracing an ever-growing number of victims of the economy: middle-class homeowners who live near toxic dumps; renters and young families who cannot afford to ride out the recession and real estate speculation; and single parents who shoulder the burdens of raising their families alone.

All these constituencies are mass in the sense that they often cut across class, economic, and racial lines. They are not politically marginal groups; they add up to an overwhelming majority. They are the core of the new coalitions of the 1980s.

Against the political avalanche of right-wing policies, local organizations are demonstrating a strengthened resolve to participate actively in efforts to reverse or protest programs. The above constituencies are proving to be the groups that are entering those alliances. The following examples are but a few of the important organizing efforts directed against conservative policies.

The Greater Los Angeles Labor-Community Coalition has steadily been campaigning against county cuts in health and welfare services since June 1981. As a result of its efforts, the cuts have not yet been implemented. On the contrary, the eight clinics which were closed, the thirty-two clinics which suffered cuts in services, and the county hospitals which experienced a 10 percent service cut have had their services restored temporarily pending further public hearings.

Following a carefully wrought strategy, organizers initially convened a coalition which became the County Health Alliance with a broad base to oppose health and welfare cuts. This group built an effective organization by convening when rumors of the proposed health and welfare cuts began to circulate. As a result of such critical timing, the Alliance was in a position to consider strategies and anticipate alternative plans and scenarios. There was also ample time to broaden the base of the coalition to include groups which did not represent low-income populations—an important strategy for gaining widespread support for any organization.

Members of the Alliance next searched the law and determined that a California state law, the Beilinson Act, prevents cuts in county services until public hearings are held. The law also requires that after the hearings the county must present evidence that any cutbacks will not have a detrimental effect on the needs of indigent people in the county.[9] Using this knowledge, the alliance called for public hearings and organized an impressive array of people and groups throughout Los Angeles to testify at them.

Having established a broad base of support for acting against the county cuts, the County Health Alliance advanced to an advocacy position and engaged the Western Center on Law and Poverty to initiate a lawsuit requesting the Superior Court to restore services to their former level. In less than one

[9]*California Senate, The Beilinson Act, Sections 1442 and 1442.5, Health and Safety Code Relating to Health Care for Indigents, 1974.*

month, an unprecedented period of time for litigation, the Superior Court judge ruled temporarily in favor of the County Health Alliance pending a second round of public hearings under the Beilinson Act. What is clear from the decision, despite its qualifying clause, is that the County Health Alliance won a victory. Participatory activities quickly emerged, and people affected by the cuts mobilized an effective coalition, employing campaigning and advocacy strategies to ensure government attention to their concerns.

Another group in California met for the first time in the fall of 1981 to formulate an alternative agenda to conservative policies. The Campaign for Human Development convened under the auspices of the Catholic Committee of Urban Ministry and the Protestant Committee on Urban Ministry. It brought together groups of church activists from across the nation but concentrated on attracting people from neighborhoods and citizen groups that reflected the fullest possible diversity of languages, color, and class background. Over 750 people were present, including many organizers from networks which had hardly any prior contact.

The sponsorship and concern of religious groups are proving to be a powerful resource for coalition building. Religious coalitions in various parts of the country have begun to devise strategies to combat what they see as harmful proposals on both state and local levels. Some of their tactics have been effective in Wisconsin and California, where cuts have been restored. Of particular significance is that churches in many areas, like Wisconsin and California, are joining forces with unions and with advocacy groups like welfare rights organizations. They are effectively following up their strategy of protest by meeting with legislators.

Similarly, a meeting of the Citizen/Labor Energy Coalition was held in Cincinnati in November 1981. This coalition brought together groups of diverse trade unionists, neighborhood activists, public interest advocates, and a variety of interested people for the first time. Their agenda is clearly to cooperate in dealing with all threats to their special interests, despite their past history of going it alone.[10] A major strategy for this group is the same as that of the Los Angeles County Health Alliance—to plan before events overtake them.

In Baltimore, the Southeast Community Organization of Baltimore (SECO) has used diversity as an organizing asset. Formed ten years ago in a mixed racial and ethnic community on Baltimore's South Side, when community residents joined to block a planned highway project, SECO has a long record of successes on neighborhood issues such as housing, street repair, and city services. It has also begun a neighborhood corporation for economic development and a community family service program to integrate social service agencies with community networks.[11] In SECO's case, the community organi-

[10] *"A New Spirit from the Neighborhood Networks,"* Social Policy, *January–February 1981,* p. 31.
    [11]Ibid., *p. 31.*

zation strategy of building a broad-based organization after successfully dealing with a single issue of crisis dimensions has proven its efficacy.

An umbrella organization of nine autonomous groups on the West Side of Chicago, the West Town Concerned Citizen Organization, threatened to block the city's $95 million general revenue sharing allotment as a means of securing construction jobs for its Hispanic constituents and by claiming that the city was discriminating against Hispanics in hiring construction workers. The coalition is notable for the fact that Hispanic people comprise 20 percent of the city's employees. To deal with the conflict, they filed a complaint with the United States Treasury Department, alleging employment discrimination, and accompanied this with mass marches on City Hall. The result was that the mayor of Chicago met with the coalition in late 1981 at a meeting attended by over seven hundred people and announced the creation of an affirmative action program to promote equal employment. Strategies employed by this program included mass demonstration and organization, confrontation, and legal action.

In New York City in January 1982 more than two thousand elderly, poor, and disabled people convened to discuss the devastating effects of the Reagan budget cuts on their lives. The gathering, convened under the auspices of the Community Council of Greater New York, was for the purpose of forming a coalition that would make these feelings and concerns known to Congress and the administration. Eleven members of the New York congressional delegation were present and spoke of letting Congress know how drastic the effects of the budget cuts are. A petition to that effect was signed by everyone present. Such an expressive gathering in the midst of crisis reflects the best of the community organization political-action model.

As a final example of coalition building, new charity coalitions are emerging throughout the country in direct challenge to the United Way. Their strategy is to parallel the United Way's efforts by soliciting donations in the workplace. These new coalitions, largely black united funds and women's coalitions, are forming in reaction to funding constraints on the United Way; but the reactions to federal cutbacks and the Reagan administration's efforts to pass along greater responsibility to the private sector have abetted their growth. Despite their nascent state, they are beginning to make an impact on the United Way, which view them as a threat, according to United Way officials.

There is sufficient evidence to believe that local coalitions have begun to come to grips with the tide of conservative policies and current retrenchment and that the conservative years ahead can be a focus for renewed community organizing to ensure that the democratic impulse of participation and equality does not disappear. Activism has surfaced as an American way of life that cannot be repealed by legislation. This momentum, along with the imperatives of political pragmatism, will provide important stimuli for community organization types of social work practice.

What becomes important is the form of such activism. Individual organizations, no matter how powerful, cannot compete with each other in attempts to obtain resources during these difficult times. Polarization along right- and left-wing lines is becoming entrenched in American life. Only coalitions of groups which can sufficiently agree in their analysis of issues and selection of strategies can return a sense of balance to the nation.

A final question remains unresolved and could pose a major obstacle in building the coalitions of the 1980s. At the core of all discussions about coalition strategies is the dilemma of whether to work through the Democratic party as it builds its new agenda, to begin new parties, or to eschew electoral politics altogether. The force of this dilemma is sufficiently strong that it could erode the expansion of coalitions in their nascent stage. Whatever the decision, resolution of this problem must occur as the result of sophisticated analysis, a careful reading of history, and must be soon. If no resolution can be found, then the issue must not be allowed to deter the basic agenda of new coalitions—to stem the conservative tide.

An Approach to Liability Concerns: Standards for Practice

WILLIAM VINCENT GRIFFIN

You are a child protection caseworker, and you closely follow agency policy on all cases. After completing an investigation of a child reported as abused, your assessment is that the child will remain at home while services will be provided to the family. While the case is open, the child dies of injuries allegedly inflicted by a family member. You are called to testify about the case before a grand jury. The next day you are arrested and charged with criminal malfeasance of your public duties.

This fictitious case is based on actual experience. In the investigative role, child protection workers constantly face the possibility of a civil suit (being held accountable for damages resulting from action), or criminal charges (being arrested for poor performance in a public role). In the past, it was the rule that the child protection agency and not the individual worker was named as the defendant in such cases. Today, individual workers are being held accountable. Recent court cases have determined the level of accountability to be the worker in Colorado, Texas, New York, and Massachusetts. The decisions reached have ranged from dismissal of the charges (Texas), to conviction of official misconduct (Colorado), to a grand jury finding of guilt for "neglect or nonfeasance in public office" (New York).

Since the mid-1960s every state in the Union has enacted laws mandating the report of child abuse and neglect, but these laws are generally unclear in relation to standards for child protection workers. The specifics of the statutes, in most instances, deal with the imposed civil or criminal liability for failure to *report* such cases, if there was reasonable cause to suspect a child may have been in need of protection. Most statutes place the requirement to report upon individuals who have "reasonable cause to suspect that a child coming before them in their professional or official capacity is an abused or maltreated child."[1] These statutes then usually designate which professionals are liable under the requirements for reporting.

WILLIAM VINCENT GRIFFIN is Senior Field Instructor, Child Protective Services Training Institute, Cornell University, Ithaca, N.Y.

[1] *New York State S.S.L., Section 413.*

The first and most important case imposing civil liability for a failure to report a child abuse case is *Landeros v. Flood* (1976). In this case the court upheld the liability of a physician, stating that the doctor should have recognized the "battered child syndrome" which, the court said, "has become an accepted medical diagnosis."

To date, no one has been criminally convicted for failure to report a case of suspected child abuse and neglect, but we are aware of three investigations (Colorado and New York) regarding this offense. These situations involved a teacher, a doctor, and a child protection worker, and all were resolved without criminal sanctions being imposed.

The statutory requirements to report set by state legislatures are based on two assumptions. First, the state traditionally has had some input into the job performance of a mandated reporter; the practice of these professions usually requires a license. Second, the professionals designated as mandated reporters generally have a strong set of criteria within their own disciplines that establish standards for job performance. Traditionally, in civil courts, the standard of conduct has been "adequate professional practice as defined by the profession itself." Thus, imposition of penalties for failure to report suspected cases of child abuse and neglect has been established based upon the standards of practice of the professionals themselves. Where the group involved is mandated to report, but lacks the strong traditional background of being a "profession," the state has in most instances established the standards through licensing procedures, as it has done with day care providers.

Most statutes require that upon receipt of a report of suspected child abuse or maltreatment, the central registry, or responsible state agency, will then transmit the allegations to a field worker who must follow up the transmittal with an adequate investigation and intervene when the child is endangered. The laws specify definitions, procedures, and consequences of a report of suspected child abuse and neglect, but they only outline the investigative process.

The failure of the statutes to reflect clear standards for *all* child protective service activities is a fundamental problem. This issue must be dealt with before more cases arise in which the malfeasance of public employees is charged.

How does a worker go about performing an "adequate investigation"? When is "intervention" needed to protect an endangered child? Is a response to the person who reported the situation sufficient? Should the children be seen? Does a report involving three children under the age of five get the same response as a report involving a child of sixteen? Does a field visit constitute an adequate investigation? There are hundreds of these questions that remain unanswered by state statutes. Yet, workers are being taken to task for failing to respond "adequately" to reports of suspected child abuse and neglect and to the broad requirements of their own state laws. Are we negligent for action we did not take? Can we be held liable for the actions taken? William L. Prosser summarizes negligent action as follows:

1. A duty or obligation, recognized by the law, requiring the actor to conform to a certain *standard* of conduct
2. A failure on his part to conform to the *standard* required
3. A reasonably close causal connection between the conduct and the resulting injury
4. Actual loss or damage resulting to the interests (health, finances, and emotional or psychological ability) of another.[2]

What is the standard of conduct when the state has not defined adequate practice for child protective services?

At one time, the standard of care was measured by the norm within a particular locality. Increasingly, however, the trend of the courts is to impose a higher standard of care. Prosser states that the higher standard of care imposes a higher standard of training: "Professional(s) in general, and those who undertake any work calling for special skill, are required not only to exercise reasonable care in what they do, but also to possess a standard minimum of special knowledge and ability."[3]

Some states have incorporated into their legislation a rather broad framework, requiring that the state agency responsible for child protection implementation be the designated body for directing educational and training programs for those individuals who will be enforcing the statutory requirements.[4] Yet few states have made use of this opportunity to establish and train workers to basic standards for child protection. Instead, they have let out for bid contracts that allow for generic social work training rather than developing a comprehensive and coordinated statewide curriculum for basic training of child protection workers. The question should be raised constantly as to how poorly trained, inadequately prepared, and virtually unsupervised child protective workers can be asked to make decisions about endangered children and their families.

The Massachusetts Committee for Children and Youth (MCCY), under the leadership of Dr. Eli H. Newberger, recently filed suit against the Commonwealth of Massachusetts, alleging that the *state* does not fulfill its constitutional and statutory mandate to protect abused and neglected children. The relief sought by MCCY encompasses the entire protection service system: policy, budget, administration, supervision, and delivery of services. The suit also specifically addresses the "inadequate numbers of properly trained protective service caseworkers . . . employed by the Department."[5] MCCY asks that

---

[2]*William L. Prosser, Handbook of the Law of Torts* (4th ed.; St. Paul: West Publishing, 1971), p. 30.

[3]*Ibid., p. 161.*

[4]*New York State S.S.L. Section 421.*

[5]*Massachusetts Committee for Children and Youth Inc. versus Commonwealth of Massachusetts, Superior Court Department of the Trial Court, Civil Action, Suffolk, September 24, 1979.*

the defendant, the Commonwealth of Massachusetts, be *ordered* to establish specific guidelines and standards related to child protective services.

Vincent DeFrances states: "Where adequacy of service delivery is challenged, a strong case can be made upon a showing of agency operation at a level substantially below accepted national standards in the specific areas cited."[6] Thus, if a worker is held accountable for not performing at a proper capacity and this impairment is due to an agency's failure to establish standards of practice, the worker should involve the agency as codefendant. The state and the individual workers share the responsibility and the liability concerning the provision of services. Workers must be accountable, but a logical sequence of state and agency responsibility must also be established. This can occur only with the establishment of standardized criteria for the minimum of service.

STANDARDS—AN HISTORICAL PERSPECTIVE

Many professional organizations involved in the development of child protection services consider improving practice through standard-setting as a major priority: "Setting standards and improving practice in all social services for children have been major functions of the Child Welfare League of America since its formation more than 50 years ago."[7]

In 1977 the American Humane Association, by virtue of 100 years of experience in protecting children, developed standards for agencies which carry out child protective service responsibilities. These standards were operational in nature and were developed mainly as a result of the many requests the association had received from participants in its training workshops across the United States and Canada.[8] The view of the association is that these standards are the core subject of much broader discussions and definitions expressed by groups of individuals concerned with the more global world of child welfare. Hence, it has undertaken training and evaluation of communities based upon these standards. The Child Protection Certification Curriculum developed and delivered by the American Humane Association has been utilized in South Carolina, West Virginia, Vermont, and Edmonton (Canada) to certify that the states and province have received training based upon established standards particular to operational and functional definitions.

The National Association of Social Workers (NASW) in 1979 appointed a Task Force on Social Work Practice in Child Protection. This group was established to meet one of the maximum-priority association goals set by their 1979 National Delegate Assembly: "To develop standards for the delivery of social services in relevant delivery systems."[9] The standards developed by

[6]*Vincent DeFrances*, American Humane Association Newsletter, *Winter 1979, guest editorial.*

[7]*Child Welfare League of America*, Standards for Child Protection *(New York: the League, 1960), p. v.*

[8]*The American Humane Association*, Child Protective Services Standards *(Englewood, Colo.: the Association, 1977).*

[9]*"Protective Services Standards Published,"* NASW News, *April 1981.*

the task force became known as NASW Standards for Social Work Practice in Child Protection, which set forth "models of behavior for social workers who endeavor to alleviate the occurrence and root out the causes of child abuse and neglect."[10] These standards, approved by the NASW Board of Directors, represent the professional commitment to establish a *level of competence* expected of all social workers employed by child protective services agencies and those who supplement these agencies. This attempt is along more functional than operational lines; it addresses requirements of knowledge of such fields as personality development, child rearing, and family culture. The workers are also asked to have knowledge of the laws which might affect the performance of their jobs (child abuse and neglect legislation, child custody, guardianship, and adoption laws), as well as knowledge of the legal and judicial systems which adjudicate child abuse and neglect cases.

In May of 1981 the American Public Welfare Association (APWA) published a *Guide*[11] prepared by the APWA National Resource Center on Child Abuse and Neglect. The Guide is intended to provide child protective services agency administrators and supervisors with a vehicle for enhancing the competency of agency social workers and supervisors.

James A. Harrell, Director, National Center on Child Abuse and Neglect, Children's Bureau, reflects on this work as

> a document [that] aspires to provide a flexible framework within which states and localities can analyze the tasks performed by child protective service workers and supervisors. The *Guide* furnishes agencies with a detailed checklist to assess knowledge and skills needed by their staffs in carrying out their child protective tasks.
>
> This document is especially timely. *The number of legal suits aimed at child protective workers and their agencies* has increased during the last year. A number of jurisdictions have experienced an increase of child deaths involving children *known* to protective agencies. The challenge of child protection continues to outstrip our capacity to meet them. This *Guide* can become an important aspect in improving services to abused and neglected children and their families.[12]

These standards could be utilized by states to develop a model for their own system that could be the basis for good child protection practice. In 1979 the New York State Department of Social Services developed a Title XX contract to establish the Childhood Protective Services Training Institute to implement a standardized, comprehensive training program for all child protection service workers, supervisors, and county attorneys. This program,

---

[10]Ibid.

[11]*Joanne Secinske,* A Guide for Improved Service Delivery: Analysis of the Tasks, Knowledge, and Skill Requisites and Performance Criteria of the Child Protective Functions *(Washington, D.C.: American Public Welfare Association, 1981), Introduction letter.*

[12]*James A. Harrell, Introduction letter,* ibid. *(emphasis added).*

administered by Cornell University, has begun to bring a standardized approach to the problems of child abuse and neglect throughout New York State. Since the states themselves have assumed the legal responsibility to protect endangered children, it follows that action such as this must be taken by the state-level agencies before any standardization of service on a statewide basis can be established. Such standardization, insofar as it delineates the responsibilities and the accountability of caseworkers, will decrease their concerns about liability and improve child protection services for families in the community.

PRESCRIPTION FOR PROGRESS

The comparison of these sets of standards shows that there have been two important developments. The first occurred during the 1950s and 1960s when operational standards were established. The Child Welfare League of America and the American Humane Association were the first groups to establish procedures to put the delivery of child protective services into operation organizationally. What became apparent to both these groups and to NASW, APWA, and the National Center on Child Abuse and Neglect was that the functional aspects desperately needed attention. Within a few years (1975–81), a wealth of information and standard-setting activity along functional lines took place.

The American Humane Association in 1980 published *Helping in Child Protective Services*,[13] and through field experiences additionally formalized the Child Protection Certification Curriculum:

> Child protective service has become a highly specialized area of social work within the broad field of child welfare. In most communities it represents the front line of defense in the system of services aimed at protecting children from neglect and abuse. While the total child protective effort calls for *multidisciplinary capability and coordination*, this book is designed to address the *vital and distinctive tasks* of the child protective caseworker. It represents the wealth of experience and knowledge gained from the field of practice in CPS and *sets a standard for performance.*[14]

The NASW published the previously mentioned standards for social work practice in child protection, documenting the ethics, values, knowledge requirements, and skills needed by all social workers engaged in the services, including administrators, supervisors, and child protection workers.

The APWA drafted its guide to provide a foundation for agency personnel

---

[13]*Wayne M. Holder and Cynthia Mohr, eds.*, Helping in Child Protective Services *(Englewood, Colo.: the Association, 1980).*

[14]*National Association of Social Workers*, NASW Standards for Social Work Practice in Child Protection *(Washington, D.C.: the Association, 1981), p. 4 (emphasis added).*

and academicians to continue their work toward establishing a valid and reliable means for certifying the competency of child protection workers and supervisors in *public* agencies.

What is needed now is a unified approach in bringing together the available operational and functional standards so that a cohesive program encompassing all the aspects of child protective services can be achieved. Numerous states and counties have established handbooks (Colorado), procedure manuals (Hennepin County, Minnesota, and Utah), model standards and guidelines for particular aspects (multidisciplinary child abuse teams in Pennsylvania and in New Haven, Connecticut), directories of agencies that provide child abuse services (Michigan, Connecticut), and so on. However, the National Center on Child Abuse and Neglect and the American Humane Association are the only organizations that have published works that could be viewed as attempting to universalize the approach to child protective services today.

Individual states now need to glean the available materials and formulate a comprehensive statewide approach to the establishment of standards. These standards will be the foundation for the comprehensive development of a functional, worker-supportive protection system. We have placed much emphasis on getting appropriate services in place and have not been heedful enough of the role of a competent worker in putting into operation approaches to problems of child abuse and neglect.

If workers' thoughts are squarely on ameliorating the problems of maltreatment encountered in a given situation rather than on personal liability issues, they will more likely be able to complete their mandated tasks. We cannot afford to have front-line workers who are hesitant in approaching situations of abuse and neglect. Established standards will help to ensure a solid footing for competent job performance.

The occurrence of a child protection investigation constitutes a turning point in the personal history of a caseworker as well as the subjects of the worker's report. Like other pivotal events, its resolution can dramatically affect the course of the future. Just as the subjects should be made aware of their rights to privacy, confidentiality, and legal recourse, so must caseworkers, supervisors, and administrators. Additionally, it is of paramount importance that what occurs in the interaction between subjects and agency be firmly grounded in consistent, responsible policy and regulation. The development of objective standards is the ultimate goal for those intervention strategies.

The organizations mentioned in this article are taking a national leadership role in developing just such criteria for child protective services. If agencies and workers can parallel their actions with these standards, their ability to withstand subjective scrutiny and ensure the protection of professional social work practice can only be enhanced. Accordingly, program administrators will no longer be able to separate themselves from the actions of their agents. They will instead have to become a party to the defense of those actions.

Many agencies across the nation have not felt the effects of a civil or criminal action against any employees. Those agencies that have, will continue to feel the reverbations for many years to come. Even those agencies that have not been affected will not go unscathed, for with each new instance of questioned actions, the chances of further movement in the direction of litigation will be inevitable.

We do not wish to become so stringent in our approach to protective services that workers become robotlike in their daily activities. However, we must give both the untrained, inexperienced worker and the veteran of many protective encounters the same message: their actions are based upon clear, established criteria. When a situation of family violence involving a child occurs, they will be intervening in a professional, positive manner, and not with a subjective, literally ad hoc approach that is detrimental both to subjects and worker over the course of time.

THE SOCIAL WELFARE FORUM, 1983

PART II

OFFICIAL PROCEEDINGS, 110TH ANNUAL FORUM
NATIONAL CONFERENCE ON SOCIAL WELFARE
HOUSTON, TEXAS
MAY 22–25, 1983

Published 1985 by the
National Conference on Social Welfare

Foreword

The 110th Annual Forum of the National Conference on Social Welfare convened in Houston, Texas, from May 22 to May 25, 1983. The theme of the Annual Forum, "Mobilizing Society to Meet New Realities," is well represented in the contents of *The Social Welfare Forum, 1983*. In broad perspective, the theme is reflected widely in today's world by the desperate efforts of social welfare workers, advocates, and agencies to meet urgent societal needs despite pressing economic, political, and social constraints. In a more immediate and apparent sense, it is evidenced by the fact that now is the time to combine two editions of *Social Welfare Forum*, namely, the 1982 and 1983 issues, into a dual volume and, also, to distribute the volume in offset form and under the imprimatur of NCSW. In many respects, therefore, the practices as well as the preachments of this year's National Conference on Social Welfare testify to societal mobilization to meet new realities.

The Honorable J. J. Pickle, chairman of the Subcommittee on Social Security, Committee on Ways and Means, United States House of Representatives, was the keynote speaker at the opening plenary session of the Forum. His speech constituted a strong defense of America's Social Security system, yet one tempered by a sober analysis of contemporary political and economic trends. In the following plenary session, Robert J. Lampman, Professor of Economics at the University of Wisconsin, Madison, presented an innovative technique for assessing the effects of a wide range of social welfare problems upon the economy of the United States.

Among the topics discussed at the 1983 Annual Forum were the "new federalism," volunteerism, private-sector contributions to social welfare, employee assistance programs, Social Security assistance, immigrant and minority families, the elderly, the homeless, correctional programs, long-term care and hospital care, women's and children's issues, protective services, youth unemployment, health promotion and health care costs, information management, and knowledge dissemination. Although not all the foregoing topics are represented in this volume, many of them are reviewed succinctly in the SCAN listings that are published in the newsletter of the NCSW.

Appreciation is extended to the efficient and hard-working members of the Editorial Committee: Esther Wattenberg (chairperson-elect), Assistant Director, School of Social Work, University of Minnesota, Minneapolis; Bill B. Benton, Director, Human Services Division, Urban Systems Research and Engineering, Washington, D.C.; Jane Collins (Program Committee representative), Director, Department of Clinical Social Work, Denver Department of Health and Hospitals; Ronald B. Dear, Associate Professor, School of Social Work, University of Washington; Jeanne Giovannoni, Professor,

School of Social Welfare, University of California, Los Angeles; Martin Sundel, Roy E. Dulak Professor, Graduate School of Social Work, University of Texas, Arlington; Mark R. Yessian, Editor, *New England Journal of Human Services*. The committee especially expresses its appreciation for superb editorial assistance to Maureen Herman, Senior Staff Associate, NCSW.

It was our high honor to serve the National Conference on Social Welfare. The Editorial Committee hopes that the contents of *The Social Welfare Forum, 1983* will be of interest and of value to its many readers. Even further, it hopes that this volume will represent a significant step toward implementing the theme of the 110th Annual Forum, namely, mobilizing societal resources to meet new realities.

RONALD A. FELDMAN
Chairperson,
Editorial Committee

Remarks of the NCSW President

DUIRA B. WARD

My brief remarks are intended to be an accounting, covering the past two years of the long life of the National Conference on Social Welfare. They have been spent in seeking appropriate means by which the organization might perform the role for which it is uniquely suited. This is not a new role, but it was clearly reaffirmed by board action two years ago in San Francisco just before Mitch Ginsberg handed me the gavel. That role is to act as a continuing national forum in which the major social issues of the day can be addressed together by citizens of good will who come from *varying* backgrounds and experiences.

Accordingly, we have attempted to widen our membership in kind, as well as in numbers. The effort has coincided with a time of strong competing pressures, but it continues and needs your participation. It is perhaps a sign of the times that among those who have joined us have been some major national and international corporations: Champion International, Gulf and Western, Northeast Utilities, Xerox, and Systems Development Corporation. We need more corporations like these who believe, with the Business Round-table's Committee on Corporate Responsibility, that: "Business and society have a symbiotic relationship: the long-term viability of the corporation depends upon its responsibility to the society of which it is a part."

In turn, board membership itself has become more diversified. For surely we have learned over the past three difficult years that the public base on which systematic attention to the meeting of human needs must rest can never again be taken for granted. Surely we have learned that we providers and volunteer advocates cannot hope to reestablish that base by talking only among ourselves.

And so our 109th Annual Forum in Boston in April 1982 reflected that lesson learned. It was designed to expose participants to clear expositions of varying views of the social role of government. By its close, I believe, issues had been sharpened, but we could not leave it there.

As the gap between human need and national government provisions to meet it widened; as state legislatures demonstrated their reluctance to fill it in spite of those vaunted new revenue resources returned to them in the form of federal income tax reductions; as the New Federalism thus was revealed as only Old Localism, after all; as the resources and problems of localities became themselves ever more unequal, we decided that the time called out for a concentrated, sober study of the federal social role, a study which by enlisting the participation of influential representatives of academe, business, labor, and government, as well as of the human services community, might have some impact on policy-makers.

The Ittleson Foundation quickly understood the need for, and the timeliness of, such an endeavor, and therefore gave NCSW initial support in the form of a grant which we were permitted to use as planning and sustaining money. Fortunately for us, Alan Pifer—whose classic exposition of the federal social role opened our Boston Forum—was on the point of retiring as president of the Carnegie Corporation in order to contribute his time to just such undertakings of his own choosing. To our joy, he agreed to chair the study, indeed to contribute half of his time to it, and to support us in our approaches to foundations for continuing funding of the operation. His first act was to locate a full-time director of the project, Forrest Chisman. Mr. Chisman holds his bachelor's degree, summa cum laude, from Harvard, his doctorate in politics from Oxford, has taught political theory and American government at the University of Toronto, and has worked with the Aspen Institute Program on Communications and Society, the Markle Foundation, and the National Telecommunications and Information Administration.

Armed with funding for the exploratory stage of the project by the Edna McConnell Clark Foundation, the Carnegie Corporation, the Kaiser Foundation, and the Ford Foundation, these two gentlemen have worked out of our offices since early February in personal interviews with some two hundred leading citizens and institutions of many persuasions—some of them members of NCSW, some of them suggested by NCSW members, and some of them suggested by others.

There has been no shortage of enthusiasm for the study and its timeliness, or of eagerness to be involved.

The advice they have received can be summarized as: review the federal social role from the perspectives of both history and philosophy, and then look to those discernible future trends which will shape that role inevitably, regardless of shifting ideologies. They have been aware that there is already an abundance of material to work with scattered over the landscape, and so the major effort in the first instance is planned to be one of synthesis and evaluation. It is expected that the entire effort will continue for from two to three years. Funding is being applied for in three stages: the present exploratory stage, already in hand, with two substantive stages to follow, consisting first of collection, collation, integration, and evaluation of material, and, second, the convening of a commission to develop the final report. We hope to direct public attention to both the process and the product.

In the end, we hope to have contributed usefully to the national sobering up which must follow ever-so-charmingly rationalized federal social irresponsibility.

It was in keeping with this effort, as well as with the ongoing mission of NCSW, that we selected the somewhat presumptuous theme of this Forum: "Mobilizing Society to Meet New Realities."

Now I must comment on the successive crises which have afflicted NCSW over these same two years. The strained budgets of member agencies have been reflected in ours. The drying up of federal research grants and projects have removed important pieces from the jigsaw puzzle solving which has been our traditional budgeting process. It has adversely affected our ability to provide adequate staffing to the Forum on Long Term Care. It has ended the ability of NCSW to continue to serve the Coalition for Refugee Resettlement—both painful developments for areas which continue to need the brokering skills of NCSW staff. We have been distracted by repeated lifeboat drills. Our staff has suffered and sacrificed. Their patience and generosity have been our secret weapon.

At our darkest moment last September, we were forced to send out an SOS to our membership. Your generous response at a time of your own financial stresses pulled us through.

And so the National Conference on Social Welfare lives on. I believe its historic mission is more relevant than ever to the ultimate social health of this nation. We must restore and maintain a coherent national presence during this period of creeping Balkanization of a country increasingly, paradoxically, characterized by mobility and interdependence. Let us admit that this Balkanization has followed a period of fragmentation within our own human services community.

I am told that NCSW has been called "the mother of social welfare organizations." Indeed, we take pride in those which have sprung from our forums and from among our member activists. As a plaintive mother of independent children myself, I have no difficulty at all in formulating the question which I would like now to send to the members of these organizational offspring. That question is: "Have you called you mother lately?"

It has been a privilege to work with NCSW during these two years. I shall transfer this office to Bertram Beck on Wednesday confidently and joyfully. More about that gentleman then.

Now, for the main event of the evening.

National Conference on Social Welfare Distinguished Service Awards

THE NATIONAL CONFERENCE on Social Welfare Distinguished Service Awards for 1983 were awarded to the following:

THE NATIONAL COUNCIL OF JEWISH WOMEN AND THE NATIONAL COUNCIL OF JUVENILE AND FAMILY COURT JUDGES FOR THE NATIONAL COURT APPOINTED SPECIAL ADVOCATE PROJECT. The Project focuses on the group of children found to be neglected, abused, or dependent. Under the CASA Project, trained and professionally supervised volunteers function as court-appointed guardians *ad litem* and are charged with investigating circumstances of alleged child abuse or neglect, independent evaluation and recommendations for further action in the best interest of the child, and for monitoring the child's progress through the child welfare system until permanent placement is achieved.

The Court Appointed Special Advocate Project has demonstrated that involvement of volunteers in working with the juvenile justice and child welfare systems can help to provide more permanent placements for children and to make the child welfare system more responsive to the best needs of the child and to ensure that every child has the opportunity to have a safe, loving, and legally protected home.

MELVIN A. GLASSER, Social worker, educator, author, effective negotiator and administrator in the labor movement, and advocate for improved health and welfare services in the United States and in other countries; and pioneer in the shaping of national social policy; innovator in the development of worker benefits for labor and consumers; and leader in national and international social welfare organizations; consultant to Presidents, members of Congress, and to governments in other countries; strong and persuasive advocate for a system of national health care for the United States.

NATIONAL CONFERENCE ON SOCIAL WELFARE
DISTINGUISHED SERVICE AWARDS, 1955 – 1983

1955 EDITH M. BAKER, Washington, D.C.
FEDELE F. FAURI, Ann Arbor, Mich.
ELIZABETH WICKENDEN, New York

1956 TIAC (Temporary Inter-Association Council) PLANNING COMMITTEE, New York

1957 THE REVEREND MARTIN LUTHER KING, JR., Montgomery, Ala.
WILBUR J. COHEN, Ann Arbor, Mich.

1958 THE HONORABLE JOHN E. FOGARTY, R.I.
LEONARD W. MAYO, New York

1959 ELISABETH SHIRLEY ENOCHS, Washington, D.C.
OLLIE A. RANDALL, New York

1960 LOULA DUNN, Chicago
RALPH BLANCHARD, New York
HELEN HALL, New York

1961 THE HONORABLE AIME J. FORAND, R.I.

1962 JOSEPH P. ANDERSON, New York
THE ATLANTA *Constitution*, Ralph McGill and Jack Nelson, Atlanta, Ga.
CHARLOTTE TOWLE, Chicago

1963 HARRIET M. BARTLETT, Cambridge, Mass.
ERNEST JOHN BOHN, Cleveland
FLORENCE G. HELLER, Glencoe, Ill.
Special Award: Television Documentary, "The Battle of Newburgh," IRVING GITLIN and the NATIONAL BROADCASTING Company, New York
Special Citation (Posthumous): ANNA ELEANOR ROOSEVELT, "First Lady of the World"

1964 DR. ROBERT M. FELIX, Bethesda, Md.
Special Citation (Posthumous): JOHN FITZGERALD KENNEDY, "Man of Destiny"

1965 JAMES V. BENNETT, Washington, D.C.
SIDNEY HOLLANDER, Baltimore
CORA KASIUS, New York

1966 REPRESENTATIVE WILBUR D. MILLS, Ark.

1967 THE HONORABLE HUBERT H. HUMPHREY, Washington, D.C.
PLANNED PARENTHOOD — WORLD POPULATION
Special Awards (Posthumous):
HOWARD F. GUSTAFSON, Indianapolis
RUTH M. WILLIAMS, New York

1968 LOMA MOYER ALLEN, Rochester, N.Y.
KENNETH BANCROFT CLARK, New York

1969   THE HONORABLE ELMER L. ANDERSEN, St. Paul, Minn.
       HARRY L. LURIE, New York
       IDA C. MERRIAM, Washington, D.C.
1970   No award
1971   SAM S. GRAIS, St. Paul, Minn.
       DOROTHY I. HEIGHT, New York
1972   WHITNEY M. YOUNG, JR. *(Posthumous)*
1973   WINSLOW CARLTON, New York
       THE HONORABLE JAMES CHARLES EVERS, Fayette, Miss.
       JOE R. HOFFER, Columbus, Ohio
       NATIONAL COUNCIL OF JEWISH WOMEN, New York
1974   ASSOCIATION OF AMERICAN INDIAN SOCIAL WORKERS
1975   MITCHELL I. GINSBERG, New York
1976   BERTRAM S. BROWN, M.D., Rockville, Md.
       THE HONORABLE BARBARA JORDAN, Washington, D.C.
       THE HONORABLE WALTER F. MONDALE, Washington, D.C.
       WILLIAM A. MORRILL, Washington, D.C.
1977   ROY WILKINS, New York
1978   COY EKLUND, New York
       VERNON E. JORDAN, JR., New York
       CYNTHIA C. WEDEL, Washington, D.C.
1979   JAMES R. DUMPSON, New York
       GISELA KONOPKA, Minneapolis
       NORMAN V. LOURIE, Harrisburg, Pa.
       GEORGE M. NISHINAKA, Los Angeles
1980   *Special Citation (Posthumous)*: JUSTICE WILLIAM O. DOUGLAS
       DOUGLAS A. FRASER
1981   EVELINE M. BURNS, New York
       LOIS AND SAMUEL SILBERMAN FUND, New York
       NATIONAL URBAN COALITION and M. CARL HOLMAN, President,
       New York
1982   ROGER N. BALDWIN *(Posthumous)*
       CHARLES I. SCHOTTLAND, Tucson, Ariz.
1983   MELVIN A. GLASSER, Washington, D.C.
       NATIONAL COUNCIL OF JEWISH WOMEN, New York and NATIONAL
       COUNCIL OF JUVENILE AND FAMILY COURT JUDGES, Reno, Nev.

Greetings to the Conference from President Ronald Reagan

I AM happy to extend my warm greetings to members and guests of the National Conference on Social Welfare as you gather for your 110th Annual Forum.

This occasion provides me with a most welcome opportunity to salute the work of your members in helping the less fortunate people in our nation. Your conference theme, "Mobilizing Society to Meet New Realities," reflects very well the concern we all have for addressing the challenges we face today.

Your organization represents a spirit and commitment of generosity and compassion. You attempt to bring the blessings of America to all our people, and to overcome problems to assist in the fulfillment of individual potential. You have set a fine standard for the rest of us, and it is appreciated.

You have my best wishes for a most productive and successful forum. By working together, we all—whether professionals in the field, volunteers, or representatives of government—can continue to strive to improve the quality of life for all Americans.

Contents

152   *Contents*

Mobilizing Society to Meet New Realities

J. J. PICKLE

I MUST confess that I was not comfortable with the prospect of standing before a conference entitled "Social Welfare." In Washington, some of my colleagues—and maybe some members of the National Conference— call me a redneck conservative. In my district, however, some folks call me a flaming liberal. And there are those who have tried to pin other labels on me. But of all the things I have been called, I have never thought of myself as a social welfare worker.

But I shall let you in on a secret. I worked for the National Youth Administration for three and a half years, closely allied to the WPA. If that makes me a social welfare worker, I am proud of it.

And I shall let you in on another secret. As a member of the U.S. Congress, I am one of the most constant of all social workers. The casework performed by Congressmen is something we deal with every day, every hour. We do not ask for this, and sometimes we feel discomfort at the constant demands— but my last secret is that nothing gives greater lasting pleasure than to know we have helped someone who needed it. It is the most worthwhile part of our job.

Here at the Forum we come from many different backgrounds, many different professions, and many different political persuasions, but our challenge, and the challenge always of the NCSW, is the same—to provide for society's needs against ever-changing realities. The job of social welfare is to balance human needs between the *challenge* that society ought to provide its members to work to provide for themselves and the *security* that society ought to provide when we need it.

No nation ever becomes a great nation or stays great unless it provides for those who are less advantaged. A great nation must have a great heart. I think our nation has shown this to the world over and over.

The irony is that we cannot become great unless we give an essential part of our assets to help the unfortunate; but history also has taught us that if we go beyond that which is proper or appropriate we weaken the strength of our nation. Not all of us are subject to a higher calling. We might prefer to go fishing if we did not have to hold a job to keep a roof over our heads and

The Honorable J. J. PICKLE is a member of the U.S. House of Representatives Washington, D.C.

provide for our families. We can become poor and waste our nation's minds and energies if we give too much help.

The fact is, society must do what is expected and proper. It must find what will help the individual but will not keep him in bondage. It is with a bit of melancholy that we realize we do not know where that line is. Perhaps it is not a stationary line. But that does not excuse us from the effort.

The NCSW itself is in adjustment. The strength of this organization over the years is that it has shifted its focus and its activities many times as the challenges facing social welfare have shifted. The continuing debate over just what NCSW should be about has enabled it to change what it is about as that was needed.

I see this kind of debate not only as healthy but as necessary. In recent decades the impulse has been to turn to the federal government for money, hope, and direction. Throughout the 1960s and early 1970s the moral dicta disseminating from Washington and the open federal purse taxed the ingenuity of social organizations just to figure out ways to put this largesse to work. Some of the things we came up with worked pretty well—others did not. But, with increasing outcries from the middle class about tax burdens, followed now by the prospect of $200 billion federal deficits, we clearly must find new responses.

Entitlements are being limited more and more—and will have to be limited beyond current restraints before we are through. But most are not being eliminated. The nation is still turning to the federal government to provide benefits such as extra aid for the jobless and health care for the unemployed.

Entitlements have been the Blessed Assurance of our less fortunate that they have not been forgotten, that help is not just on the way but that help will continue. But entitlements have been such a continuing, ongoing annual increase in expenditure that Congress must reckon both with the direction and the growth of entitlements.

Congress has not yet come to grips with this question. However, very soon Congress must confront this matter. I hope we can do it with grace—with Amazing Grace.

Those who are in social programs, and particularly those who depend so religiously on entitlements, must recognize that we must make some kind of evaluation of these programs, too. When our nation is facing $200 billion deficits, we can be sure that Congress is not going to authorize a 10 percent net increase in defense spending. As patriotically as that might appeal to some citizens, Congress will not do it. Similarly, I must say that neither is the Congress going to increase social expenditures very much, if at all.

I hope the social work profession accepts the fact that we must agree on a direction that will help us reduce the huge deficits, for if we do not find an answer to that we cannot do good works anywhere—neither in defense nor on the domestic front. In other words, the dollar amount that social welfare programs receive from the government is not the most important decision to be made—most important is the kind of help we provide and the direction of programs we approve.

There is a definite shift, and it is more than just in money. The government is asked to respond to crises such as joblessness, but there is a growing leadership vaccuum in overall social welfare policy. We no longer look to the federal government alone to set the overall social welfare agenda. That job is being disseminated—and the question is, to where?

We will need in the future more intergovernmental cooperation. We will need more communication and coordination of government and private-sector efforts. We will need to focus more on how to provide for the general welfare than on the dollars needed.

A prime example is Medicare. Like Casey Jones' freight train, it is going downhill ninety miles per hour, and in another valley we can already hear the whistle screaming. We all know that we must make major changes in this field. I know that those changes are not likely to occur until at least one more Congress convenes, but that gives us precious little time. From groups like the NCSW must come the innovative answers that will enable us to continue to provide health care to our needy and our elderly. Medicare and Medicaid are not fanciful dreams; they are absolute necessities. The solutions that Congress settles on will be only as good as the ideas which come from concerned people in social welfare.

I implore you to think about this.

Groups like the NCSW must help provide the cooperative leadership, and must pioneer new consensus-building mechanisms, not just in the health field but in those that will further social welfare efforts at all levels of society. No one has a higher calling than the social work profession. The purpose of social welfare as I see it is to provide for the well-being of our community. It is not just a laundry list of the needs of the unfortunate: and social workers limit *themselves* if they treat it that way. Social welfare is the whole community. It gets at the guts of humanity.

It has been my high privilege to be associated for the past several years with the most successful of all our social programs, and that is Social Security. This is a program that better than any I know meets that balance between the challenge and the security society must provide. It rewards the worker, but it provides security to those who lose their income whether they are middle class or poor or whatever.

After almost a decade of growing alarm about the health and solvency of our Social Security program, the lack of daily Social Security headlines since the new bill became law is a welcome relief. The country—especially our elderly and our young—deserves this respite. Social Security will always be there; no government will ever let it go broke. In this new Social Security bill, Congress showed that the government can make the substantive changes necessary to keep the program sound.

The Social Security program now pays out over $200 billion in benefits annually to over 36 million beneficiaries, not counting Medicare payments. Clearly, it affects every American family and business, and it is no wonder that enacting changes in this program is a difficult, politically sensitive process.

No one claims that the new law will solve every problem that may arise in Social Security, but it gives us a much stronger foundation than we had before. The new Social Security law will raise $166.2 billion for the years 1983 through 1989. Even under relatively pessimistic assumptions, this will keep reserves above minimum levels for the next several years and allow them to begin to climb to more comfortable levels at the end of this decade.

Congress also included important backup procedures should trouble still arise in the next few years. These include allowing the three trust funds to borrow from each other, limiting cost-of-living increases to the percentage increase in average wages when trust fund reserves are low and inflation is higher than wage increases, and a requirement that the administration accompany any report of an unexpected shortfall with recommendations on how to deal with it.

The new law also drops the current long-term Social Security deficit from 2.09 percent of payroll to a *flat zero*.

The money to reach the goals of solvency and greater stability now and in the future must come from many sectors. By using the National Commission proposals as a base, Congress spread the burden around so that no one will be hit unduly or harshly.

The law is important for what it does not do as much as for what it does do:

It does not raise the wage base or raise tax rates beyond those already scheduled in law.

It does not rely on tax increases to close the long-term gap.

It avoids reductions in benefits except in the cost-of-living (COLA) adjustments and through taxing benefits of beneficiaries with incomes above $25,000 (single people) and $32,000 (married, filing jointly).

It avoids wholesale alterations in the program.

It does affect us all: retired workers, present workers, self-employed workers, employers, Congressmen, federal and nonprofit workers never before covered under Social Security, and future retirees. And *all* of these changes were difficult. There was not an easy one in the bunch. After years of favorable economies and easy votes, the Congress has in recent years had to step up to the line and prove its real commitment to Social Security with tough, unpleasant votes, both providing extra funds and making necessary structural changes in the program to keep it sound in the future.

The challenge in Social Security was to make changes in a rational and humane manner. Similar challenges will *always* face this group in other areas. I say that because I think it is hard sometimes not to feel besieged by change. But the challenge of change is not new to the field of social welfare; it is the *nature* of that field because it is *human nature*. Never should your profession coast and feel that your job is done—and never should you feel discouraged. NCSW more than most organizations, is part of the process of society and the process of community itself, and I salute you.

The Effects of Social Provision on the Economy

ROBERT J. LAMPMAN

SOCIAL welfare expenditures under public programs by federal, state, and local governments combined equaled 20.4 percent of GNP in 1978. These expenditures were for income maintenance, health care, education, and other welfare goods and services.[1] Another 8.0 percent of GNP went for these same purposes via supplements or alternatives to public social welfare expenditures. These include certain elements of "tax expenditures" which benefit specific families under the federal individual income tax; private group insurance for pensions and health care; expenditures of philanthropic organizations which accept voluntary contributions from one family and deliver benefits to another; and direct interfamily giving.[2]

These expenditures flow through public and private channels as secondary income. This flow is distinct from that between business firms and households. The taking of such income by recipient families is made possible by the giving in the form of taxes paid and private contributions made by families. The flow is one of interfamily transfers. Transfer income is distinct from primary or producer income, which is distributed by the market; it comes as a gift or without a reciprocal exchange of goods or services in the current period. However, I do not include all transfers. Excluded are intranuclear family transfers, transfers such as investment subsidies, which are intended to enhance production in the business sector, and transfers which are not targeted to specific families but flow to all residents in the form of such public goods as national defense and law and order.

I call this combination of income flows secondary consumer income (SCI). In 1978 the SCI cash and in-kind benefits received amounted to $580 billion or $2,655 per person. I assume that these benefits were paid for by $580 billion funded by taxes, wage diversions for pensions and health insurance, gifts to philanthropic organizations, and gifts made directly from one family to another.

A substantial part of the population receives one or more SCI benefits in any one year. However, the benefits are tilted toward those who are old and

ROBERT J. LAMPMAN is Professor of Economics, University of Wisconsin-Madison.

[1]*Alma W. McMillan and Ann K. Bixby, "Social Welfare Expenditures, Fiscal Year 1978,"* Social Security Bulletin *(1980)*, 43(5):3–17.
[2]*Robert J. Lampman, preliminary, unpublished manuscript.*

those who are poor. Families with children and those who experience illness are also favored. The combined pattern of benefits and payments for the benefits results in a net transfer from the top half of families to the bottom half in any one year.

Between 1950 and 1978 the ratio of SCI to GNP rose from 18.8 percent to 28.4 percent. What effects did this increase have on the economy? Was the national enterprise as a whole better off or worse off as a result of the change? Did the nation's well-being rise faster or slower than it would have if the increase in the SCI ratio had not occurred? To answer that question requires that we imagine what the nation would have been like without that expansion. It also requires that we identify, measure, and weigh the *social* benefits and *social* costs which may flow from the increase of SCI.

SOCIAL BENEFITS OF THE INCREASED SCALE OF SCI

The table lists benefits and costs. Benefits are seen as improvements in the degree of attainment of goals. The four explicit goals of the SCI system are, I assert, reduction of insecurity with respect to income loss and with respect to irregular and extraordinary expenditure, reduction of income poverty, and fair sharing of SCI taxes and contributions. These four goals are listed as items 1–4 in the table. Side benefits may flow from reduction of income inequality (item 5), improvement of the social and political environment (item 6), production increases due to improved education, health, and economic security of the work force (item 8), and production increases from more effective automatic stabilization of the economy (item 9).

The question is: Do these benefits exceed the social costs listed as items 10–13? The question is complicated by the fact that most of the social benefits are nonquantifiable. Let us begin by discussing the six possible but nonquantifiable benefits. Reduction of insecurity with respect to income loss is claimed as a social benefit of the increase in the SCI ratio. Cash benefits, which are the chief means of offsetting income loss due to retirement, disability, loss of breadwinner, and unemployment, increased 1.5 times as fast as GNP. This provided protection for more people against more risks. Hence, we can mark this down as an added social benefit with a plus sign in the first right-hand column.

Item 2 refers to the goal of reducing insecurity with respect to irregular and extraordinary expenditures. The greatest change here has been in the field of health care. SCI expenditures for health care increased three times as fast as GNP, primarily because of the expansion of private insurance and the introduction of Medicare and Medicaid. SCI expenditures for education increased 1.5 times as fast as GNP, and those for food, housing, and other welfare services increased slightly less than GNP. SCI expenditures for health, education, food, housing, and other welfare services combined increased 1.6 times as fast as GNP. Hence, we can conclude that more people have been made more secure with respect to unpredictable and "lumpy" purchases.

TABLE 1

SOCIAL BENEFITS AND SOCIAL COSTS IN 1978 ATTRIBUTABLE TO 1950–1978 CHANGES IN SCI

Item	Added Benefit	Added Cost
Nonquantifiable Items		
1. Reduction of insecurity with respect to income loss	+	
2. Reduction of insecurity with respect to irregular and extraordinary expenditure	+	
3. Reduction of income poverty	+	
4. Fair sharing of SCI taxes and contributions	0	
5. Reduction of income inequality	+	
6. Improvement of the social and political environment	+ or −	
7. Total of nonquantifiable benefits (items 1–6)	+	
Quantifiable Items		
8. Production increases due to improved education, health, economic security of the work force	4 percent of GNP	
9. Production increases from more effective automatic stabilization of the economy	0	
10. Collection, compliance, and administrative costs		1 percent of GNP
11. Loss of GNP due to reduction of hours at work, adjusted for positive value of extra nonmarketed time		2 percent of GNP
12. Loss of GNP due to reduction of productivity per hour at work from less intensity of work and less capital per worker		+ or −
13. Reallocation of resources to selected goods, adjusted for consumer valuation of selected goods		2 percent of GNP
Summary Items		
14. Quantifiable benefits (items 8 and 9) and quantifiable costs (items 10–13)	4 percent of GNP	5 percent + or − ? of GNP
15. Total of nonquantifiable and quantifiable benefits (items 7–9) and total costs (items 10–13)	4 percent + ? of GNP	5 percent + or − ? of GNP

The SCI system is also responsive to the goal of reducing income poverty. In 1978 about one third of all SCI benefits—as compared to only 2 percent of primary income—went to the 20 percent of the population who were pretransfer poor. Government cash transfers reduce the number counted as officially posttransfer poor to only 12 percent of the population. If in-kind government transfers of food, public housing, and health care are counted as income, then "adjusted income poverty" affected only 6.5 percent in 1978.[3] The pretransfer poverty rate did not fall consistently after 1965 but remained near 20 percent of the population. This would appear to reflect the slow growth of the economy during the 1970s, the accelerating divorce rate, and the increasing propensity of the young and old to form their own households. On the other hand, it may be due to the disincentives to earn primary incomes set up by the increased levels of SCI benefits and taxes. However, the increase in cash transfers is associated with reduction in the posttransfer poverty rate from 16 percent to 12 percent. The most dramatic improvement was the sharp reduction in the number of aged poor. Overall, then, we can say that the growth of the SCI system has had a positive contribution to the goal of reducing income poverty.

Item 4 points to the explicit goal of fair sharing of SCI taxes and contributions. The funding system which most people seem to accept is one that is regressive against primary incomes. Cash benefits and health care benefits are largely paid for by payroll taxes and wage diversions. On the other hand, education and food, housing, and other welfare services are mostly paid for out of income, sales, and property taxes. Philanthropy and interfamily direct giving provide about 20 percent of the funds. The justification offered for regressivity on the tax and contribution side is that SCI benefits are progressively distributed to those who are, at time of receipt of benefit, in the lower income class. Since there has been no sharp change in the pattern of burden among contributors, I will enter a zero with regard to added benefits for item 4.

I turn now to some benefits that are not explicit goals of the SCI system but which can be called side benefits. The first of these is reduction of income inequality. There have been some reductions of differences in income between young and old, white and black, residents of North and South. It would seem plausible that some reduction of such differences is due to the growth of SCI benefits. On the other hand, there has been virtually no change over time in the degree of inequality in the size distribution of income. Hence, it seems doubtful that SCI can be assigned a high mark for that. However, I place a plus sign alongside item 5.

I also find it hard to say whether there has been progress with respect to the social goal of improving the social and political environment. One difficulty is that this goal overlaps goals 1, 2, 3, and 4. Moreover, there is considerable controversy in the welfare state literature about the definition of this goal and

[3]G. William Hoagland, "The Effectiveness of Current Transfer Programs in Reducing Poverty," in Paul M. Sommers (ed), Welfare Reform in America *(Boston: Kluwer-Nijhoff Publishing, 1983), pp.53–75.*

little attention to how to measure the degree of attainment. Some argue that lessened inequality of opportunity and more economic security will reduce social tensions and interclass hostilities and, at the same time, expand the freedom to enjoy traditional social and political liberties—a freedom that is effectively denied to some by the market distribution of income and property. Others assert that the SCI system is destructive of freedom *from* certain interferences by government—or what can be called negative freedom.[4] I see some merit in both sides of this argument but I do not know how to measure the outcomes that they predict.

Two side benefits of the expansion of SCI are stated in terms of added GNP and are therefore quantifiable. These are shown in items 8 and 9. Item 8 is stated as production increases due to improved education, health, and economic security of the work force. The most studied of these relationships is that between education and production. The cost of education may be equated with human capital. A team of researchers at Northwestern University calculates that the nation's stock of such capital was $1.1 trillion in 1945 and $4.5 trillion in 1976, all in 1972 dollars,[5] an increase of $3.4 trillion. If we can say that half of the increase occurred because of the sustained rise in the percentage of GNP devoted to SCI for education, and if the rate of return to human capital is 5 percent, then we can say that $1.7 trillion times .05, or $85 billion, is the amount by which the 1978 GNP was increased due to the rise in SCI for education. This $85 billion is 4.2 percent of the 1978 GNP. This rough calculation is similar to the outcome of applying parallel assumptions to the contribution that increased education makes to the growth of national income, namely 0.41 percentage points per year.[6] I enter 4 percent of GNP as the added benefit for item 8.

I am not clear about the added benefit from a higher SCI ratio with respect to automatic stabilization of the economy. Keynesian economists point out that SCI benefits and taxes, without discretionary changes by legislative bodies, will produce deficits in recessions and surpluses in booms, and hence alternately and appropriately restrain unemployment and inflation. As we know, Keynesian economics is less popular now than it was before the advent of stagflation, in which inflation and high unemployment occur at the same time. The final verdict is still out on whether the SCI system's automatic responses are appropriate in a period of stagflation. Hence, I enter a zero for item 9.

This is a good place to note that we have run through the list of identified social benefits that might be attributed to the 1950–78 rise in the SCI ratio. Most of the benefits resist quantification, but I suggest that those benefits are

[4]Journal of Social Policy, *1982, Vol. II, Part 2 is largely devoted to a discussion of freedom and the welfare state with articles by Albert Weale, Robert E. Goodin, Joan Higgins, Robert Sugden, Peter Jones, and David M. Green.*

[5]*Robert Eisner et al., "Total Incomes in the United States" (unpublished manuscript, table 15).*

[6]*Edward Denison.* Accounting for Slower Economic Growth: U.S. in the 1970s. *(Washington, D.C.: Brookings Institution, 1979), Table 8–1.*

positive on balance. Your own measurement or weighting of the several benefits may differ from my own and hence you may not agree with the plus sign I put on item 7. Only two of the benefits are quantifiable and only one of these is clearly positive, at 4 percent of GNP.

Let us look now at the social costs of the increase in the SCI ratio. It is important to note at the outset that taxes and contributions paid to finance cash SCI benefits are not good indicators of the burden or social cost of the SCI system. The flow of cash from one part of the household sector to another does not have a direct effect on the total or average level of private consumption. The outcome is quite different from that of a program which draws money out of the household sector and, by exhaustive expenditures on, say, national defense, reduces the ability of households to consume. The point here is that case transfers are not really "burdens" on the private economy in any simple or direct sense. Social cost is best thought of as a reallocation of resources that results in less output or lower value of consumer goods. In accord with that thought, I consider social cost to arise from: resources used up to expand collection, compliance, and administrative activities of both cash and in-kind SCI programs (item 10); the shifting of potential labor time induced by the expansion of the SCI system from the labor market to such nonmarketed uses as schooling, home production, and leisure (item 11); loss of productivity per work hour (item 12); and reallocation of resources to the provision of additional health care, education, and other SCI goods and services (item 13).

Item 10 refers to the overhead costs of SCI benefits. They include the use of land, labor, and capital to raise the funds and make and implement decisions about who should and who should not receive benefits. They also include the time and effort that private citizens and their lawyers and accountants expend in complying with rules and regulations concerning taxes and contributions on the one hand and the receipt of benefits on the other hand. The overhead costs form a wedge between what is paid into the SCI system and what the beneficiaries receive. There appears to be great variability on collection and compliance costs among the several public and private programs, but I hazard the guess that they amount to about 5 percent of the total funds collected for all SCI purposes. On the delivery side, there are also compliance costs and, additionally, administrative costs. It is hard to draw a sensible line between administrative expense and the provision of an SCI benefit. However, I conclude that such expense is about 5 percent of total SCI expenditures. That may be added to the 5 percent I estimated would cover collection and compliance costs for a grand total of 10 percent. That 10 percent of SCI revenues was equal to $58 billion in 1978, which accounted for 3 percent of GNP. If the scope and scale of the SCI system in 1978 had been the same as in 1950, such costs might have been only 2 percent of GNP. The one percent difference between 3 percent and 2 percent, is a social cost of the 1950–78 expansion of the SCI system.

I conclude that one of the greatest social costs of the increase in SCI is to be found in the reduction of market labor time which it induces. It is argued that SCI may reduce work effort at two points, one where the beneficiary receives nonlabor income and the other where the worker suffers a wage loss because of the tax or contribution. The research question is: Without the rise in SCI, would the labor supply of men have declined less and/or would that of women have increased more than it actually did between 1950 and 1978? Cross sections of hours worked by people with different levels of nonlabor income and at different wage rates give us an entrée to this question, although they only give indirect evidence of doubtful applicability.[7] Such studies tell us most clearly that some groups of people respond more clearly to work disincentives than others. The most responsive groups include older workers, disabled persons, female heads of families, and married women. Prime-age men are least responsive. By combining this information with knowledge about who pays for and who receives the extra SCI benefits we are able to paint a picture of changes in labor supply due to the increase in the SCI ratio. Additional evidence is supplied by empirical studies of specific SCI programs.[8] I suggest that the 1978 market labor supply might have been 6 percent larger than it actually was if the SCI ratio had remained at the 1950 level. One-half of that loss is allocable to women other than heads of families and to the aged. Most of the rest of the loss is identified with the disabled, female household heads, and young people.

This 6 percent of market labor time translates into a 4 percent loss of GNP. GNP does not assign a value to such nonmarketed uses of time as home production, schooling, or leisure. But why is not the loss of GNP fully offset by the value of hours gained for nonmarket activity? The quick answer is that the consumers of the extra hours did not make a free and individual choice of the quantities of leisure they were consuming. They were, in effect, "bribed" to consume the extra amounts. That does not necessarily mean that there should be no offset at all; the issue is whether the offset should be a high or low percentage of the 4 percent of GNP. I select an offset rate of 50 percent and enter 2 percent of GNP as the social cost of the induced reduction of market work (item 11).

Item 12 recognizes the claim that is often made, that increased SCI reduces intensity of work and the stock of capital per worker and thereby cuts the rate of increase in productivity per hour worked. I can find no good evidence on causes of change in intensity of work. The evidence on changes in saving and hence in capital formation is mixed, so I put down a mark of + or − for this item.[9]

[7]*Stanley Masters and Irwin Garfinkel,* Estimating the Labor Supply Effects of Income Maintenance Alternatives (New York: Academic Press, 1977).

[8]Sheldon Danziger, Robert Haveman, and Robert Plotnick, "How Income Transfer Programs Affect Work, Savings, and the Income Distribution: A Critical Review," *Journal of Economic Literature* (1981), 19, 975–1028.

[9]Henry J. Aaron. Economic Effects of Social Security *(Washington, D.C.: Brookings Institution, 1982), ch. 4.*

Item 13 refers to the extra resources reallocated by SCI to education, health care, food, housing, and other welfare services. This means we are looking at noncash benefits which in effect "bribe" consumers to take more of the selected goods. My best guess is that the reallocation due to expansion of in-kind benefits is a total of 4 percent of GNP: health care, 2.5 percentage points; education, one point; and food, housing, and other welfare services 0.5 point. This reallocation or distortion would not have occurred if these in-kind benefits had been converted to cash. Here, as in the case of induced leisure, we have the question of what offset to use in recognition that beneficiaries get some consumer benefit. Again, I suggest an offset ratio of 50 percent and therefore enter 2 percent of GNP as social cost for item 13.

This brings us near the end of our story about the effects of social provision on the economy. The quantifiable social costs of increasing the SCI ratio from 18 percent to 28 percent of GNP are 5 percent of GNP. The one quantifiable social benefit, namely, more GNP due to more education, almost offsets the social costs. To get a strong, positive, benefit-to-cost ratio, one has to believe that the six nonquantifiable social benefits are sufficiently valuable to more than offset the remaining one percent of net quantifiable social costs shown in item 14. I, for one, have no trouble in believing that the reductions in insecurity and in income poverty (items, 1, 2, and 3) are sufficiently valuable to do that. However, the main point of this exercise is to move you, the reader, to make your own benefit-cost calculation and to come to your own conclusions about whether the nation as a whole is better off or worse off as a result of the great rise in SCI which occurred in the years 1950–1978.

Developing a System of Income Maintenance for the United States*

MARTHA N. OZAWA

NEVER in the history of American social welfare have we needed more than we do now a coherent and compelling vision for an income maintenance policy. Both Social Security and welfare—which are important parts of our system of income maintenance—have come under severe attack in recent years. The bankruptcy of Social Security funds has been predicted unless present rates and regulations are changed, and there have been threats of reduced Social Security benefits. Welfare expenditures have been cut, and other reductions have been suggested. Public social welfare expenditures are often blamed for our economic malaise in which we find ourselves losing, on a number of fronts, the competitive economic edge that we long enjoyed.

If social welfare expenditures are in fact creating adverse effects on the American economy—even though they are having less impact than other factors—policy-makers would be wise to try to correct the faults that make such expenditures extremely susceptible to criticism. And at a time when the economy is flagging, it is surely incumbent upon policymakers not to create work disincentives through the setup and the operation of the income maintenance system.

Nevertheless, for the United States to sustain itself, the nation needs to provide a basic floor of income to vulnerable groups: children, the elderly, and the disabled. It is the policy-maker who is responsible for seeing that this is done. How, then, can one envision a system that provides adequately for these vulnerable groups of individuals but at the same time does not erode the incentive structure of the American economy? Furthermore, how can one plan this system so that it embraces the divergent ideologies at the root of our income maintenance policy? How can one plan this system so that it will have elements appealing to the diverse social and economic philosophies of the American people?

MARTHA N. OZAWA, is Professor, George Warren Brown School of Social Work, Washington University, St. Louis

*This paper was adapted from Martha N. Ozawa, *Income Maintenance and Work Incentives: Toward a Synthesis* (New York: Praeger, 1982).

In order to leap into the future with a new vision for a system of income maintenance, one needs to deal with the problems in the present program that have aroused strong opposition; that is, the problems involving welfare and Social Security. Any proposed system must solve current problems in both these areas besides achieving the broad objectives already mentioned; these goals are not mutually exclusive.

IDEOLOGICAL ROOTS OF AMERICAN INCOME MAINTENANCE POLICY

The income maintenance policy of the United States has two ideological roots. One of them is Old Liberalism. This view upholds the virtues of individual freedom, a free market, a minimum government, and the natural selection of the fittest. Those who adhere to this view assume that if these virtues are upheld and implemented, a society will not only be efficient in its use of limited resources but will also be a stronger society, with individuals maximizing their talents to their own best interests and ultimately to the best interests of society. Old Liberalism is one of the pillars of conservatism in contemporary America. It assumes that each human being can be treated as an entity rather than as a member of a collectivity, that society is at its best when individuals can strive for their own best interest, and that people should be left alone, either to thrive or perish.

The ideology surrounding the welfare system (comprised of Aid to Families with Dependent Children (AFDC), Supplemental Security Income (SSI), general assistance, and a variety of income-tested in-kind programs) is a spin-off of Old Liberalism. Welfare recipients are perceived as a fall-out from the private-sector economy. They are seen as having failed in their pursuit of economic independence. As a result, stigmatization of welfare is considered to be justified in order to draw a clear boundary between the world of work and the world of welfare and also to minimize the number of people who cross that boundary. However harmful its effects on welfare recipients may be, stigmatization is considered a necessary evil to keep the American enterprise system functioning. Furthermore, stigmatization is directly related to a societal attempt to maintain work incentives.

New Liberalism—the other root of income maintenance policy in the United States—projects a totally different view of how society can best function. Advocates of New Liberalism emphasize the importance of interdependence among individuals, cooperation in human endeavor, egalitarianism in the allocation of resources, and willingness to accept a certain amount of governmental intervention for redistributing resources from one segment of society to another. Unlike old liberals, new liberals believe that many of the causes of poverty are beyond the control of the poor. Economic risks of old age, disability, and the death of the breadwinner are recognized as strongly related to becoming poor. New liberals believe that the misery of poverty can be prevented for many people if society is better organized. Society can pool economic resources to help individuals meet risks.

New liberal thinking was behind the movement to develop various types of social insurance programs both in Britain and the United States. Social Security, unemployment insurance, and workers' compensation are examples of social insurance. John R. Commons, a pioneering student of social insurance, defined insurance as "an arrangement for distribution among many of the loss of a few."[1] Social insurance incorporates into an insurance program compulsion for all to participate; this distinguishes it from private insurance, which operates on the basis of voluntary participation. Social insurance, then, provides a deliberate way for society to distribute income to individuals and families who experience specific social and economic hazards identified by law, such as unemployment, old age, disability, and the death of the breadwinner. Although social insurance does not prevent hazards, it helps individuals and families who encounter them to meet the consequences. It offers an organized way for all to contribute to the system and for all to benefit from it in case such events strike.

As described, the American system of income maintenance has Old Liberalism and New Liberalism as its ideological roots. Old Liberalism espouses individualism, and New Liberalism espouses egalitarianism. These apparently opposite ideologies dictate the types of income maintenance that this nation develops and implements. Thus, in fashioning a system of income maintenance for the United States, one hopes that these ideologies not only are embraced but also are incorporated in such a way that they complement each other. It seems crucial for a proposed system of income maintenance to embrace these ideologies constructively if it is to be widely accepted by the American public.

PROBLEMS IN WELFARE

One of the major problems in welfare revolves around the issue of work incentives. Since all welfare programs are income-tested, welfare payments decrease as recipients increase their earnings. Rates of reduction in benefits differ, depending on the type of program, but the rates are normally much higher than the rates at which American families pay federal income taxes. When families receive welfare payments from multiple programs, implicit tax rates on their earnings become prohibitive. Under some circumstances, welfare families may, in fact, face a loss in net income if they increase their work effort.

Related to the issue of work incentives are the policy concerns for program costs and for target efficiency. With the aim of minimizing public outlays, policy-makers attempt to target welfare payments to the needy. Targeting payments, however, requires that benefits be reduced at a relatively high rate as recipient families increase their earnings. Only in this way can payments

[1]*John R. Commons and John Andrews,* Principles of Labor Legislation *(3d ed.; New York: Harper, 1920), p. 382.*

to not-so-poor (working poor) families be minimized. But the price for targeting payments to needy families is the weakening of work incentives. The dilemma is clear. Work incentives of welfare recipients cannot be enhanced without sacrificing the policy goals of target efficiency and minimum expenditures. The only way out of this dilemma is to reduce the level of basic benefits for families with no income of their own.[2]

Past welfare reforms, including those attempted by Presidents Nixon and Carter, seem to have been trapped in this dilemma. In order to enhance work incentives among welfare mothers, AFDC in 1967 decreased the implicit tax rate from 100 percent to 67 percent. It further allowed a disregard of income spent for work expenses and child care. Subsequently developed programs— the food stamp program and Supplemental Security Income (SSI), for example—incorporated benefit withdrawal rates that were lower than 100 percent. These policy measures were taken to achieve a goal of minimizing expenditures for welfare programs by improving work incentives. Instead, the result has been greater expenditures.

Stigmatization of welfare recipients is another problem that concerns policy-makers. As argued before, stigmatization seems to have a function to fulfill in free-enterprise America. But is is also true that stigmatization limits the spiritual and intellectual horizons of those who are stigmatized. One can only guess the extent to which stigmatization is preventing welfare children from growing to their fullest potential.

Another serious problem in welfare is the adverse effect that the dual receipt of SSI payments and Social Security benefits is creating. Because SSI payments are offset dollar for dollar against Social Security benefits, with the exception of $20 per month, SSI in effect is eroding the value of Social Security. For those who receive benefits from both programs, past contributions to the Social Security system become almost meaningless. Thus SSI encourages marginal workers to retire early and to cheat on Social Security contributions; furthermore, it dampens their motivation to work.

In summary, major problems in welfare are: (1) concern for work incentives; (2) a conflicting relationship between the work incentive issue on the one hand and target efficiency and minimization of welfare expenditures on the other; (3) stigmatization of welfare recipients; and (4) linkage between SSI and Social Security.

Underlying all these problems is the gap between the way wages are paid and the way welfare payments are paid. Wages are paid according to the *individual's contribution* to the economy, but welfare payments are made according to *family need*. Put another way, welfare payments are sensitive to family size, but wages are not. Because welfare provides assistance according to family size, many welfare families in high-paying states often receive from

---

[2]*The Reagan administration, through the Omibus Budget Reconciliation Act of 1981, cut welfare expenditures by targeting welfare payments to "the truly needy," but this entailed sacrificing work incentives.*

various programs combined benefits that are larger than working families can earn. Therefore, as long as there is a gap between what the breadwinner is paid on the basis of individual productivity and what is provided to welfare recipients on the basis of family need, there will always be tension in the system of income maintenance in the United States. One important item on the agenda for a proposed system of income maintenance, therefore, is to find a way to close that gap or counteract its effects.

PROBLEMS IN SOCIAL SECURITY

Just as there are structural problems in welfare, there are some difficult structural problems in Social Security. They pertain to distribution of subsidies through Social Security, the earnings test, and treatment of women under Social Security.

As discussed elsewhere, the major part of current Social Security benefits is a subsidy by the working population.[3] The subsidy varies, however, depending on earnings, sex, and marital status. Other things being equal, low-paid workers receive proportionately greater subsidies. But in absolute terms (that is, in exact dollar amounts), highly paid workers receive greater subsidies. Subsidies for married workers with dependent spouses are far greater than those for single workers, both proportionately and absolutely. Subsidies for female workers are greater both proportionately and absolutely than those for their male counterparts because of the longer life expectancy of women.

The policy issue in regard to the distribution of subsidies is the question of whether subsidies should be distributed equally to all retired workers regardless of their earnings level or whether they should be distributed in relation to past earnings records. It is my opinion that these subsidies should be distributed equally to all retired workers, because subsidies represent the welfare component of Social Security.

The earnings test (or the retirement test) is another controversial issue in Social Security. As of 1983, retirees aged 70 or over are allowed to earn without restriction. Those aged 65 through 69 are allowed to earn up to $6,600 a year without having their benefits reduced. (The exempt amount of $4,920 applies for those under 65.) Earnings in excess of the exempt amount are subject to the reduction of benefits at the rate of fifty cents for each dollar of excess earnings. The elderly who wish to earn extra income feel that they are subjected to an unreasonably high implicit tax rate on their earnings. Several studies indicate that the earnings test is related to early retirement or

[3]*Martha N. Ozawa, "Who Receives Subsidies through Social Security and How Much?"* Social Work *(March 1982), 27(2): 129–34; Orlo R. Nichols and Richard G. Schreitmueller, "Some Comparisons of the Value of a Worker's Social Security Taxes and Benefits," Actuarial Note No. 95 (Washington, D.C.: U.S. Department of Health, Education, and Welfare, Social Security Administration, Office of the Actuary, 1978).*

to limited work after retirement.[4] Thus, if the policy goal is to enhance work incentives among the elderly, the earnings test should be repealed. However, if the test was repealed, there would be even greater subsidies in Social Security benefits, most of which would accrue to high-income elderly persons. It would be unfair to ask the working population to bear the burden of higher payroll taxes— a regressive form of tax. Therefore, it seems that the repeal of the test requires a structural reform in Social Security.[5]

The last but not the least important issue confronting Social Security is how women should be treated under it. When the Social Security Act was passed in 1935, most females were homemakers. Now, over one half of all women work, and in over one half of all households both the husband and the wife are working.[6] As a result, inequity in Social Security benefits for single working, married working, and married nonworking women is becoming more visible. To compound the situation, the rising rate of divorce is leaving many women without the protection of Social Security in old age, unless they have been married ten years or more, or have worked long enough to receive benefits on their own. Thus, women in old age are in a complex situation of financial security, one that depends on their work history and marital status. It is a challenge to reform Social Security so that women of different backgrounds are given more equitable consideration than at present. The changing role of women provides an opportunity, however, for designing a more equitable and efficient Social Security program.[7]

---

[4]*See, for example, Michael J. Boskin, "Social Security Retirement Decisions,"* Economic Inquiry *(1977) 15(1): 1–25; Michael J. Boskin and Michael D. Hurd, "The Effect of Social Security on Early Retirement,"* Journal of Public Economics *(December 1978), 10(3): 361–78; Anthony Pellechio, "The Social Security Earnings Test, Labor Supply Distortions and Foregone Payroll Tax Revenue," National Bureau of Economic Research Working Paper 272, August 1978; Virginia Reno, "Retirement Patterns of Men," in* Reaching Retirement Age: Findings from a Survey of Newly Entitled Workers, 1968–70, *Research Report No. 4, U.S. Department of Health, Education, and Welfare, Social Security Administration (Washington, D.C.: Social Security Administration, Office of Research and Statistics, 1976), p. 32.*

[5]*Short of a drastic reform in Social Security, policy-makers could improve work incentives of the elderly either by further liberalizing the earnings test or by providing a partially refundable income tax credit for persons sixty-five and over who forego Social Security benefits under the earnings test. The National Commission on Social Security recommended that workers sixty-five and older be allowed to claim a fraction of foregone benefits as a credit against federal income taxes. See U.S. Congress, National Commission on Social Security,* Social Security in America's Future: Final Report of the National Commission on Social Security *(Washington, D.C.: U.S. Government Printing Office, 1981), p. 146.*

[6]*Richard V. Burkhauser, "Earnings Sharing: Incremental and Fundamental Reform" (a paper presented at the Conference on Social Security and the Changing Roles of Women, University of Wisconsin, 1980).*

[7]*The problem of the changing roles of women was extensively studied by the U.S. Department of Health and Human Services. The department also studied two alternative Social Security plans that deal with the treatment of women under Social Security. See U.S. Department of Health, Education, and Welfare,* Social Security and the Changing Roles of Men and Women *(Washington, D.C.: U.S. Department of Health, Education, and Welfare, 1979); see also Martha N. Ozawa, "An Analysis of HEW's Proposals on Social Security,"* Social Service Review *(March 1980), 54(1): 92–107.*

How can Social Security be reformed so that the multiple goals of a more equitable distribution of benefits across earnings levels, elimination of the earnings test, and fair treatment of women with different backgrounds can be achieved concurrently? I believe these goals can be achieved if the nation adopts a double-decker system of Social Security that incorporates the sharing between spouses of credits for contributions. Under the double-decker system I have proposed, all elderly individuals would receive a universal flat-amount pension that would amount to a guaranteed income at the poverty line.[8] On top of this, the retired worker would receive an annuity based on that person's past contributions plus interest. Under this plan, credits for contributions would be shared between spouses when calculating retirement benefits. Incidentally, the plan would encompass the disabled as well as the elderly. All disabled persons would also receive the flat-amount benefits plus contributions-related benefits.

If such a double-decker plan were adopted, the three policy goals could be concurrently achieved. First, since the universal flat-amount pension represents subsidy under Social Security, all elderly individuals in the United States would receive the same subsidy from Social Security. Absolute equality in subsidy payments seems more equitable than equal subsidy payments that depend on the level of earnings.

Second, since the proposed double-decker plan allows the sharing of credits for contributions between spouses, equitable treatment of women would be assured. Under the plan, there would no longer be benefits for dependents. All women would be considered to be workers, whether they were homemakers or worked outside their home. The annuities of married women would be financed by the sharing of credits for contributions between spouses.

Third, since Social Security benefits under the plan would be made up of an annuity (paid for by past contributions plus interest) and a universal pension, neither an earnings test nor an income test would be necessary. All elderly persons would be left alone to pursue their economic activities. They would receive all that they were entitled to from Social Security, whether they worked or not, after the retirement age.

DEVELOPING A SYSTEM OF INCOME MAINTENANCE

It is now appropriate to recommend a system of income maintenance for the United States which would achieve the two policy goals of (*a*) providing adequately for children, the elderly, and the disabled, and (*b*) enhancing work incentives for the rest of the population; address major problems in welfare and reform issues in social security; and constructively embrace the divergent ideologies of income maintenance.

---

[8]*See Martha N. Ozawa,* Income Maintenance and Work Incentives: Toward a Synthesis *(New York: Praeger, 1982).*

In recommending this system of income maintenance, I start out by dividing the total population into children and adults. For children, I recommend a program of children's allowances at the poverty line. For the adult population, minimum wages, social insurance, and noncategorical public assistance will deal with their income insecurity. These three layers of income provisions will be placed in a clear hierarchical order, with minimum wages at the top. That is, year-round, minimum-wage workers will earn twice the poverty-line income; social insurance beneficiaries will receive benefits at least at the poverty line; and noncategorical public assistance recipients with no income from other sources will receive benefits at one half of the poverty line. This way, all income maintenance programs in the system will be coordinated by the differential national minima of income security that they provide in relation to the poverty line. Noncategorical public assistance recipients will be subjected to a 50 percent implicit tax rate on earnings and a 100 percent implicit tax rate on unearned income.

Notice that providing for children independently of adults will mean that my proposed plan closes the current gap between the units of income provision through minimum wages and income-transfer programs. Since children are dealt with separately under my recommended system, all other income provisions could deal with individuals not families. The unit of income provision under minimum wages is also the individual. Closing the gap in this way is the key to rationalizing and streamlining the treatment of the adult population and solving problems with respect to work incentives. It is also the key to being able to provide adequately for children without concern about destroying the work incentives of their parents. Furthermore, I believe that the proposed system would attain the policy goals set forth.

ADEQUATE INCOME FOR CHILDREN, THE ELDERLY, AND THE DISABLED

In the proposed system, the income insecurity of children would be adequately dealt with through children's allowances. All children in the nation would be paid allowances equivalent to 100 percent of the poverty-line income deemed necessary to support a dependent living in a family. The income insecurity of the elderly and the disabled is adequately dealt with through Social Security (and Worker's Compensation for work-related injury and diseases). All these groups of individuals would be guaranteed at least poverty-line income.

ENHANCEMENT OF WORK INCENTIVES

Enhancement of work incentives is pursued on many fronts:
1. Providing for children quite independently of their parents' employment status or earnings levels would improve the work incentives of their parents. Currently, AFDC is provided only when parents cannot earn, or earn little, thus creating the possibility that some children are adequately provided for only when their parents do not work. Such a

possibility would not arise if children's allowances were provided instead, because allowances would be paid whether parents work or not.
2. Placing income maintenance provisions for adults in hierarchical order would also assure that work always brings more income to those who work than to those who do not. This, too, would be an inducement for more work effort.
3. Elimination of overlaps between minimum wages, Social Security benefits, and noncategorical public assistance payments would eliminate the possibility of adults receiving benefits from more than one program, again resulting in an enhancement of work incentives.
4. The double-decker plan would ensure that those who have contributed to the Social Security system would always receive a greater combined amount of benefits from the universal pension and the annuity than those who have not worked. This, too, would translate into an enhancement of work incentives. The absence of an earnings test or an income test in the proposed plan of Social Security would also encourage the elderly to work.

SOLUTIONS TO PROBLEMS IN WELFARE AND SOCIAL SECURITY

Many of the problems in welfare would simply vanish because public assistance as such would play only a small role in the recommended system. Only adults who did not work or who did not receive social insurance benefits would have to resort to public assistance. Incidentally, SSI would be preempted by the double-decker Social Security system. Further, the problem of cumulative implicit tax rates would not arise because no one adult would receive benefits from more than one program.[9] Of course, the same family might receive children's allowances and one type of adult benefits. But even here, the cumulative tax rates should be relatively low because children's allowances would be provided no matter what happened to their parents' work status or earnings levels. More important, the level of stigmatization would be low in the proposed system of income maintenance because so few families would need to resort to income-tested public assistance.

DIVERGENT IDEOLOGIES OF INCOME MAINTENANCE POLICY

For a system of income maintenance to be adopted, it needs to be compatible with the divergent ideologies at the root of income maintenance policy in the United States. As mentioned earlier, there are two divergent ideologies. It is

[9]*A question can be raised about income-tested, in-kind programs. How can one make sure that each adult benefits from only one type of program? As I suggested in* Income Maintenance and Work Incentives, *the policy-maker might decide to make in-kind benefits a substitute for cash benefits. Under this scheme, the recipient of aid from a noncategorical public assistance program would be given a chance to choose either cash payments or in-kind benefits of equivalent value.*

a challenge to incorporate these ideologies in the system in a constructive manner. The recommended system of income maintenance appears to meet this challenge. Guaranteeing a minimum income to three vulnerable groups of individuals—children, the elderly, and the disabled—should satisfy those who believe in New Liberalism, which espouses egalitarianism. Placing in a hierarchical order the levels of national minima of income security under minimum wages, social insurance, and noncategorical public assistance should satisfy old liberals, who emphasize individualism and the work ethic. In effect, this is a reactivation of the old poor-law doctrine known as "less eligibility," meaning that those who do not work should not fare better than those who do. Implementation of the doctrine of less eligibility in the recommended system would not bring about cruel treatment of poor families with children—as was the case when the doctrine was put into practice widely in England and the United States—because in the recommended system children are not entangled in the treatment of the adult population. Focusing on the Social Security component, the universal pension reflects the principle of social adequacy, satisfying new liberals; on the other hand, the annuity reflects the individual equity principle, satisfying old liberals. And yet there does not seem to be ideological conflict between the components in any particular program or between the various income maintenance programs proposed.

The spirit of Old Liberalism and the spirit of New Liberalism have contributed significant ideas and attitudes toward life that have furthered the development of this nation and enhanced its well-being. Many Americans adhere steadfastly to the philosophy of Old Liberalism; many are just as unswerving in their devotion to the tenets of New Liberalism. Therefore, any proposed system of income maintenance must keep alive the spirit of both ideologies, must bring together both ideas in such a way that they do not contradict each other, and must present program elements that can win legislative and public approval and that can be made to function smoothly together as the plan is implemented.

If the policy-maker devises a system of income maintenance that activates the principles of the two divergent ideologies along these lines, then this system should help develop a society which provides adequately and willingly for its vulnerable citizens. At the same time, this system should bring about conditions that stimulate rather than weaken the incentive to work—thus encouraging the society as a whole to be more productive economically rather than less so. This discussion is one attempt to establish such a system.

Civil Rights vs. States' Rights in the 1980s

JOSÉ A. RIVERA

THE passage of the Omnibus Budget Reconciliation Act of 1981 by the 97th Congress[1] ushered in wholesale changes destined to affect federal and state government relations through the 1980s and perhaps beyond. The change in government roles and responsibilities immediately began the unfolding of a new chapter on the administration of civil rights. As the cornerstone policy of President Reagan's New Federalism, the block grant programs authorized in the act altered the course of civil rights history by shifting the brunt of civil rights oversight away from a single and central federal system to a decentralized program in each of the fifty states plus the two hundred or so state implementing agencies.

While initial reaction to the block-grant proposals focused on budget cutbacks, recent attention has shifted to the political realities of program decentralization. Piven and Cloward, for example, charge that Reagan's New Federalism in effect launched a "class war" which threatens to breathe new life in the once discredited doctrine of separation: "One way is by attempting to decentralize authority over programs inaugurated in response to popular pressures—to strengthen some of the [institutional] arrangements that once restricted popular political participation and influence to the local level."[2] Piven and Cloward forewarn that a successful policy of decentralization will deflect popular economic demands from the national arena as constituency organizations become fragmented and channel all their energies into the competitive politics at the state and local levels.[3]

Other critics of New Federalism echo Piven and Cloward and charge that the Reagan administration seeks to undermine the community organizations of minorities and of the poor in every way possible. "Behind the apparently capricious and arbitrary cutbacks," claims Harry C. Boyte, "a political pattern

JOSÉ RIVERA is Director, Southwest Hispanic Research Institute, and Assistant Professor, University of New Mexico, Division of Public Administration, Albuquerque.

[1]*U.S. Congress*, Omnibus Budget Reconciliation Act of 1981, *Public Law 97–35, 97th Congress, August 13, 1981.*

[2]*Frances Fox Piven and Richard A. Cloward, The New Class War (New York: Pantheon Books, 1982), pp. 128–29.*

[3]*Ibid., p. 130.*

is evident. . . . it is this grassroots democratic movement [of community organizations] that the Reagan administration, despite its rhetoric, cannot tolerate"[4] Boyte furnishes an extensive list of assistance programs terminated or targeted for severe cutbacks by the administration, programs which in the past had spearheaded community advocacy, initiative, and self-help: VISTA, CETA, Legal Services, the Neighborhood Self-Help Development Program, the National Consumer Coop Bank, the Economic Development Administration, the Farmers Home Administration, and the Solar Energy and Conservation Bank.

To Ira Glasser of the American Civil Liberties Union, the disdain of the administration for neighborhood programs such as Legal Services is symbolic of the grander scheme of New Federalism to resurrect states' rights by limiting federal intervention in the area of civil rights:

President Reagan has attempted to erode federal standards and remedies governing race discrimination and has tried to shift discretion in this area back to the states, whose discretion first caused—and still causes—the problem. The resurrection of the discredited ideology of states' rights is a direct assault on the principles of the Fourteenth Amendment.[5]

THE ADMINISTRATION OF CIVIL RIGHTS

Block grant implementation has been under study by a variety of sources practically since the issuance of the first group of block grants on October 1, 1981. The most widely circulated materials at the start focused on the cutback aspects, comparing the new grants with the categorical programs they replaced. The runner-up topic soon afterward became the process and speed of transition as states exercised the option to accept or postpone acceptance of each block grant. The "sleeper issue" of civil rights vs. states' rights only surfaced recently, is gaining momentum, and promises to be the main issue of debate for some time to come—the rest of 1983 certainly and perhaps well into the 1980s. For minorities and other disadvantaged groups, the gains of the past eighteen years are very much at stake as the federal civil rights establishment applies the brakes to the central system of administration and as the states begin to muddle through their newly acquired discretion.

Evidence that a battle over the administration of civil rights was in the making began in May 1982 when the Senate Subcommittee on Intergovernmental Affairs conducted hearings on the first round of block-grant implementation. Among the witnesses presenting testimony was the National Association of Social Workers. The NASW staff raised objections to the discretionary nature of civil rights monitoring as described in the OBR act and in the subsequent

[4]Harry C. Boyte, "Ronald Reagan and America's Neighborhoods: Undermining Community Initiative," in Alan Gartner, Colin Greer, and Frank Riessman, eds., in What Reagan Is Doing to Us, (New York: Harper & Row, 1982), p. 122.
[5]Ira Glasser, "The Coming Assault on Civil Liberties," ibid., pp. 241–42.

implementing regulations issued by the federal departments. To correct the perceived weaknesses, NASW called for new federal requirements: (*a*) a uniform reporting system as to the race, ethnicity, age, sex, handicapping condition, and income level of service recipients; (*b*) a mandated state procedure for the conduct of impartial hearing of complaints; and (*c*) a readiness on the part of the U.S. Attorney General to exercise federal nondiscrimination laws in cases of noncompliance, including action to withold further block grant funds from the state.[6]

A few months later, the results of a state-by-state survey of block-grant implementation prompted the Center for Law and Social Policy to issue a report with the telling headline "New Federalism or Old Hoax?: Block Grants in FY 1982." The report listed civil rights protections and grievance procedures among the top four issues which emerged as results from a lengthy survey instrument.[7] While the Center's report was based on a mail questionnaire, the General Accounting Office also conducted field visits in thirteen states in 1982, leading to the release of a special report to the Congress by the Comptroller General on August 24, 1982. Whereas most of the report is lenient in its judgments about state progress in transition from categorical grants to block grants, the Comptroller General did reveal some poignant observations: "Federal agencies have adhered to a policy of minimum involvement. . . . In several cases Federal authority is limited by statute; *but even where agencies have discretion, they often have passed it on to the States*" (emphasis added).[8] With respect to statutory requirements for the administration of civil rights, the Comptroller General continued by reporting that "[Federal] agencies are developing procedures for fulfilling their compliance and enforcement responsibilities in such areas as nondiscrimination and *have stated their intent to rely heavily on States' interpretation of the statutes*" (emphasis added).[9]

CIVIL RIGHTS PROGESS AND THE FEDERAL GIVEAWAY

The flap over the new state discretion on civil rights matters and other areas originated with the wholesale giveaway embodied in the language of the Omnibus Budget Reconciliation Act and the subsequent implementing regulations of the administering federal departments. The Reagan-supported statute relinquished federal control in three short paragraphs contained in Title XVII, Sec. 1742: to receive any of the nine initial block grants, states need only to (*a*) submit a report on intended use of funds; (*b*) make the report public to

---

[6]*U.S. Congress, Senate,* Block Grant Implementation, *hearings before a subcommittee of the Senate Committee on Governmental Affairs, 97th Congress, 2d Sess., May 5 and 11, 1982, pp. 187, 193–94.*

[7]*"New Federalism or Old Hoax? Block Grants in FY 1982" (Washington, D.C.: Center for Law and Social Policy, 1982) p. 18.*

[8]*Comptroller General, "Early Observations on Block Grant Implementation," report to the Congress of the United States, August 24, 1982, p. 44.*

[9]Ibid.

facilitate comments; and (*c*) hold one public hearing. For compliance purposes, Sec. 1745 simply called for each state to conduct audits of all its block-grant funds according *"insofar as is practicable . . .* with standards established by the Comptroller General." (emphasis added).[10]

Conspicuous by absence in Title XVII were any record-keeping or monitoring requirements with regard to civil rights protections guaranteed by all previous legislation: Civil Rights Act of 1964 (Title VI), Education Amendments of 1972 (Title IX), the Rehabilitation Act of 1973 (Section 504), and the Age Discrimination Act of 1975. Title XVII, under Subtitle C, Chapter 2, was the only part of the OBR act that established uniform requirements of any kind for all nine of the block grants. Yet no mention was made of civil rights assurances. Instead, each title in the act pursued its own course, causing confusion as to intent, consistency, applicability, and so forth.

Five of the block grants prohibited discrimination on the basis of race and color, national origin, sex, age, handicap, or religion. Two others contained the same prohibitions except for religion. Another two (social services; elementary and secondary education) did *not* include a nondiscrimination section. As a clean-up gesture, the respective U.S. Secretaries for these two block grants eventually issued regulations clarifying that all federal civil rights laws would be applicable. Concommitantly, however, the Secretary of Health and Human Services took pains to demonstrate the federal decision to provide *maximum* discretion to the states: "We will not burden the States' administration of the programs with definitions of permissible and prohibited activities, procedural rules, paperwork and recordkeeping requirements, or other regulatory provisions."[11]

The Secretary made it clear that the specific provisions in the act to prohibit discrimination would indeed be passed on as a responsibility of the states. As with other provisions in the act, the Secretary interpreted federal enforcement powers with the blanket statement that rang out as the harbinger of a new reality:

> When an issue arises as to whether a State has complied with its assurances and the statutory provisions, the Department will ordinarily defer to the State's interpretation of its assurances and the statutory provisions. *Unless the interpretation is clearly erroneous, State action based on that interpretation will not be challenged by the Department* (emphasis added).[12]

Should a state err in is own interpretation of the standing civil rights laws,[13]

---

[10]*U.S. Congress,* Omnibus Budget Reconciliation Act of 1981, *Sec. 1745, p. 764.*

[11]*Department of Health and Human Services, "Block Grant Programs; Final Rules,"* Federal Register, *July 6, 1982, p. 29472.*

[12]*Department of Health and Human Services, "Block Grant Programs; Final Rules on Implementation,"* Federal Register, *October 1, 1981, p. 48585.*

[13]*Included in some titles of the OBR act are references to the Civil Rights Act of 1964 (Title VI), the Education Amendments of 1972 (Title IX), the Rehabilitation Act of 1973 (Section 504), and the Age Discrimination Act of 1975.*

the chief executive officer of the state would still have up to sixty days to comply voluntarily. Only in the event of refusal to comply would the Secretary ostensibly initiate federal enforcement actions provided for in prior nondiscrimination statutes. To civil rights advocates, while the boilerplate may have been preserved, the federal civil rights establishment would no longer remain at the helm.

THE VIEW FROM THE SOUTHWEST

The State advisory committees to the Southwestern Regional Office of the U.S. Commission on Civil Rights felt compelled to assess the extent of civil rights concerns in the spring and summer of 1982 by holding a series of consultations at the state capitals of Texas, New Mexico, Oklahoma, Louisiana, and Arkansas. In each case the respective advisory committee requested and received testimony from federal and state officials, legislators, community leaders, heads of human services organizations, provider group representatives, tribal officers, civil rights advocates, and others. All testimony was documented by professional court reporters, resulting in five separate transcripts. The staff of the Southwestern Regional Office coordinated the consultations and produced a final report on behalf of the advisory committees.[14]

The transcripts of the five consultations document the expected lament over cutbacks in program funding. However, as requested by the advisory committees, the majority of the testimony focused on civil rights and related issues. The contest between civil rights and states' rights sparked debate and surfaced two major points of view: those of the "believers" and those of the "skeptics"— federal and state officials on the one hand and seasoned community advocates on the other.

The federal officials were unanimous in their claim that civil rights protection would not be jeopardized by the block grant program. One official from the Office of Management and Budget (OMB), in fact, credited the Reagan administration with having been calculated and deliberate in its efforts to guarantee *no* slippage of past federal policies and law:

The statutes and regulations definitely call for a very, very strong civil rights provision. They were built into the intitial proposals that the administration provided. . . . The administration . . . clearly wanted to demonstrate their commitment to the civil rights guarantees *and to make sure that all of the federal requirements would continue in this area unchanged* (emphasis added).[15]

---

[14]The New Wave of Federalism: Block Granting and Civil Rights in the Southwest Region, *a report of the State Advisory Committees to the U.S. Commission on Civil Rights, Southwestern Regional Office, 1983.*

[15]*Testimony before the Louisiana Advisory Committee to the U.S. Commission on Civil Rights in Baton Rouge, April 15, 1982 (hereafter cited as* LA. Transcript*), pp. 26, 30. (Note: The transcripts utilized in this article had not been edited for legal considerations and should not be utilized for purposes of official citation or attributed to the U.S. Commission on Civil Rights or the various State Advisory Committees.)*

Apart from the OMB official, many federal department administrators were present at the consultations, all of whom testified that the federal civil rights enforcement role would continue. Even though the states have the first opportunity to ensure voluntary compliance, clarified a representative from the Department of Health and Human Services (DHHS), the Secretary still retains the power to enforce the civil rights statutes: "We have delegated certain authorities to the states, but we have not given up our enforcement powers."[16] A branch chief from the Dallas Regional Office of Civil Rights (DHHS) described the partial delegation as a "partnership" whereby the states will be provided an opportunity "to voluntarily resolve their problems, to investigate, to propose remedy, and to consult with [the HHS] department in order to finalize," and where voluntary compliance does not solve the problem, she continued, "the responsibility for initiating enforcement will remain with our office . . . . the [DHHS] Office for Civil Rights is not abdicating its responsibility."[17]

The "believers" also included the cadre of state executives from governors and their aides to the top administrators of state agencies in charge of implementing the block-grant programs. All five governors' offices professed a moral commitment to equal opportunity and assured their intent to comply with civil rights laws. The state agency administrators as a group indicated that all procedures from the past, such as record keeping, monitoring techniques, complaint processes, and so on, would continue via in-place systems that had already been required under the federal categorical programs.

At the Oklahoma consultation, for example, the Coordinator of Federal and State Regulations for one of the agencies assured the advisory committee that no changes had been made in data collection or in record keeping. "The department has always been involved in assuring compliance with civil rights," reflected the Coordinator, and we have "a fair hearing process which permits an aggrieved individual the opportunity to appeal agency decisions. The Department's Office of Inspector General investigates and assures compliance."[18]

In Arkansas the Legislative and Budgetary Affairs Director claimed that in that state each agency handled its own complaints as they developed "Primarily, if someone has a complaint about a program, they make it to the State agency which administers that program, and the procedure is usually handled within each agency."[19] Some state agencies reported very specific review, monitoring, and compliance procedures from the categorical programs of the past and were unequivocal in the faith they placed in established mechanisms.

[16]*Testimony before the New Mexico Advisory Committee to the U.S. Commission on Civil Rights in Santa Fe, July 22, 1982 (hereafter cited as* NM. Transcript*), II, 247.*

[17]*Testimony before the Texas Advisory Committee to the U.S. Commission on Civil Rights in Austin, Texas, May 27, 1982 (hereafter cited as* TX. Transcript*), pp. 127–28, 132.*

[18]*Testimony before the Oklahoma Advisory Committee to the U.S. Commission on Civil Rights in Oklahoma City, June 21–22, 1982 (hereafter cited as* OK. Transcript*), p. 295.*

[19]*Testimony before the Arkansas Advisory Committee to the U.S. Commission on Civil Rights in Little Rock, March 24, 1982 (hereafter cited as* AR. Transcript*), Panel III, p. 5.*

In Texas, for example, the Department of Human Resources has had an in-house Civil Rights Division since 1976 staffed by a statewide network of a dozen or so civil rights officers. The Deputy Commissioner of that department assured the Texas advisory committee that Title VI (Civil Rights Act of 1964) compliance procedures were still in place and that they "provide for a formal and extensive review of complaints of discrimination in service delivery filed by a recipient."[20]

Juxtaposed to the affirmations that poured out in the statements of federal and state government officials was the testimony expressing disbelief by a multitude of other speakers throughout the five states. The "skeptics" included leaders of block-grant coalition groups, directors and staffs of programs for the elderly and the handicapped, legal services advocates, representatives of women's organizations, and tribal government officials and spokespersons for Hispanic civil rights organizations.

The League of United Latin American Citizens (LULAC) presented testimony at the consultations in two of the states. In Texas, the past State LULAC Director reminded the advisory committee that his state "has historically been far less sensitive to minorities and civil rights than has the federal government" and should not be made responsible for *both* service delivery *and* enforcement of nondiscrimination provisions; the latter function should remain a federal charge in order to "insure impartial enforcement divorced from control by the state agencies administering the block grants."[21]

Two other Hispanic organizations testified at the Texas consultation. The San Antonio director of the Mexican Legal Defense and Educational Fund (MALDEF) expressed general opposition by the organization to the block-grant program as a whole. At the heart of her testimony, she raised a number of unanswered questions directed at the state of Texas and concluded that:

We at MALDEF feel the only avenue left to service agencies and advocates is watchdog monitoring. We have no alternative but to monitor the devastating effects and to begin looking at ways to challenge enforcement problems inevitable with the block grant programs.[22]

The American G.I. Forum representative was no more assured of a good-faith effort on the part of Texas officials. "State and local authorities will do what is politically expedient," he predicted, and "the poor, elderly, needy, the minorities and handicapped are not a loud voice in the political process"; and even the voices of advocates for disadvantaged groups "will be drowned out by citizen groups that want local control, want states rights . . . civil rights compliance will be left to the good conscience of managers and supervisors under pressure of sometimes unconscionable political office holder."[23]

[20]TX. Transcript, *p. 205.*
[21]Ibid., *pp. 331–32.*
[22]Ibid., *p. 345.*
[23]Ibid., *pp. 372–73.*

From among the five states in the Southwestern region, Texas was one of three that reportedly did not have à statewide, central, and independent agency to hear alleged discrimination complaints. The consultations in Oklahoma and New Mexico noted the existence there of state-level mechanisms to handle human rights issues. Despite this reputed advantage, in New Mexico at least, the State Human Rights Commission was not perceived as a viable replacement for its federal equivalents. "Every time the Legislature meets," said the Executive Director of the Albuquerque Human Rights Office, "a major effort is made to abolish the [state] Commission," a signal that "a significant number of our legislators have not taken seriously the need to protect our Civil Rights, or the enforcement of nondiscrimination."[24] To reinforce his point, the Director reminded the advisory committee of the 1982 reapportionment plan that was passed by the Legislature only to be ruled unconstitutional by the federal courts a few months later. With this fresh example, "it is plain to see that the states, left to their own discretion will without federal guidelines, continually resort to formulas and measures that are not only in violation of federal statutes, but also in violation of the United States Constitution.[25]

Both the Omnibus Budget Reconciliation Act and the implementing regulations of the Department provided for direct funding of some of the block grant programs to Indian tribes and tribal organizations. Five were made available for direct funding: community services, preventive health and health services, alcohol and drug abuse and mental health services, primary care, and low-income home energy assistance. The act itself simply stated that the Secretary held discretion to determine whether a petitioning tribe would be "better served" by means of a direct grant versus state administration of all allotted block-grant funds in that state. To be eligible, the tribe or tribal organization has to meet the requirements of the Indian Self-Determination and Education Assistance Act. The one stipulation for the requesting tribe, however, was that the funding amount reserved for the tribe would be on a formula basis as a ratio amount applied against the initial allottment granted to the state.

The implementing rules of the department included an elaborate statement saying that the Secretary determined that "members of Indian tribes and tribal organizations would be *better served by direct Federal funding* than by funding through the states *in every instance* that the Indian tribe or tribal organization requests direct funding" (emphasis added).[26] The ruling was prefaced by reference to the act's provision which recognized the government-to-government relationship between the federal government and tribes as well as the provision for implementing the standing policy on Indian self-determination.[27]

---

[24]NM. Transcript, *1, 13.*

[25]Ibid., *14.*

[26]*Department of Health and Human Services, "Block Grant Programs; Final Rules,"* Federal Register, *July 6, 1982. p. 29480.*

[27]Ibid.

Despite the regulation seemingly in favor of direct tribal participation in the block grant program, the consultations in New Mexico and Oklahoma produced a long list of complaints from the invited tribal governors and other representatives:

1. Tribes were not eligible for four of the block grants at all.
2. Only the community services and low-income assistance programs were automatic since the three health block grants required prior funding under the categorical programs, a condition that excluded the majority of tribes.
3. Eligibility by itself did not provide a great deal of incentive to apply since many tribes could not afford to share the administrative costs of implementing the programs, a distinct disadvantage when compared with the tax bases of state and local governments.
4. For the smaller tribes, the funding formula channeled awards of worthless amounts; e.g., the Fort Sill Apache tribe in Oklahoma reported an allottment of $149 from the community services block grant.[28]
5. Urban Indian organizations were not eligible for direct funding due to the Secretary's determination in the regulations that such organizations do not have a government-to government relationship with the United States.

With the many problems associated with eligibility rules and implementation requirements, tribes could elect, of course, not to apply for direct funding but to be served instead by state agencies and their network of provider groups. But this prospect did not generate much enthusiasm either. According to the chairman of the Eight Northern Indian Pueblos Council in New Mexico,

Indians have traditionally had a hard time getting funds and services from some State agencies. The only recourse [in the past] was to apply directly to the Federal Government for categorical funds or to amass enough evidence of discrimination to force changes at the legislative level. . . . With fewer Federal controls on State actions, we expect to hear that "no" more often.[29]

One arrangement allowed for in the block grants was the possibility of provider subcontracts from the state to tribal organizations. This option, however, drew wide opposition. At stake, tribal officials reported, was the foremost priority of all tribes: retain sovereignty as nations via a continued government-to-government relationship with the federal government. "I fear that the Federal government has again approached the Indian people with a plan to further alienate itself from carrying out its trust responsibility," said one tribal governor in New Mexico, and if this trend continues and we approve such Block Grant Programs to be allocated by the State, then I believe we would soon become

[28]OK. Transcript, *p. 265.*
[29]NM. Transcript, *l. 137.*

wards of the State. . . . if those Block Grant Programs fail, where does that leave us?"[30]

In Oklahoma, the perceived loss of sovereignty was likewise the main issue in that the block grant program threatened to erase two centuries of unique tribal status:

> The administration . . . has failed to recognize tribal governments. The treaties and agreements and congressional actions, the court decisions that have transpired for the past two hundred years have verified over and over again that our existence is a true sovereign entity yet we were only given passing recognition in this new federalism.[31]

Tribes in both states were leery of state government requirements that all provider groups form nonprofit corporations in order to receive block grant funds legally. "Right now the state . . . is dangling dollars before the tribes," claimed a representative of the United Indian Tribes of Western Oklahoma and Kansas; "they are saying if you want this money you come in as a private nonprofit organization or we keep the money."[32] "The States approach of funding Tribes essentially relegates Tribes to the status of a non-profit corporation,"[33] echoed the Mescalero tribe of New Mexico.

REALITIES AND ALTERNATIVES FOR THE 1980s

The Comptroller General's report to the Congress cited earlier established that the initial period of transition from categorical to block grants did not produce significant changes in the delivery systems at the state level, except, of course, for the impact of cutbacks. In the years ahead, however, states stand to gain more experience and confidence in their ability to manage block-grant programs. "States can be expected to institute more programmatic and administrative changes."[34]

With experience will come the exercise of discretion over many areas of concern to the ethnic and racial minorities, women, the handicapped, and the elderly. Experimentation and subsequent controversy can be expected in critical issues such as:

Eligibility standards and definitions

Imposition of fee for service schedules and other user burdens

Design of program activities and service mix

Targeting of funds, including set-aside provisions

Fund distribution formulas

[30]Ibid., *p. 128.*
[31]OK. Transcript, *p. 265.*
[32]Ibid., *p. 261.*
[33]NM. Transcript, *I, 145.*
[34]*Comptroller General, "Early Observations on Block Grant Implementation," report to the Congress of the United States, Washington, D.C., August 24, 1982, p. i.*

Transfer of funds from block grant to block grant
Subcontracting opportunities, costs, and trade-offs
Citizen participation processes and mechanisms
Civil rights monitoring, compliance, and enforcement systems.

At a minimum, civil rights and other community advocacy groups in the Southwest and elsewhere can be expected to play watchdog roles as changes around the many flexible areas are made in each state. With 50 different state systems and 200 implementing agencies, odds are that mistakes and arbitrary decisions will be made. Block-grant coalition groups have been formed at the national level and in most states with monitoring as their principal mission. Some organizations, especially in the provider category, no doubt will be co-opted and find themselves bidding for and accepting subcontracts from the state agencies, serving on state program advisory bodies, influencing state legislatures for more favorable treatment of social programs, and generally buying into New Federalism and the system of state control. Little support can be expected from national service organizations and support networks as they are eliminated or substantially crippled.

Only the die-hard civil rights organizations that are independently financed can be expected to confront New Federalism through other channels. Some may turn to the courts as they find that the protections called for in the statutes become increasingly jeopardized. This scenario envisions a series of test cases challenging state actions on key issues such as recipient eligibility, targeting criteria, funding cutoffs, citizen participation, access to services and information, adequacy of state systems for the filing and disposition of complaints, due process, uniform standards, and others. Litigation could be costly.

To challenge or to buy-in seems to be the choice of minority and other organizations of the disadvantaged through the rest of the 1980s. The provider organizations of services to the elderly, handicapped, farmworkers, and other disadvantaged groups will have no choice but to buy into the system unless, of course, they opt to dissolve and thereby leave their clients with one less support group. Ongoing and short-term needs no doubt will persuade these organizations to remain in business and strike the best deal they can with the state implementing agencies. Only the most effective programs, politically and in terms of performance, will survive the decade.

The new politics of civil rights will be left to an even smaller group of advocacy organizations, fueled largely by membership contributions, private funds, and a lot of volunteer time and in-kind services. By the middle of 1984 the advocates will have mobilized against the cumulative actions of the Reagan administration, from the initial efforts to dilute the Voting Rights Act of 1965 to the more recent attempt by the OMB to debar nonprofit organizations who engage in routine advocacy activities while receiving federal funds. As proposed by the administration, nonprofit organizations would face debarment or suspension should they directly or indirectly use federal funds to influence administrative processes, government decisions, regulations, guidelines, and

policy statements of *any* level of government, federal, state, or local![35] This
proposed regulation jolted the entire nonprofit sector when it was published
in the January 24, 1983, issue of the *Federal Register*, and pressure soon
began to mount overwhelmingly to defeat its adoption.

What's next? Civil rights or states' rights? Can we have both? The 1980s
will tell the story. Stay tuned.

---

[35]*See Office of Management and Budget, "Cost Principles for Non-Profit Organizations,"*
Federal Register, *January 24, 1983, pp. 3348–51.*

Trends and Changes in Income Support for the Disabled

NANCY R. MUDRICK

NEARLY 17 percent of noninstitutionalized adults in the United States report that they have impairments which limit their activities sufficiently to constitute disability.[1] Among the elderly population, the proportion is higher. The disabling impact of these impairments includes not only a lessened ability to work for wages, but greater demands for health care, social services, and income support. Analysis of the social and economic status of the disabled have consistently found that their utilization of, and expenditures for, medical care are higher and their household income considerably lower than that of the nondisabled.[2]

Since colonial times, needy disabled persons have been considered among "the deserving poor." As a result, numerous federal and state-financed social programs have been developed to provide income support, special training, and living assistance. More recently, legislation has been enacted to protect the rights of the disabled and ensure their access to public facilities. Despite these long-standing efforts, the public provision for the disabled is currently undergoing reassessment. While this reassessment began during the Carter administration, the pace of policy modifications in response to these studies has accelerated under President Reagan. The primary focus of reassessment and modification of the programs serving the disabled has been the Social Security Disability Insurance (DI) and Supplemental Security Income (SSI)

NANCY R. MUDRICK is Associate Professor, School of Social Work, and Senior Research Associate, Health Studies Program, The Maxwell School, Syracuse University, Syracuse, N.Y.
The author is grateful for the assistance of Michael McGuirl, Tod Porter, and Claire Rudulph.

[1] *U.S. Department of Health and Human Services*, Work Disability in the United States: A Chartbook *(Washington, D.C.: Social Security Administration, Office of Policy, Office of Research and Statistics 1980).*

[2] *Harold S. Luft*, Poverty and Health *(Cambridge, Mass.: Ballinger, 1979); Sandra Duchnok*, Health Care Coverage and Medical Care Utilization, 1972, *Disability Survey '72, Disabled and Non-Disabled Adults, Report no. 11 (Washington, D.C.: Social Security Administration 1978); Monroe Berkowitz, William G. Johnson, and Edward H. Murphy, Jr.*, Public Policy Toward Disability *(New York: Praeger, 1976); U.S. Department of Health and Human Services*, Work Disability.

programs. Additionally, recent changes in the economy and in related income-support programs have also affected the disabled.

ELIGIBILITY, APPLICATION, AND ACCEPTANCE FOR DISABILITY TRANS-FERS

The definition of disability is a problem which continually plagues not only those researching and writing in the area of disability, but the income support programs which must select participants on the basis of disability.[3] The Social Security Disability Insurance and Supplemental Security Income programs have developed a definition to determine who is disabled which states that an "inability to engage in any kind of substantial gainful activity (SGA) by reason of any medically determinable physical or mental impairment which can result in death or be expected to last for a continuous period of not less than 12 months" constitutes disability. This definition has been implemented in the eligibility criteria by considering not only the nature of the medical problem, but the impact of its associated impairment in light of an individual's age, level of education, prior work experience, morale, and the labor market he or she faces. Consideration of these nonmedical factors in addition to the medical factors has two consequences. First, the decision to apply for and accept income transfers on the basis of disability may be a function of both the medical condition and social and economic factors. Second, whether or not an *impaired* individual is a *disabled* individual is often a matter of judgment and dispute.

DETERMINANTS OF DISABILITY APPLICATIONS

Applying for disability-related income support requires that an individual be willing to consider himself or herself disabled. The distribution of the demographic characteristics of the disabled suggests that the decision to define oneself as disabled is the result of the interaction of personal characteristics and economic and medical conditions. Studies of the disabled have consistently found that the probability of impairment and subsequent disability increases with age;[4] that women report a slightly higher incidence and more severe disability with younger ages of onset than men;[5] that nonmarried persons

---

[3]Lance Liebman, *"The Definition of Disability in Social Security and Supplemental Security Income: Drawing the Bounds of Social Welfare Estates,"* Harvard Law Review *(March 1976),* 89(5):833–67; James W. Singer, *"It Isn't Easy to Cure the Ailments of the Disability Insurance Program,"* National Journal *(May 6, 1978),* 10:715–19; Nancy R. Mudrick, *"Disabled Women,"* Society *(March/April 1983),* 20(3):51–55.

[4]Lawrence D. Haber, *"Age and Capacity Devaluation,"* Journal of Health and Social Behavior *(September 1970),* 11(3):167–82; Kathryn Allan, *"First Findings of the 1972 Survey of the Disabled: General Characteristics,"* Social Security Bulletin *(October 1976),* 39(10):18–37.

[5]Lois M. Verbrugge, *"Females and Illness: Recent Trends in Sex Differences in the United States,"* Journal of Health and Social Behavior *(December 1976),* 17(4):387–403; Constance A. Nathanson, *"Sex, Illness, and Medical Care,"* Social Science and Medicine *(January 1977),* 11(1):13–25; Allan, *"First Findings of the 1972 Survey."*

report a higher incidence than married persons;[6] that blacks experience a greater incidence of disability than whites;[7] and that low-skill, poorly educated persons have a higher incidence of disability than well-educated white-collar workers.[8] The most common medical problems that lead to disability are cardiovascular (heart conditions and other circulatory problems) and musculoskeletal (bad backs, pain and stiffness in joints) conditions.[9] It should be evident from the characteristics of the disabled that the perception and determination of disability are not merely the results of an objective medical examination. This complication is one of the reasons that the determinants of application and acceptance for disability transfer benefits are topics which have received considerable attention from researchers, policy analysts, and congressional committees.

Several factors have been identified as influencing the decision to label oneself disabled and apply for disability transfers given the presence of an impairment. Among them are: (1) the level of disability benefits with respect to expected wages in the labor market; (2) work opportunities, especially when the unemployment rate is high; (3) knowledge of, and stigma associated with, beneficiary status; and (4) the legitimacy of being disabled (a variant of the "sick role") as a reason for not working.

Level of benefits. Analyses of the replacement rates of Disability Insurance benefits (the ratio of transfer benefits to prior wage income) have found that from 10 percent to 23 percent of beneficiaries (depending upon the method of computation) have replacement rates in excess of 80 percent.[10] This means that disability benefits may exceed predisability take-home pay. One possible consequence of this may be the creation of an incentive to withdraw from the labor force to be eligible for DI benefits. One study found that nonmarried men and women may be most influenced to withdraw from the labor force by the size and stability of disability benefits.[11] Studies of prime-age males have found that at best, their labor force participation is mildly influenced by the replacement rate of DI benefits.[12]

Work opportunities. The relationship between the unemployment rate and disability transfer applications has also been investigated on the assumption

[6]*Lois M. Verbrugge, "Marital Status and Health,"* Journal of Marriage and the Family *(May 1979), 41(2):267–85.*

[7]*U.S. Department of Health and Human Services,* Work Disability.

[8]*Luft,* Poverty and Health.

[9]*U.S. Department of Health and Human Services,* Work Disability.

[10]*U.S. Senate Committee on Finance,* Issues Related to Social Security Act Disability Programs, *Committee Print, CP96-23 (Washington, D.C.: U.S. Government Printing Office, 1979).*

[11]*William G. Johnson, Nancy R. Mudrick, and Hoi Sing Wai, "Social Security Disability Insurance or Work for Wages: the Choices of Impaired Men and Women," Health Studies Program Working Paper no. W-80-12 (Syracuse, N.Y.: Maxwell Graduate School of Citizenship and Public Affairs, Syracuse University, 1980).*

[12]*Donald O. Parsons, "The Decline in Male Labor Force Participation,"* Journal of Political Economy *(February 1980), 88(1):117–34; Sheldon Danziger and Robert Haveman, "How Income Transfer Programs Affect Work, Savings, and the Income Distribution: A Critical Review,"* Journal of Economic Literature *(September1981), 19(3):975–1028.*

that unemployed persons with impairments may give up the job search and seek income from disability transfers. Two studies have found modest evidence that disability claims rise with the unemployment rate while a third found no relationship.[13]

Knowledge and stigma. It has been suggested that the stigma of receiving disability transfer benefits has diminished since the implementation of SSI.[14] Increases in the number of DI applicants in the mid-1970s have been attributed in part to SSI because the publicity surrounding SSI increased public knowledge of both programs. Since both are administered by the Social Security Administration, persons who apply for one program are screened for eligibility in both.

Disability as a role. Finally, sex and social roles have been discussed as factors which influence the self-perception of disability. Especially with respect to women, it has been suggested that the "sick role" or the label "disabled" may be taken on by impaired women who consider themselves to have failed at other roles.[15] Thus, women who are not in paid employment and no longer engaged in full-time homemaking and child care activities may account for their time in terms of disability. This explanation has found only modest empirical support. At best, it appears that the disability status of women under age 50 may be influenced by "failure" in other sex roles.[16] Although this model has not been investigated with respect to men, it has been noted that between ages 55 and 64, a large proportion of men experience the onset of severe disability. This age range can be a difficult time for men who have stopped advancing in their careers or whose skills have become obsolete.[17] They are too young to retire, yet too old to retool easily for a new occupation.

ACCEPTANCE FOR DISABILITY BENEFITS

Once an individual applies for transfer benefits on the basis of disability, several criteria must be met in order to be found eligible. DI applicants must have worked in employment covered by Social Security and must meet the recency-of-employment criterion (employed twenty of the past forty quarters). SSI applicants must show that income and assets are below the means-test standard. The most difficult and disputed standard is the definition of disability previously quoted. Although a number of specific practices have been adopted

[13]*Mordechai Lando, Malcolm G. Coate, and Ruth Kraus, "Disability Benefit Applications and the Economy,"* Social Security Bulletin *(May 1976), 39(5):3–10.*

[14]*U.S. Senate Special Committee on Aging,* Social Security Disability: Past, Present, and Future, *Committee Print (Washington, D.C.: U.S. Government Printing Office, 1982).*

[15]*Stephen Cole and Robert LeJeune, "Illness and the Legitimation of Failure,"* American Sociological Review *(1972), 37(3):347–56.*

[16]*Ibid.; Nancy R. Mudrick, "Disability Among Women from a Life Course Perspective: A Test of the Influence of Sex Roles,"* Health Studies Program Working Paper no. W-83-2 (Syracuse, N.Y.: Maxwell Graduate School of Citizenship and Public Affairs, Syracuse University, 1983).

[17]*Mudrick, "Disability Among Women."*

to facilitate the assessment of disability, there is wide agreement that the disability determination process has thus far produced inconsistent decisions.[18]

The initial decision regarding the presence of a "medically determinable impairment" that prevents "substantial gainful activity" is made for the Social Security Administration by the state offices that also determine disability for state vocational rehabilitation programs. The decision to allow benefits at the initial (state) review may be overturned by the Social Security Administration. An applicant denied at this level may appeal the denial; the appeal is heard by an administrative law judge (ALJ) who may affirm or overturn the denial. A claimant who is denied benefits by an ALJ, may ask the Appeals Council to hear the case. The Appeals Council, which is responsible to the Social Security Administration, may decide whether or not to hear the case.

Several recent studies of the allowance process have verified that significant differences exist between the decisions made by state examiners and those made by ALJ's.[19] As part of a congressionally mandated study, the Social Security Administration compared the decision on the same set of cases as they would be made by the state offices and by the ALJ's. They found that the ALJ's allowed 64 percent of the cases sampled, the Appeals Council using ALJ standards allowed 48 percent, and the state offices allowed 13 percent. Further, only a small percentage of these same cases were allowed at each level for the same reasons.[20] The report suggested that this inconsistency may be the result of: (1) different standards at each level of review (the state offices use SSA regulations, and the ALJ's use the statute); (2) the impact of face-to-face encounters (state determiners use only records, ALJ's see the claimant); and (3) errors, especially on the part of ALJ's, in the interpretation of the criteria. The ALJ's dispute this assessment of their accuracy. They find the state decisions faulty. Their reversal rate of appealed state denials is approximately 47 percent, a rate slightly up from the early 1970s when state examiners were under less pressure to "tighten" the disability determination process.[21]

The main source of variation in disability judgments results from the difficulty of judging the presence of an "eligible" disability. Not only have agents of the Social Security Administration disputed among themselves an individual's eligibility, but they have increasingly disputed with the claimants'

---

[18]*U.S. General Accounting Office,* A Plan for Improving the Disability Determination Process by Bringing It Under Complete Federal Management Should Be Developed, report by the Comptroller General of the United States, HRD 78–146 (Washington, D.C.: 1978); U.S. House of Representatives, Subcommittee on Social Security, Status of the Disability Insurance Program, *Committee on Ways and Means, Committee Print, Wmcp:97-3 (Washington, D.C.: U.S. Government Printing Office, 1981); U.S. Department of Health and Human Services, "The Bellmon Report,"* Social Security Bulletin *(May 1982), 45(5):3–27.*

[19]*U.S. Department of Health and Human Services, "The Bellmon Report"; U.S. General Accounting Office,* A Plan for Improving the Disability Determination Process.

[20]*U.S. Department of Health and Human Services, "The Bellmon Report."*

[21]*Mordechai Lando, Alice V. Farley, and Mary A. Brown, "Recent Trends in the Social Security Disability Insurance Program,"* Social Security Bulletin *(August 1982), 45(8):3–14.*

lawyers in the federal courts. Between 1955 and 1970 the total number of disability appeals in Federal District Court was approximately 10,000; there were nearly 15,000 such cases pending in 1978 alone.[22]

Once an individual is awarded benefits on the basis of disability, the Social Security Administration is responsible for ensuring that eligibility continues, terminating benefits if recovery occurs or income exceeds the level of the means test. Until recently, recertification of eligibility was rarely initiated by the Social Security Administration. A General Accounting Office (GAO) study in 1981 estimated that as many as 584,000 persons were receiving DI benefits for which they were no longer eligible.[23]

The inconsistency in determination judgments in combination with the GAO estimates of the large number of ineligible beneficiaries has led many in and out of government to charge the Social Security Administration with poor management of the disability transfer programs. As a result, both the executive branch and Congress have recently tightened the procedures utilized to determine disability and manage the disability transfer programs.

OTHER PROGRAMS WHICH AFFECT INCOME SUPPORT OF THE DISABLED

Whether a disabled person requires income support from one of the disability transfer programs is in part related to employment opportunities in other sectors of the economy. Approximately 80 percent of severely disabled men and 16 percent of severely disabled women work either full or part-time.[24] However, the employed disabled are especially vulnerable to wage discrimination, employment discrimination, and unemployment. To the extent that these problems reduce labor force participation or wages, they may lead to an increase in application for, and utilization of, disability transfers. Discrimination against the handicapped in terms of hiring, promotion, and wage rates is believed to be commonplace although there are few empirical studies of its magnitude. A recent assessment of the extent of wage discrimination concluded that such discrimination against impaired persons reduces their wages by approximately twenty-one cents an hour after accounting for productivity and skill levels.[25] The number of cases of discrimination reported under the 1973 Rehabilitation Act has also been very small, and probably not a good indication of the actual number of persons experiencing discrimination in hiring and promotion.[26] Thus, while there is general agreement that impaired

[22]*U.S. Senate*, Social Security Disability: Past, Present and Future.

[23]*U.S. General Accounting Office*, More Diligent Follow-up Needed to Weed Out Ineligible SSA Disability Beneficiaries, *HRD 81-48 (Washington, D.C., 1981).*

[24]*U.S. Department of Health and Human Services*, Work Disability.

[25]*William G. Johnson and James Lambrinos*, "A Theoretical and Empirical Investigation of Discrimination Against the Handicapped," Health Studies Program Working Paper no. W-81-5 (Syracuse, N.Y.: Maxwell Graduate School of Citizenship and Public Affairs, Syracuse University, 1981).

[26]*Frank Bowe*, Rehabilitating America *(New York: Harper and Row, 1980).*

persons are disproportionately unemployed, underemployed, and underpaid, estimates of the impact of these factors on the demand for transfer income are not available.

Recent policy trends in these areas are in conflict. On the one hand, regulations implementing the equal employment and affirmative action requirements of the 1973 Rehabilitation Act (Sections 503 and 504 of 93–112) were promulgated and enforced starting in April 1977. These regulations are responsible for the continuing efforts to ensure the disabled physical access to public buildings, schools, and employment, as well as the increasing efforts toward affirmative action for the disabled with respect to employment. Section 503 of the Rehabiliation Act has been interpreted as requiring employers to ensure that personnel offices and some sections of the job site are accessible to the disabled, even if this means that architectural modifications must be made.[27] On the other hand, the Reagan administration has made it clear that it supports a "loosening" of affirmative action requirements; especially when they impose additional costs on employers.

High rates of unemployment also affect the transfer programs that serve the disabled. When impaired workers exhaust their unemployment insurance benefits they may turn to disability transfers for support. Thus, discouraged workers become disabled workers. High unemployment may also slow the termination rate from disability transfers. Finally, it has been suggested that Social Security early retirement benefits often function as a disability transfer program for persons whose ill health makes continued employment extremely difficult, but whose impairments are not severe enough to meet the disability criteria of DI or SSI.[28] Thus the recently passed Social Security reforms which raise the retirement age in the next century may produce increased numbers of early retirees despite the reduced benefits awarded those who retire early.

TRENDS AND CHANGES IN INCOME SUPPORT PROGRAMS

Recently proposed legislative and programmatic changes in income support of the disabled emphasize employment for persons with impairments. This goal is evident in program liberalizations which are intended to facilitate the maintenance of employment and, in the conservative proposal, to award disability benefits solely on the basis of medical factors. Recently enacted changes in the allowance process, benefit calculation, and coverage for Social Security disability benefits reenforce this by reducing the availability and size of disability transfers.

The main program liberalizations were included in the Disability Amendments of 1980. They included the maintenance of Medicare eligibility of DI beneficiaries for a period of two years after termination of disability benefits due to return to work, automatic SSI and DI reentitlement for a period of

[27]Ibid.
[28]*U.S. Senate,* Social Security Disability: Past, Present, and Future.

fifteen months after cessation of benefits due to employment should the work attempt fail, and allowed the deduction of extraordinary work expenses from earnings before estimating whether earnings exceed the substantial gainful activity (SGA) limit.[29] Medicare eligibility after termination of DI benefits due to employment has been extended so that possible loss of health insurance does not act as a disincentive to employment. Health care costs of the disabled are higher than those of the nondisabled, and health insurance is difficult to obtain when severe health problems exist. By extending Medicare eligibility, it is hoped that not only will DI beneficiaries be encouraged to seek and maintain employment, but that after a period of sustained employment, they will have been able to make arrangements to be covered either individually or through an employer group plan.[30]

Automatic reentitlement for SSI and DI benefits is another work incentive of the 1980 amendments. Prior to these amendments, an individual who maintained employment for a period of nine months at wages above the SGA standard was terminated from cash benefits and no longer considered disabled. If the individual subsequently found it impossible to continue working or the medical condition worsened, reinstatement of disability transfer benefits could occur only after the five-month waiting period imposed on first-time applicants. Thus, there was a substantial risk that no income would be received for a considerable period if the work attempt failed, posing a "sizable impediment to disabled beneficiaries contemplating a return to work."[31] The fifteen-month automatic reentitlement period extends to two years the period in which employment must be maintained before both cash benefits and status as a disabled person under the Social Security Act are terminated.

The final liberalization with respect to work incentives allows both SSI and DI recipients to exclude from wages the costs of attendant care services, medical devices, protheses, and similar items and services needed to enable employment. This is important because one of the tests of disability is the size of earnings. Earnings in excess of a specified monthly amount (now $300) are considered evidence of the ability to engage in substantial gainful activity, indicating that an impaired individual is not disabled. Under the new law, earnings are measured against the SGA limit net of the special costs of working. Those whose earnings net of work expenses are below the SGA will remain fully eligible for disability transfers. It is hoped that this provision will encourage disabled persons to venture into the labor force so that eventually they may earn enought to support themselves without the aid of disability transfer benefits.

---

[29]U.S. Department of Health and Human Services, "Social Security Disability Amendments of 1980: Legislative History and Summary of Provisions," Social Security Bulletin (April 1981), 44(4):14–31.

[30]U.S. Department of Health and Human Services, "Disability Amendments of 1980."

[31]Senate Finance Committee, quoted in U.S. Department of Health and Human Services, "Disability Amendments of 1980," p. 27.

Measures tightening the administration of the disability transfer programs and restricting the access to, and size of, benefits were included in the 1980 amendments to the Social Security Act, the Omnibus Reconciliation Act of 1981, and recent revisions in the regulations governing SSI and DI. The major benefit restrictions cap benefits and alter the way in which coverage is determined for younger workers. The 1980 amendments limit a family benefit under DI to 85 percent of the averaged indexed monthly earnings of 150 percent of the primary insurance amount, whichever is less (as long as that amount is at least 100 percent of the primary amount). This change is intended to eliminate the receipt of DI benefits which exceed predisability net earnings. It is intended to counteract the potential work disincentive of high replacement rates. A further cap on benefits was included in the Omnibus Reconciliation Act of 1981. Called the disability megacap, it requires a reduction in a person's DI benefits (including those for spouse and children) so that the sum of all disability benefits from certain federal, state, and local public programs will not exceed 80 percent of a person's "average current earnings."[32] The 1980 amendments also reduced the benefits of some new DI recipients. The 1980 legislation eliminated the minimum benefit (first for all beneficiaries, later amended to affect only new beneficiaries); persons whose DI payments based on the benefit formula are very low will now have to supplement their low income via SSI. Also included in this legislation was a provision to reduce the DI benefit of young workers by allowing fewer drop-out years in the calculation of their benefits.

Finally, because of changes in administrative processes and both explicit and implicit pressure from the Social Security Administration, fewer persons have recently been found to meet the disability criteria than was the case five years ago. Additionally, more current beneficiaries have been terminated from the programs for failure to remain disabled under the program definition. In fact, the abrupt termination of DI benefits, prior to appeal, caused such an outcry that administrative reforms of the administrative reforms were initiated in late 1982. These reforms include requiring face-to-face interviews at the beginning of the review procedure (called a Continuing Disability Investigation), and a reduction in the number of cases to be reviewed in 1983.[33] Additionally, Congress revised the requirements of the 1980 disability amendments by passing legislation requiring that the opportunity for face-to-face evidentiary hearings be provided at the reconsideration level of review of state agency decisions and continuing DI and Medicare benefits during the initial appeals of benefits terminated via the continuing disability investigation review. These recent reforms were in response to benefit denials and terminations which appeared to many as unjustified or based on poor evidence. Their

---

[32]John A. Svahn, *"Omnibus Reconciliation Act of 1981: Legislative History and Summary of OASDI and Medicare Provisions,"* Social Security Bulletin *(October 1981)*, 44(10):3–24.

[33]U.S. Department of Health and Human Services, *"Social Security in Review,"* Social Security Bulletin *(October 1982)*, 45(10):1.

intent is to protect disability applicants and beneficiaries by encouraging a more complete assessment of the evidence and shifting the responsibility for proof of disability from the beneficiary to the Social Security Administration. Rather than allow benefits to be abruptly terminated and only reinstated following a successful appeal, benefits will now be continued for those appealing termination until the outcome of the appeal is also known.

There are several other changes in disability transfer programs which are presently under discussion. The first is a proposal to base disability determinations on medical evidence alone. Although benefit allowances based on vocational factors consititute, at most, 25 percent of allowed cases, the Reagan administration believes that the use of medical evidence alone would reduce the number of beneficiaries and produce a more consistent outcome from the disability determination proccss.[34] Critics argue that this change would be harshest on persons between the ages of fifty-five and sixty-four since they are the least likely to be able to work in the face of an impairment.[35] The second proposal is to change the definition of disability so that qualified impairments must be expected to last at least twenty-four instead of twelve months as at present. Related to this is the proposal that the waiting period before DI benefits can be received be increased from five months to six months. Each proposal is suggested as a means of reducing program size and cost. Disabled persons made ineligible for DI by this change would be expected to support themselves through savings, privately financed temporary disability programs, or the means-tested SSI program.

The final proposal is to increase the recency-of-employment standard for eligibility for DI. Currently, recency of employment is defined as work covered by Social Security during at least twenty of the preceding forty quarters (the requirement is scaled down for workers under age thirty-one). The Reagan administration proposal would change the standard to six of the past thirteen quarters and thirty of the past forty quarters of covered employment, to be applied simultaneously. These stricter standards are intended to eliminate from eligibility persons whose recent employment was not covered by Social Security. However, a congressional study points out that these standards would adversely affect women, minorities, and persons with slowly progressive illnesses. Women would be adversely affected since if they spent more than twenty-one months out of the labor force for childbearing or child care, they would need to work steadily for seven years to regain their coverage for DI. Persons with intermittent employment and persons forced to withdraw from the labor force before their impairments are severe enough to meet the

---

[34]*U.S. House of Representatives, Subcommittee on Social Security, Committee on Ways and Means,* Reagan Administration Disability Proposals, *Committee Print WMCP:97-23 (Washington, D.C.: U.S. Government Printing Office, 1981).*

[35] *U.S. Senate,* Social Security Disability: Past, Present, and Future.

DI medical criteria might also fail to meet the proposed recency of employment test.[36]

THE NEW REALITY

Income-support programs for disabled persons changed slowly from their inception to 1980. Nearly all the amendments to these programs in that period had the effect of liberalizing eligibility criteria and enlarging the target population. Notable among these changes was the development of a disability insurance program (as opposed to the earlier "disability freeze") which covered impaired workers of all ages and the substitution of SSI for the state categorical Aid to the Blind and Aid to the Permanently and Totally Disabled. Throughout this century, public attitudes and consequently public income-support programs considered disabled persons the "deserving poor." Both the wage-based DI program and the means-tested SSI program paid little attention to work incentives, workfare measures, or encouraged recipients to obtain income from employment. Once a person was declared disabled under the standards, there was little expectation and little pressure to obtain employment. Since the presence of earnings is used to indicate the absence of disability it was conceptually awkward to encourage work among the disabled. This is not to say that rehabilitation services were not offered recipients or that many persons did not obtain employment. Once deemed rehabilitated or employed, these persons were no longer considered disabled. It was not possible to be an employed disabled person. Since 1980, legislation amending the income-support programs for disability has altered this stance. Needy disabled persons are no longer necessarily among the deserving poor. The political support for, and public attitude toward, income-support programs serving the disabled are much less differentiated than in the past from programs that serve other needy persons. Similar to other transfer programs, recent legislation has added work incentives and rigorous recertification procedures.

The changes in the income-support programs implemented over the past three years, as well as those still under discussion, contain benefits, as well as drawbacks. The drawbacks come from the more conservative interpretation of the definition of disability and the requirement that persons whose impairements are not classified as permanent must undergo a complete review every three years. Not only is accumulation of the data required for the review costly and inconvenient, when it involves new medical tests, it may also be hazardous to the health of the beneficiary.[37] While they decrease the chances that ineligibles will receive benefits, these new standards also increase the

---

[36]*U.S. House of Representatives, Subcommittee on Social Security*, Reagan Administration Disability Proposals.

[37]*Burt Schorr, "Congress Considers Revising Review Procedures for Disability Payments to Aid the Beneficiaries,"* Wall Street Journal, *August 18, 1982.*

chances that eligibles are denied benefits. For the needy eligible who are denied benefits these new measures have a high cost.

The recent modifications of disability transfer programs have some benefits, however. For the first time, impaired persons are, in a positive sense, encouraged to work. By excluding work expenses from the SGA test and extending medical coverage after termination of cash benefits, the risks associated with attempting employment are much reduced. This encouragement of employment is consonant with the efforts by the disabled to ensure enforcement of regulations requiring barrier-free architecture at job sites and affirmative action in employment practices. If the recent legislation contributes to the demise of expectations for the disabled based on paternalism and dependency, then it holds additional benefits for the disabled.

It is clear that the current goal of policy changes in disability transfer programs is to provide less for fewer persons. There are good reasons for disabled persons and those who sympathize with them to fight these changes. There are also, however, some challenges and new opportunities for independence made possible by this new reality.

Employment Policy and
Labor Market Reality

MICHAEL W. SHERRADEN

AT THE end of 1982, the nationwide unemployment rate had reached 10.8 percent, or about twelve million people without jobs and looking for work. If additions were made for those who had become discouraged and for those who were working part time but preferred to be working full time, the unemployment rate would have exceeded 17 percent. This was by far the highest level of joblessness since the depression. Moreover, high unemployment rates are expected to persist in the years ahead. The President's chief economic adviser has forecast an unemployment rate of 7 percent for several years from now.[1] The widespread suffering represented by these statistics is all too familiar to those of us who work in social welfare. We are shocked and outraged. Agencies are overextended. Services of all kinds are inadequate to meet the needs of the unemployed. We speak out and lobby for more humane policies, and we hope that Congress will respond. We know beforehand, however, that the policy response is not likely to be enough. At best, less than a million jobs will be created, and eight or nine million people will remain unemployed.

In the 1980s, and perhaps beyond, unemployment will be a serious problem. Under these circumstances, we must consider not only today's unemployed, but tomorrow's unemployed as well. A long-term perspective is required. What policies should be adopted in the years ahead? To begin to answer this question, it is useful to recognize that unemployment is not a single monolithic problem but rather a cluster of problems, each with different characteristics.

TYPES OF UNEMPLOYMENT

Unemployment can be categorized into four basic types: frictional, structural, cyclical, and chronic.[2] The four types are conceptually all-encompassing and

MICHAEL W. SHERRADEN is Assistant Professor, George Warren Brown School of Social Work, Washington University, St. Louis.

[1]*Martin Feldstein, chairman of the Council of Economic Advisors, "Meet the Press," NBC television, November 21, 1982.*
[2]*This general categorization is widely accepted. For example, see Eleanor Gilpatrick, "On the Classification of Unemployment: A View of the Structural-Inadequate Demand Debate,"* Industrial and Labor Relations Review, *January 1966, pp. 201–12.*

nonoverlapping, and consequently they provide a useful framework for exa-mining the nature of unemployment problems. Definitions for the four basic types of unemployment are as follows:[3] *Frictional unemployment* is caused by short-term labor market adjustments, such as seasonal fluctuations and time spent between jobs. If the economy were operating at its most efficient level, all of the remaining unemployment would be frictional. This would be unemployment resulting from inevitable shifts of capital and labor supply in a fluid economy. In this sense, frictional unemployment is not an irregularity at all but rather an essential feature of a dynamic economy.

Structural unemployment refers to deeper and more long-lasting ir-regularities in the labor market—inconsistencies between skills required in available jobs and skills possessed by available workers. Structural unemploy-ment occurs because the labor market is, in reality, many semirigid submarkets, and skills do not automatically transfer from job to job. Indeed, in the more sophisticated skill areas, years of specialized training are required to secure employment. Thus it is possible that some structural job vacancies exist for long periods, even though people are unemployed and looking for work. Factors which may contribute to structural unemployment include shifts in demand for labor, speed of labor supply adjustments, flexibility and transfera-bility of skills, and geographic rigidity in the labor market.

Cyclical unemployment is caused by labor demand deficiency during the recessionary phase of the business cycle. In other words, cyclical unemploy-ment is the unemployment difference between peak and trough periods in the cycle.

Chronic unemployment refers to labor demand deficiency above and beyond cyclical fluctuations; that is, labor demand deficiency which persists even when times are good. Chronic unemployment is sometimes called GNP-gap or growth-gap unemployment. With the major types of unemployment thus defined, it is useful to estimate how much of total unemployment belongs in each category.

Frictional and Structural Unemployment

For the purposes of this discussion, frictional and structural unemployment can be considered together.[4] The most basic approach to estimating frictional and structural unemployment together is to look at unemployment rates when the economy has been robust; that is, when labor demand has been especially high. In the postwar period, the unemployment rate for all workers fell to lows of 2.9 percent in 1952 and 3.5 percent in 1969. Thus, historically, it

---

[3]*These definitions are similar to those in Lloyd G. Reynolds,* Labor Economics and Labor Relations *(7th ed., Englewood Cliffs, N.J.: Prentice Hall, 1978), pp. 122–32), and many others.*

[4]*Frictional and structural unemployment would be easier to estimate separately if the Bureau of Labor Statistics kept systematic data on job vacancies. Unfortunately, however, the Bureau does not do so.*

can be said that when demand deficient unemployment is wiped away, or nearly wiped away, the remaining frictional and structural unemployment totals about 3 percent.[5] There is certainly considerable "face validity" in this estimation, but it is necessary to pause for a moment and consider this approach.

George Perry and others have suggested that this reasoning is not useful because both frictional and structural unemployment change as a function of aggregate demand.[6] These changes are thought to be as follows: When demand deficient unemployment falls, frictional unemployment is reduced because people spend less time looking for jobs. And when demand deficient unemployment falls, structural unemployment is reduced because obsolete skills get "melted down" and cast into new molds under the pressure of high demand. As a result of these hypothesized interdependencies, many economists, if asked to specify a level for frictional and structural unemployment, are inclined to hedge and say it probably depends on aggregate demand for labor. This line of thinking, however, obscures more than it reveals. If frictional and structural unemployment fall (or rise) as a function of labor demand, then for policy purposes, all of this decrease (or increase) is due to aggregate demand. To paraphrase an old quotation, demand deficiency is demand deficiency is demand deficiency. The way in which demand deficiency gets acted out in the labor market is not centrally important from the standpoint of policy-makers.

Thus, it is appropriate to take 3 percent as an "ordinary" historical level of frictional and structural unemployment. The word "ordinary" is used here because it is quite possible, in a rapidly changing economy, for structural unemployment to become much higher; in other words, job vacancies might exist in large numbers with workers who were not trained to fill them. This is possible, and indeed might be the case in the future, but it is clearly not the case now. Aside from very small shortages of engineers in defense industries, shortages of skilled workers in some areas of high technology, and shortages of mathematics and science teachers, no other labor markets are now looking for workers. Most labor markets are exceptionally slack, with unemployment higher than normal in nearly every occupational category. Indeed, it would be very difficult to show that even one million long-term job vacancies currently exist in the economy, which would make total structural unemployment less than one percent.

[5]*Unemployment data are from* Employment and Training Report of the President, 1982 *(Washington, D.C.: U.S. Government Printing Office, 1983), p. 194. Recently the 3 percent frictional and structural unemployment estimate has been supported in a study of job vacancy data; see Katharine G. Abraham, " 'Frictional Structural' Versus 'Demand Deficient' Unemployment: Some New Evidence," Massachusetts Institute of Technology and National Bureau of Economic Research, 1982, (unpublished).*

[6]*George L. Perry, "Unemployment Flows in the U.S. Labor Market,"* Brookings Papers on Economic Activity *(1972), no. 2, pp. 245–78; see also Gilpatrick, "On the Classification of Unemployment," and Reynolds, Labor Economics, p. 126.*

While there is significant potential for higher structural unemployment if extensive capital is rapidly invested in emerging industries, this remains only a potential until those jobs actually exist. The fact that capital investment in high technology has not in fact occurred on nearly a large enough scale in the United States is a serious economic problem, but it is not, by any stretch of the imagination, a structural unemployment problem.

The term "structural" has been somewhat abused of late, and a word of clarification may be in order. Martin Feldstein, chairman of the Council of Economic Advisors, recently referred to a "structural" unemployment rate of 7 percent.[7] What Feldstein meant by this misuse of the term "structural" is that 7 percent is the rate of unemployment now considered consistent with price stability. In other words, the Reagan administration, without wishing to say so openly, now places "the unemployment rate at full employment" at 7 percent. This definition has nothing whatever to do with the commonly accepted definition of structural unemployment. Hodding Carter, for example, has chided the administration for exploiting the term "structural" and hiding behind it as if the unemployment problem were unavoidable rather than susceptible to remedy through political action.[8]

Cyclical Unemployment

Cyclical unemployment can be estimated with a considerable degree of confidence. By definition, cyclical unemployment is the difference in unemployment rates between peak and trough years in the business cycle. Below are unemployment highs and lows for the last five complete business cycles.[9]

High Unemployment		Low Unemployment		Years in Expansionary Phase	Cyclical Difference in Unemployment Percentage
Percentage	*Year*	*Percentage*	*Year*		
5.6	1954	4.1	1956	2	1.5
6.8	1958	5.5	1959	1	1.3
6.7	1961	3.5	1969	8	3.2
5.9	1971	4.9	1973	2	1.0
8.5	1975	5.8	1979	4	2.7

As the table indicates, the cyclical unemployment rate has varied between 1.0 percent and 3.2 percent over the past five complete business cycles. The average rate has been 1.9 percent. Based on this information, an estimate of about 2 percent for cyclical unemployment is reasonable. It is also apparent

[7]*Feldstein, "Meet the Press."*
[8]*Hodding Carter III, "Don't Blame Me, Blame the Structural Problem,"* Wall Street Journal, *February 17, 1983, p. 27.*
[9]*The basic data are from* Employment and Training Report of the President, 1982, *p. 194.*

from these data that the cyclical unemployment percentage is closely related
to the length of the expansionary phase of the business cycle—the longer the
expansionary phase, the greater the cyclical decline in unemployment. (A
calculation of Pearson's r correlating length of the expansionary phase with
decline in unemployment percentage yields $r = .91$, and $r^2 = 83$. In other
words, the length of the expansionary phase explains 83 percent of the variance
in cyclical unemployment.) This relationship exists because unemployment
continues to drop as business improves. Simultaneously, inflation rises, and
the decision of when to end the expansionary phase generally depends on
how much inflation is considered tolerable. Hence, the length of the cycle,
and the total cyclical drop in unemployment, is largely a political decision,
and therefore it is preferable to take an average cyclical unemployment rate
across several business cycles rather than a single rate for any given cycle.

Chronic Unemployment

Unemployment which remains after frictional, structural, and cyclical components are subtracted is chronic (or growth-gap) unemployment. Chronic unemployment at the end of 1982 was 5 percent to 6 percent (10.8 percent total
unemployment minus about 3 percent for frictional and structural and about
2 percent for cyclical). In other words, at least half of the total unemployment
at the end of 1982 was due directly or indirectly to long-term inadequacies
in aggregate demand. We also know that this percentage rose dramatically in
the 1970s. If similar calculations are made for other peak unemployment
years, the chronic rate appears to have been about one percent in 1971 and
about 3 percent in 1975. In other words, with each successive business cycle
in the 1970s and early 1980s, a larger and larger percentage of chronic
unemployment was created.

In short, the overall demand for labor is changing dramatically in the United
States, and more and more people are being permanently pushed out of
employment. More specifically, there is a growing chronic demand deficiency
of certain types of workers. Low-skill, routine, and manufacturing jobs are
disappearing. There are numerous signs of this trend. For example, between
1947 and 1981, production workers as a percentage of total employment in
private industry declined from 87.9 percent to 81.1 percent, indicating that
an increasingly lower proportion of line (nonsupervisory) workers are required.
This trend is consistent in all industries—mining, construction, manufacturing, transportation, wholesale and retail trade, finance, and services.[10] Between 1940 and 1980 the proportion of blue-collar workers in the U.S. labor
force decreased from 57 percent to 34 percent.[11] This changing employment
pattern affects marginal workers as chronic unemployment, and the most

[10]*Calculated from 'ibid', p. 241.*

[11]*Eli Ginzberg, "The Mechanization of Work,"* Scientific American, *September 1982, pp.
66–75.*

marginal workers are nonwhites and young people. In 1970, for example, nonwhites accounted for 19.8 percent of all long-term unemployment; by 1981, however, this figure had reached 29.1 percent.[12] Among teenage black workers, the official unemployment rate is now 45 percent to 50 percent. This unemployment is largely chronic. A large number of these young people will never—not in their entire lives—hold a steady job in the traditional labor market.

GALE OF CREATIVE DESTRUCTION?

The major reason for the recent dramatic change in U.S. labor demand is a changing world economy. The United States has become more vulnerable to competitive pressures throughout the world. This case is made convincingly in recent analyses by Robert Reich and Amitai Etzioni. Reich points out that:

> The globe is fast becoming a single marketplace. Goods are being made wherever they can be made the cheapest, regardless of national boundaries. . . . Every year between 1980 and 2000, 36 million people will enter the world labor force, and 85 percent of them will be from developing nations. The newly integrated world market will put many of them to work at America's old speciality of high-volume, standardized production.[13]

In other words, low-skill and routine jobs will be moving elsewhere—to Korea, Malaysia, Brazil, and other industrializing nations. Reich argues that the United States, if it is to compete economically, must switch from an emphasis on standardized production to "flexible systems" of production which depend on "sophisticated skills" of their employees. Etzioni's views about the changing economic order are essentially the same as Reich's. He refers to "a tendency to underdevelop, a kind of industrialization in reverse."[14] By "underdeveloping" Etzioni means that the United States is poorly equipped to compete with newly industrializing nations in low-skill, routinized tasks; hence, the exodus of these jobs from the United States and the increasing rise in chronic unemployment among marginal workers.

Looked at more positively, the U.S. economy is in the midst of what Joseph Schumpeter referred to as a "gale of creative destruction."[15] Schumpeter believed such "gales" to be the inevitable mode of progress in a capitalist economy. Indeed, some observers view the current "gale" with great optimism. One such perspective is that of James Cook, who suggests that the economy

[12]Employment and Training Report of the President, 1982, *pp. 203–4. Long-term unemployment here refers to unemployment of twenty-seven weeks or longer.*

[13]*Robert B. Reich, "The Next American Frontier,"* The Atlantic, *March, 1983, pp. 43–58.*

[14]*Amitai Etzioni,* An Immodest Agenda: Rebuilding America in the 21st Century *(New York: McGraw-Hill, 1983), p. 285.*

[15]*Joseph A. Schumpeter,* Capitalism, Socialism, and Democracy *(2d ed.; New York: Harper, 1947), p. 83.*

is "molting, throwing off an old skin and growing a new one."[16] Cook sees potential for dramatic increases in productivity. He acknowledges, however, that even with the "new skin," unemployment will not necessarily be reduced. It is very doubtful that job losses will be avoided. Hence, even optimists do not foresee low unemployment in the years ahead. Low-skill jobs will continue to disappear even if the United States responds successfully to the world economic challenge. A large proportion of new jobs will be highly skilled, and there is little reason to believe that the entire labor force can be accommodated in this new economic order. Cook dismisses these problems because the disadvantaged, unskilled, ill-educated, and unhealthy are not his focus. Those of us who are concerned about poverty and equality of opportunity, however, cannot afford to take such a casual view. Combined with recent cutbacks in social programs, chronic unemployment will continue to add to an already large destitute population.

In sum, the labor market of the 1980s and beyond will be characterized by high demand for skilled workers in certain industries. Simultaneously, chronic unemployment among low-skilled workers and workers in declining manufacturing industries is likely to increase with each successive business cycle. Although it seems unthinkable today, it is altogether possible that total unemployment at the bottom of the next business cycle will reach 12 percent or 13 percent, and perhaps 14 percent in the cycle following.

Assuming that the economy does successfully invest in new industries, unemployment in the years ahead will have both structural and chronic components. To address the structural issues successfully, large numbers of workers will have to be trained or retrained for new kinds of jobs. This is a great challenge to the nation, and our economic future depends on investment in, and training for, new industries. But this is not the only challenge. Chronic unemployment will present an equal or greater challenge. In a democratic society, where employment is the principal mode of income distribution, and where self-esteem is closely tied to employment, massive chronic unemployment is not only morally unacceptable, but socially, politically, and economically unmanageable as well. Each one percent increase in unemployment adds direct costs of $25 to $30 billion to the federal budget (tax revenues lost and expenditures for benefits). Indirect costs from increased crime, alcoholism, child abuse, physical illness, mental illness, and other social problems add billions more to the total cost. Although most policy-makers are today not acknowledging the scope of this problem, sooner or later it must be faced. And contrary to many fantasies, dealing with the structural problems will not *ipso facto* solve the chronic problems. The chronic problems will remain and very likely grow worse. Because Reich and Etzioni and so many others focus almost exclusively on the structural issues, and because so little attention is paid to the massive chronic unemployment which the nation now faces, the

---

[16]James Cook, *"The Molting of America,"* Forbes, *November 22, 1982, pp. 161–67.*

remainder of this discussion deals with policy choices related to chronic unemployment.

PUBLIC POLICY AND CHRONIC UNEMPLOYMENT

Chronic unemployment was, of course, the principal focus of employment policy during the depression years. President Roosevelt recognized that the private economy, left to itself, would not generate sufficient demand for labor. He created the Works Progress Administration (WPA), Civilian Conservation Corps (CCC), and several other programs which hired workers on government-created projects. Altogether, more than twenty million chronically unemployed people worked on such jobs in the decade between 1933 and 1943.

In contrast, U.S. employment policy in recent years has had a different focus. The modern era of employment policy in the United States began with the Manpower Development and Training Act (MDTA) of 1962.[17] MDTA and most other employment policy during the past twenty years, including the Comprehensive Employment and Training Act (CETA), have emphasized job training. The roots of this emphasis are entwined in the "automation scare" which accompanied the 1958 recession. In the late 1950s and early 1960s the nation was in a post-Sputnik panic, not only about the Soviet threat, but also about jobs. A common perception was that science and technology would rapidly automate production processes and employment would become increasingly more skilled.[18] Job training was therefore recommended. All of this sounds very familiar to us in 1983. Unemployment has been higher than at any time since the depression, and *Time* has selected the computer as 1982s "man of the year." We are in the midst of a "technology scare," and once again there is concern about training for a more skilled labor market. Future observers, looking back at this period, will see the technology scare of the early 1980s as similar to the automation scare of the early 1960s. The period between has been an interlude in the intensity of concern, but the issue has not been forgotten. Job training has dominated federal employment policy during this period. Occasionally, job training has been supplemented by job-creation efforts, such as public service employment, but job creation consistently has been viewed as a countercyclical measure.

In short, the implicit assumption in the employment and training policy has been that jobs are available in the traditional labor market for properly trained workers, at least during good times. Chronic unemployment has not, to any significant extent, been acknowledged in public policy in the postwar period. However, as previously noted, it is now apparent that an increasing proportion of total unemployment is due to chronic demand deficiency. This

---

[17]*Following World War II there were no significant federal efforts toward employment and job-training programs until the early 1960s.*

[18]*See, for example, Seymour Wolfbein, "Automation and Skill," in* The Annals of the American Academy of Political and Social Science *(1962), 340: 53–59.*

chronic unemployment is not likely to disappear with any amount of job training or with the next swing in the business cycle. If the United States is to adapt successfully to the changing world economy, this reality must be acknowledged.

At present, U.S. policy is long way from acknowledging chronic unemployment. The Reagan administration is reluctant to acknowledge even cyclical demand deficiency. In spite of a very deep recession, there have been few significant federal proposals for job creation. President Reagan has completely eliminated public service employment under the former CETA program, and has left intact only some job-training efforts tied to private industry. For example, the "jobs bill" which moved through the Congress in the spring of 1983 increased employment in the construction trades, but offered very little to the low-skilled chronically unemployed. Chronic unemployment was virtually ignored by this legislation except for an extension in unemployment benefits. In this regard, Representative (California, D.) Augustus Hawkins asserted that Reagan's proposal is not a "jobs bill" at all, but rather an extension of unemployment benefits and a stimulus to the construction industry.[19]

POLICY CHOICES

If President Reagan and most members of the Congress choose not to face the problems of chronic unemployment, it is up to the social welfare profession to call attention to this callous—and economically shortsighted—disregard of large numbers of Americans. As Harry Hopkins said during a period of even greater hardship, "we have to deal with the simple truth that the majority of people have associated the chance to earn their living with self-respect."[20] If self-respect and economic well-being are to be restored to the chronically unemployed, and to the nation, additional policy approaches will be required.

Basically, there are three types of approaches to chronic unemployment. The first is the private approach, responses within established private industry. The private approach has two variations: growth and no growth. The growth theme is captured by the "all boats rising with the rising tide" homily which many economic conservatives are fond of quoting. This perspective is deficient in two respects. First, there are limits to growth, and especially limits to the amount of inflation that society is willing to accept in exchange for growth. In other words, there is virtually no prospect that the economy will grow rapidly enough to eliminate demand deficient unemployment. And second, not everyone has a boat. The chronically unemployed will be left to sink to the bottom. While economic growth will be essential in the years ahead, it will not, by itself, solve the chronic unemployment problem.

[19]*Augustus Hawkins, cited in Sar Levitan and Clifford Johnson, "A Cynical, Ineffectual Jobs Bill," New York* Times, *February 15, 1983, p. A27.*

[20]*Harry Hopkins, "Relief Through Work Demanded by Hopkins," New York* Times, *March 10, 1935, p. E7.*

In contrast, the no-growth theme might take the form of more labor-intensive methods of production—hiring ten workers instead of one worker and a machine, for example. Within the private sector, this approach would be a possibility whenever labor could be efficiently substituted for energy and/or capital. This general idea appears in the writings of Hazel Henderson and other limits-to-growth advocates.[21] Unfortunately, this approach, applied to the United States, is wishful thinking. Whatever the price of labor here, labor is less expensive in Singapore or Brazil or elsewhere, and these international dynamics cannot be ignored. Unless substantially subsidized, private industry in the United States is unlikely to revert to more labor-intensive methods of production.

The second type of approach is public stimulus to the private sector. In this category are several proposals offered by the Reagan administration: an alternative minimum wage for teenagers, a subsidy for hiring disadvantaged workers, and enterprise zones. Each of these proposals is designed to increase employment in areas where chronic unemployment is highest, and each deserves careful consideration, but again the potential appears limited. Regarding a subminimum wage and a subsidy for hiring the disadvantaged (which, from the employer's perspective, is the equivalent of a subminimum wage), considerable displacement would occur; that is, higher priced workers would be bumped from their jobs. The net new jobs created would be small. And once again, international dynamics would play a role; even a subminimum wage would not make U.S. labor competitive internationally, and thus there is little potential for massive job creation over the long term. Regarding enterprise zones, several misgivings have been raised. These include evidence that tax incentives usually do not play a major role in business location decisions; doubts that the chronically unemployed in enterprise zones would be affected by new business development; and added demands on deteriorating urban infrastructures with no accompanying tax base to cope with these added demands.[22] Overall, the enterprise zone idea does not seem to hold much promise.

A third type of approach is the public approach. In this category are all types of public employment, and especially that which directly affects the disadvantaged. Public employment includes more than "employment programs." Currently, for example, the U.S. military establishment is by far the largest employer of disadvantaged young people. Considering nonmilitary employment, expansion of traditional governmental activities or public service employment are the alternatives. Expanding most traditional governmental activities would not do much for the chronically unemployed, but public service employment remains a possibility. As already noted, public service employment was the major focus of employment policy during the New Deal

[21]See Hazel Henderson, Creating Alternative Futures *(New York: Berkley, 1978).*

[22]*National Urban Coalition,* Report on the Working Conference on the Proposed Urban Jobs and Enterprise Zone Legislation *(Washington D.C.: National Urban Coalition, 1981).*

era. In 1983, however, there are not many voices calling for large-scale public service employment. The currently accepted view is that such programs are "make work" and a waste of money. This view, however, is shortsighted, lacking both historical perspective and imagination.

Public service employment can be productive. The most striking example is the CCC (1933–42) which, among many other accomplishments, developed most of the recreation areas which now exist in state and national parks and planted more than two billion trees covering twenty-one million acres, the largest single tree planting in the history of the world. Over time, the value of the CCC's efforts has paid for the original costs of the program many times over.[23] The key to the CCC's success was a genuine commitment to "the work," as President Roosevelt called it. In other words, productivity was an important goal. Although not quite so impressive as the CCC, other New Deal employment programs, such as the WPA and the National Youth Administration (NYA), also achieved respectable records in productivity. In contrast, public service employment programs in the 1960s and 1970s were not very productive. The major reason for this inadequacy was, not surprisingly, an absence of emphasis on productivity. Many of these programs were, in reality, income support programs dressed up as employment programs. This masquerade was quickly perceived by the public, and the programs suffered a great deal of criticism and were eventually eliminated altogether. (A word of clarification may be in order: there is nothing at all wrong with income support. Indeed, the author would advocate a great deal more of it for a variety of disadvantaged groups. The point here is that income support should not be confused with public service employment. Policy-makers would do well to avoid creating one and calling it the other.)

In short, the common vision of public service employment in the 1980s is negatively distorted by the misguided programs of the 1960s and 1970s. Although these recent programs were not successful, there is no reason to conclude that such programs in the future would not be successful. A more positive outlook would reflect greater historical understanding and also improve the possibility that the nation can eventually cope with chronic unemployment. It is very likely that public service employment, in a variety of forms, is the only real answer to chronic unemployment. As discussed above, labor market conditions are such that the private sector will not, at least in the decade ahead, generate enough demand to employ all those who would like to work.

Thinking about public service employment also requires imagination. Clearly, such employment would have to take forms appropriate to the needs of the nation in the 1980s and beyond. "Make work" should not be tolerated. Service projects should be selected which would be of most benefit to local communities and to the nation. One possibility is a large-scale program of

[23]Michael W. Sherraden, "The Civilian Conservation Corps: Effectiveness of the Camps" (dissertation, University of Michigan, 1979).

voluntary national service for young people. Such a program might undertake projects in natural resource conservation, weatherization of homes, disaster relief, environmental clean-up, social services, and a variety of other useful activities that are not currently addressed adequately in the private labor market. Ideally, such a program would be accompanied by postprogram educational benefits, similar to the old G.I. Bill, thus helping to deal not only with chronic unemployment but also providing education and training to cope wth long-term structural problems in the labor market as well.[24] Although all participants could benefit from a national service, the benefits to disadvantaged and minority youth, the most marginal workers, would be especially great.[25] National service would be a variation of public service employment which would simultaneously ease chronic unemployment and address other needs as well. It is encouraging that voices calling for national service are today growing more numerous.[26]

To take another possibility, the nation's rail lines, which are in a state of serious deterioration, could be rebuilt. Rail lines are a critical national resource. As energy becomes more costly—which is, sooner or later, a virtual certainty—rail transportation will become more desirable. Huge investments will be required to rebuild the rail lines. These investments are in the long-term interests of the nation, but they are far beyond the capital investment capability of private companies. A huge public project to rebuild the rail lines would require millions of person-years of effort. The work also could utilize many of the skills possessed by unemployed workers in declining "smokestack" industries.

Still a different sort of project would be to provide in-home care of older people to limit the costs and degradation of nursing home care. As the population ages, care of the elderly will become an increasing drain on the economy. Public service employment in this area could provide not only immeasurable personal benefit, but also could save billions of dollars in federal expenditures. Related to this idea is the possibility of providing in-home health care to limit the costs of hospitalization.

Other creative approaches to public service employment also should be explored, not in a "make-work" spirit, but in the spirit of imagination, cost saving, and productivity which will be essential for the nation in the years ahead. In this regard, public service employment should take a variety of forms. Experimentation at the national, state, community, and even neighborhood levels should be encouraged. For example, a forward-looking neighbor-

[24]*Michael W. Sherraden and Donald J. Eberly, ed.,* National Services: Social, Economic and Military Impacts *(New York: Pergamon Press, 1982).*

[25]*Fredrick E. Smith and Michael W. Sherraden, "National Youth Service and the Black Community," in* Social Welfare Forum, 1982–1983, Part I *(Washington, D.C.: National Conference on Social Welfare, 1985).*

[26]*In the week preceding the writing of this paper, national service was endorsed by Franklin Thomas, president of the Ford Foundation; Mayor Edward Koch of New York, and the New York* Times *on its editorial page, March 13, 1983.*

hood association in St. Louis is initiating a computerized resource exchange among unemployed residents which will allow the neighborhood to meet its own needs better and more efficiently allocate work in spite of slack demand for labor in the private market.[27] In general, at whatever level, a wide variety of opportunities must be designed for people to exercise the skills they possess, make contributions to others, and receive some means of support in return.

Connected with this, the destructive myth that public-sector employment is somehow less noble than private-sector employment must be confronted and discredited. Public intervention in the U.S. economy is not an aberration, it is the norm. The government regularly intervenes on behalf of various business interests with interest payment subsides, price supports, subsidies for nonproduction, direct loans, and a host of "tax expenditures" (benefits built into the tax laws). These measures are all contradictory to freemarket ideology and altogether cost the federal treasury more than is collected in corporate income taxes. In addition, the U.S. consumer pays higher prices for many goods because of market interventions (another form of subsidy to business). The point here is not to question the wisdom of these interventions, but simply to establish the mixed (public and private) nature of the U.S. economy. It so happens that most intervention related to economic activity is in behalf of capital. But it is not too much to ask, nor should it be considered a favor or a handout, that unemployed labor be given similar consideration. Underutilized labor is just as serious an economic problem as underutilized capital. Public service employment makes at least as much economic sense, for example, as tobacco or sugar subsidies.

Related to this point is a second myth—the myth that there is not enough work to be done. According to this view, a high level of chronic unemployment is an indication that there are not enough tasks that genuinely need to be done to keep everybody employed. One of the more informed analyses along these lines is by David Macarov.[28] This perspective assumes, however, that the private labor market is the wisest and most efficient mechanism for allocating labor. In reality, businesses make decisions oriented toward profit and survival, and not necessarily toward the long-term interests of the community and the nation. There are hundreds of tasks which private enterprise will never undertake but which are nonetheless important. These tasks include weatherization of homes and other energy-conservation efforts, environmental clean-up, literacy education, adequate day care for children of working parents, public works of all kinds, and other tasks which would, in the long run, build a stronger foundation for the future. The argument that there is not work to be done is misguided. It is not work that is in short supply but employment, the effective allocation of work.

Chronic unemployment is now a labor market reality. It is a serious problem,

[27]*Helen V. Graber and George Eberle, Jr., "Creating the New Age Settlement" (paper presented at the Annual Forum of the National Conference on Social Welfare, 1983).*
[28]*David Macarov, Work and Welfare: The Unholy Alliance (Beverly Hills, Calif.: Sage, 1980).*

and it will not go away by itself, not even with economic recovery. If the chronic unemployment problem is to be successfully dealt with in the years ahead, it is very likely that the nation will have to adopt a new perspective on public service employment. Such a perspective would be not only more humane than current policy, but also economically and politically more sound. If ignored by public policy, massive chronic unemployment will almost certainly drag down the economy and eventually will undermine political and social stability.

Similar to the perspective of Franklin Roosevelt in the 1930s, the new vision of public service employment must be creative and bold, appropriate to the times, and the work performed must be productive. The "make work" mentality must be replaced by an emphasis on accomplishment. Practical matters must take precedence over ideology and wishful thinking. The task is to create employment opportunities that will permit the disadvantaged to survive, achieve some measure of satisfaction and dignity, and contribute to the economy and to society.

The Legal Framework
for Child Protection in Two
Societies

REBECCA L. HEGAR

THE PROBLEMS of the foster care system have recently been the subject of a great deal of public and professional attention in both the United States and Great Britain. In each country, this new awareness has prompted efforts to make changes in the ways society provides substitute care for children. British and American critics of child welfare practice cite tendencies to remove children from their homes unnecessarily, to maintain children in foster care without rehabilitating their families, and to fail to provide stable, nurturing, foster and adoptive families. The poorly controlled entry of children into foster care and the difficult process of exit from care combine to trap many children in the custody of the state for indefinite periods.

The foster care "trap" is frequently treated in the professional literature as a product of the lack of supportive and rehabilitative services to families, poor case management, and a lack of planning for permanent placement. While these factors undoubtedly contribute to the problem, the laws which govern child protection and child placement pose additional barriers to permanency for foster children. The influence of these laws on the child placement system has not been adequately recognized in the literature of social work and other professions.

A framework for analyzing how child protection and child placement statutes affect the movement of children into and out of foster care is presented in this article. It helps clarify how different statutes influence the tendency for the number of children in care to build up over time. This conceptualization is applied to the child protection and placement laws of Great Britain and the United States. It is used to analyze the extent to which these laws promote the tendency to maintain children indefinitely in foster care. While the two national systems are enough alike to promote similar problems, there are also striking differences. Current proposals for legal change in each country are noted, and the conceptual framework is applied to suggest how the adoption of certain changes might affect children who would otherwise be trapped in foster care.

REBECCA L. HEGAR is Supervisor, Office of Human Development, Department of Health and Human Resources, Gretna, Louisiana.

LEGAL FRAMEWORK FOR CHILD PROTECTION IN BRITAIN

British law governing child protection, child placement, and custody has been described as "virtually incomprehensible except to the specialist."[1] The law includes certain common law principles and practices which have never been superseded by statute, as well as different Parliamentary acts that have been adopted over a period of more than a hundred years. Furthermore, several different courts, with varying rules of procedure, have jurisdiction over different types of child welfare and child custody cases. Given the complexity of the legal framework, only a cursory overview is presented here. Also, because Scotland and Northern Ireland have juvenile law and juvenile court systems different from those in England and Wales, only English law is considered.

In Great Britain, as in the United States, the work of child protection and child placement is carried out within a mixed system of public and private agencies. The local authority social service departments, similar to U.S. public child welfare departments, are central in the British system, although the private National Society for the Prevention of Cruelty to Children (NSPCC) also provides child-protective services. Like the "local authorities," voluntary child-placing agencies such as the Church of England Children's Society and the National Children's Home may place children in foster care or adoption with parental consent. However, these private organizations do not acquire parental rights over children in their care.[2]

British conceptions of parental rights and of society's responsibility to protect children from neglect or abuse are basically very similar to those in the United States. These core concepts are apparent in the legal framework within which British local authorities receive children into care and provide homes for them.

Children may enter care in Great Britain by several legal routes. The most important were established by the Children's Act of 1948 and the Children and Young Persons Act of 1969. The provisions of the former have now been incorporated in the Child Care Act of 1980 that governs voluntary placement of children by their parents. It also provides for placement of abandoned children and permits local authorities to keep in involuntary care children who were originally placed with parental consent. This is accomplished by passing an administrative "resolution," and about 18 percent of the children in the legal custody of local authorities entered care this way.[3] The resolution procedure, which transfers most parental rights from parent to public agency, is reviewed by the juvenile court only upon the objection of parents, who

[1]*Olive M. Stone*, Family Law: An Account of the Law of Domestic Relations in the Last Quarter of the 20th Century *(London: Macmillan, 1977), p. 245.*

[2]*Diana Rawstron*, Child Care Law: A Summary of the Law in England and Wales *(London: British Agencies for Adoption and Fostering, 1980), p. 9.*

[3]*Margaret Adcock and Richard White, "The Use of Section 3 Resolutions,"* Adoption and Fostering *(1982), 6(3):9–12.*

must be notified of the action if their whereabouts are known. If they do not object within one month, they still may obtain a hearing, but the burden of proof rests with them to show why they should have custody. A resolution of this type can only be passed on the following grounds: abandonment (for at least one year); permanent disability which renders the parent incapable of caring for the child; mental disorder which makes the parent unfit; being "of such habits or modes of life as to be unfit"; or having "so consistently failed without reasonable cause to discharge the obligation of a parent as to be unfit to have the care of the child."[4] In addition, it has also been possible since 1975 to pass a resolution to assume custody on the ground that the child has been in the physical care of the local authority through the preceding three years.[5]

The Children's and Young Persons Act of 1969 covers situations where children must be involuntarily removed from dangerous home situations. That act authorizes courts to issue "care orders" upon petition by police, local authorities, or the NSPCC.[6] The grounds for care orders include neglect, abuse, "moral danger," delinquency, and certain status offenses. In addition to one of these grounds, the court must find that the child is unlikely to receive care and control unless an order is issued.[7] If this dual test is met, the court may issue any of a broad range of dispositional orders, from agency supervision of the family to removal of the child.[8]

In emergency situations, the 1969 act authorizes "place of safety orders" that allow a child to be detained for up to twenty-eight days in a shelter or other suitable location. These are generally *ex parte* orders issued by any magistrate without a court hearing upon petition by anyone who has cause to believe a child may be endangered. In addition, police have special powers to remove children to places of safety for up to eight days without an order from a magistrate.[9]

In 1975 major statutory changes were enacted out of concern for the welfare of the many children who entered care and could neither return home with safety nor be freed for adoption. Both the Children's Act of 1975 and the Adoption Act of 1976 contain provisions that are designed to free for adoption or for other permanent arrangements some of the children who have been in care for long periods.[10] To this end, the 1975 act created a new type of custody order. Under certain circumstances a "custodian" for a child may be appointed who exercises most parental rights. However, a custodian does not

---

[4]*Brenda Hogett*, Parents and Children *(London: Sweet and Maxwell, 1977). pp. 175–76.*
[5]*Stone*, Family Law, *p. 252.*
[6]*Robert Dingwall and John Eekelaar, "Social and Legal Perceptions of Child Neglect: Some Preliminary Considerations,"* Child Abuse and Neglect, *(1979) 3(1):303–14.*
[7]*Stone*, Family Law, *p. 258–59.*
[8]*Ibid., p. 259.*
[9]*Rawstron*, Child Care Law, *p. 15.*
[10]*Stone*, Family Law, *p. 249.*

have the right to consent to adoption of the child, and the custodianship order is revocable.[11]

Some similar changes have been made in the law which governs adoptions, but in order to understand them a brief summary of British adoption law is necessary. Termination of parental rights can be accomplished only in an adoption proceeding. In general, the consent of each living parent is necessary before a child may be adopted. However, there are seven grounds on which the court may decide to dispense with consent, one of which was added by the 1975 act. The new ground is serious ill-treatment of the child by the parent, with rehabilitation unlikely.[12] At least one of the grounds is highly subject to court interpretation, and Stone reports that it is the most usual ground for applications to dispense with consent to adoption: that the parent or guardian "is withholding his agreement unreasonably."[13]

The Children's Act of 1975 and the Adoption Act of 1976 have made a few other changes in the old law which may facilitate adoptions. In the past, parents were required to approve each adoptive application.[14] It is now possible for parents to give a general consent to adoption and to declare their further noninvolvement with the proceedings. Also, if adults who have had a child in their home for five years apply for an order to free the child for adoption, no one may remove the child pending a hearing. A similar provision applies to all applicants for custodianship, and both safeguards have obvious implications for long-term foster parents. Unlike a custodianship order, however, grounds for dispensing with parental consent must always exist before an adoption order can be made, regardless of the time spent in the applicants' home.

LEGAL FRAMEWORK FOR CHILD PROTECTION IN THE UNITED STATES

While British law is complex, it is also difficult to portray the U.S. legal framework accurately because of the differences in state laws and court procedures. However, some general statements and representative examples can be given. Because U.S. child welfare law is reasonably familiar to American social workers, only a brief summary of the typical legal framework is included here.

When children require immediate protection, most state laws provide for emergency orders which can be issued by judges before a hearing takes place. In extremely dangerous situations, police are frequently authorized to remove children without even verbal court orders, and child-protective social workers

[11]*Hugh K. Bevan and M. L. Parry*, Children Act 1975 *(London: Butterworth, 1978), p. 115.*

[12]*Sonia Jackson, "The Children Act 1975: Parents' Rights and Children's Welfare,"* British Journal of Law and Society, *3 (1976), (3)1:87.*

[13]*Stone,* Family Law, *p. 234.*

[14]*Jackson, "The Children Act 1975," p. 87; Stone,* Family Law, *p. 231.*

occasionally have similar powers.[15] Although the legal language of state statutes varies widely, children can typically be placed involuntarily in temporary state custody if they are found to be deserted, deprived of care, or harmed by their parents. However, grounds for state intervention are frequently very broad and ill-defined. An extensive review of state laws in 1975 classified the most common grounds as "lack of proper parental care, control, or guardianship."[16] Voluntary placements may not meet even these vague standards. If parents request or agree to custody transfer, children often enter care with no judicial hearing or with only a cursory review of the situation by the judge.

As in Great Britain, exit from state custody in the United States is far more difficult than entry into care. Ideally, agencies make significant efforts to return children to their families of origin, and their work toward reunification is often promoted by the process of periodic court review of foster care cases. However, for many children, return to their own families is impossible or undesirable. For them the only route out of foster care is usually termination of parental rights and adoption. A few states also offer guardianship or permanent custody arrangements that are similar to the new British status of custodianship.[17]

One of the chief characteristics of traditional state statutes is that the requirements for involuntary termination of parental rights are different in nature from the requirements for entry into foster care. In order to terminate parental rights, different and additional charges must be proved—that the parent is "unfit" to raise the child, for example. A second difference between initial state intervention and ultimate termination of parental rights is that a different standard of proof is often applied. While the traditional civil standard of "preponderance of evidence" is often employed when children enter care, state laws and court decisions frequently mandate the more stringent test of "clear and convincing evidence" when the same case reaches the termination hearing.[18] The Supreme Court decision in *Santosky* v. *Kramer* (1982), which required the higher standard in New York's permanent neglect hearings, will further establish that standard as the appropriate test when parental rights are at stake.[19]

---

[15]*D. D. Broadhurst and J. S. Knoeller*, The Role of Law Enforcement in the Prevention and Treatment of Child Abuse and Neglect *(Washington, D.C.: U.S. Government Printing Office, 1979), see, for example, Texas Family Code 17.036.*

[16]*Sanford N. Katz, Ruth-Arlene W. Howe, and Melba McGrath, "Child Neglect Laws in America,"* Family Law Quarterly *(1975), 9(1):25, see also Michael S. Wald, "State Intervention on Behalf of 'Neglected Children': Standards for Removal of Children from Their Homes, Monitoring the Status of Children in Foster Care, and Termination of Parental Rights,"* Stanford Law Review *(1976), 28(4):623–706.*

[17]*See, for example, Texas Family Code 14.01–14.02; see also Victor A. Pike, ed.,* Permanent Planning for Children in Foster Care: A Handbook for Social Workers *(Portland, Oreg: Regional Research Institute for Human Services, 1977), pp. 76–77.*

[18]*Katz, Howe, and McGrath, "Child Neglect Laws," pp. 66–68; see, for example, Louisiana Revised Statutes 13:1601.*

[19]Santosky v. Kramer, *102 S.Ct. 1401 (1982).*

The overall effect of these differences between the requirements for foster care placement and those for termination of parental rights is to allow many more children to enter the foster car system than can ever be legally freed, should their own homes continue to be unavailable or unsafe. The result is a foster care trap that leads to the build-up of children in a system designed to provide temporary placement. In Great Britain the legal trap of foster care is perhaps even more pronounced. This is because children enter agency custody by numerous routes, including administrative decision of the agency and wardship proceedings in the High Court. No legal grounds are specified for the High Court's wardship jurisdiction.[20] On the other hand, permanent deprivation of parental rights can be accomplished only in an adoption proceeding and only with difficulty.

PROPOSALS FOR CHANGE

In the past few years, concern has been expressed frequently in both the United States and Britain about the growing foster care population and the difficulty of achieving permanence for foster children. Permanency planning efforts by child welfare agencies in the United States have demonstrated substantial success in moving children through the existing legal framework either to return them safely to their homes or to free them for other permanent placement.[21] The problems of the foster care trap have also been discussed by legal theorists and organizations. The proposals of several authors would, if adopted, substantially alter the legal framework for child protection and child placement in most jurisdictions. In general, two common thrusts of the several proposals are: to restrict initial state intervention in the parent-child relationship; and to facilitate the freeing of children for adoption after they have remained in state custody for some time.

The proposals for change discussed here include model statutes and standards developed by: Michael Wald, a legal theorist; the Joint Commission on Juvenile Justice, sponsored by the Institute for Judicial Administration and the American Bar Association (IJA-ABA); and the legal-psychoanalytic team of Joseph Goldstein, Anna Freud, and Albert J. Solnit. Several much less extensive proposals are also considered, including 1979 recommendations of the Legal Group of British Agencies for Adoption and Fostering.[22] Wald and IJA-ABA present very similar American proposals, and the well-known views of Goldstein, Freud, and Solnit are applicable to either country's system.

---

[20]*Rawstron, Child Care Law, pp. 22–24.*

[21]*Pike, Permanent Planning for Children in Foster Care, p. 5.*

[22]*Wald, "State Intervention on Behalf of 'Neglected Children' "; IJA-ABA,* Sandards Relating to Abuse and Neglect *(Cambridge, Mass.: Ballinger, 1977); Joseph Goldstein, Anna Freud, and Albert J. Solnit,* Before the Best Interests of the Child *(New York: Free Press, 1979) and* Beyond the Best Interests of the Child *(New York: Free Press, 1973); Diana Rawstron, ed.,* Care Proceedings *(London: British Agencies for Adoption and Fostering, 1979).*

Although the various proposals differ significantly, it is possible to consider how adoption of some of their common features might affect entry into, and exit from, the foster care system. Screening for out-of-home placement would be tighter, so fewer children would come into care, and the grounds for termination of parental rights would be basically the same as for placement. The length of time a child had spent in foster care would become a major criterion for termination of parental rights. Therefore, adoption of common provisions of the major proposals would eliminate the foster care trap by ensuring that fewer children entered care and that those who did could eventually be freed for permanent placement.

Entry into foster care would be restricted in several ways by some of the proposals. First, although they tend to include emergency powers to remove children without a hearing, most provide for a judicial hearing to follow quickly. This is in response to the criticism in both countries of abuse of power to take emergency custody.[23] Second, the proposals specify strict definition of the grounds for state intervention, generally stressing serious abuse or neglect that can be shown to have harmed the child. Third, stricter standards of proof are advocated at the stage of initial state intervention.

Exit from state custody would be eased by several common features of the three proposals. In court, children's interests would be given primacy, and certain rights of their long-term caretakers might be recognized. This is also true of two other model statutes that deal only with termination of parental rights.[24] All three comprehensive proposals establish lengths of time in foster care after which the rights of parents might be terminated. These time limits vary somewhat with the age of the child. Under Goldstein, Freud, and Solnit's schema, transfer of parental rights to a child's "psychological parents" would usually be semiautomatic after the time standards were met. Wald and IJA-ABA both propose that, after the time limits, the burden of proof should shift to parents to prove that termination is not in the child's best interests. Finally, IJA-ABA and Goldstein, Freud, and Solnit make it clear that voluntary placements, even when no abuse, neglect, or desertion is involved, could eventually end in termination. This is already of feature of the British system and of some U.S. state laws.[25]

PARENTAL RIGHTS

Proposals to change the bases for state intervention with the family and for termination of parental rights raise profound questions of rights and equity

---

[23]Wald, *"State Intervention," p. 630; Rawstron, ed.,* Care Proceedings, *pp. 17–18.*

[24]*James H. Lincoln, "Model Statute for Termination of Parental Rights,"* Juvenile Justice *(1976), 27(4):3–8; Ruth-Arlene W. Howe, "Development of a Model Act to Free Children for Permanent Placement: A Case Study in Law and Social Planning,"* Family Law Quarterly *(1979), 13(3):257–325.*

[25]*Joseph R. Carrieri,* The Foster Child: From Abandonment to Adoption *(New York: Practicing Law Institute, 1977).*

which cannot be ignored, even when no more than cursory consideration can be given. The three major proposals reviewed here would alter the balance of state power and individual rights in two ways. First, by restricting initial state intervention with families, they would strengthen the right to privacy in child rearing and other family matters that is a feature of English common law and that has been recognized repeatedly in U.S. Supreme Court decisions as having constitutional protection.[26] Wald and Goldstein, Freud, and Solnit are explicit about this aspect of their proposals.[27] Second, by broadening the situations under which parents may ultimately lose their parental rights, the proposals come into conflict with the view that the right to privacy requires restriction of state power to sever permanently the parent-child relationship.[28]

However, the second effect of the proposals is congruent with the views of commentators who maintain that children who have been out of the care of their own parents acquire independent rights to ties with their psychological parents.[29] The proposals for change provide mechanisms for recognizing that long tenure in foster care frequently creates separate interests for parents and their children in termination of parental rights cases. Once the original family has been long divided by placement of the children in foster care, the major model statutes favor children's interest in stable and permanent families over parental interests in reuniting the original family.

CONCLUSIONS

The child protection and child placement laws of Great Britain and the United States make an interesting comparative study because of the differences which have evolved within the Anglo-American legal heritage. For example, permanent termination or transfer of parental rights was unknown under English common law. Adoption of children was first brought into U.S. law from the Spanish law of the Southwestern states, and adoption was impossible in Great Britain until it was authorized by statute in 1924.[30] Involuntary termination of parental rights has become possible in Britain only through the device of

[26]*The Supreme Court cases include:* Meyer v. Nebraska, *262 U.S. 390 (1923);* Griswold v. Connecticut, *381 U.S. 479 (1965);* Wisconsin v. Yoder, *406 U.S. 205 (1972);* Roe v. Wade, *410 U.S. 113 (1973).*

[27]Wald, *"State Intervention," p. 638;* Goldstein, Freud, and Solnit, Beyond the Best Interests, *pp. 7–8.*

[28]*Laurence D Houlgate,* The Child and the State: A Normative Theory of Juvenile Rights *(Baltimore: Johns Hopkins University Press, 1980), p. 29; Pamela Dru Sutton, "The Fundamental Right to Family Integrity and Its Role in New York Foster Care Adjudication,"* Brooklyn Law Review *(1977), 44(1):110; Cheryl M. Browning and Michael L. Weiner, "The Right to Family Integrity: A Substantive Due Process Approach to State Removal and Termination Proceedings,"* Georgetown Law Journal *(1979), 68(1):213–248.*

[29]*Rebecca L. Hegar, "Balancing Foster Children's and Parent's Rights to a Family,"* Social Service Review, *(September, 1983, 57(3); J. Hammond Muench, "Psychological Parentage: A Natural Right,"* Family Law Quarterly, *(1979), 13 (2): 129–81.*

[30]*Grace Abbott,* The Child and the State *(Chicago: University of Chicago Press, 1938), II, 164; Stone,* Family Law, *p. 225–26.*

dispensing with consent to adoption, while in the United States many states permit termination in a separate court proceeding.

Despite such intriguing differences in law, the two legal frameworks for child protection and placement are similar enough to have led to very similar problems in the foster care system. In both countries, many children are placed in care who are unable to return home with safety and who are also unable to enter adoption. In both countries, child welfare law is changing very rapidly. Some recently adopted provisions in British law address the problem of the foster care trap, and in the United States some states have moved much further than others in resolving this problem.[31]

Advocates for children in both countries have developed reform proposals that would fundamentally change the criteria for entry into, and exit from, foster care. Adoption of some of the common features of these proposals would result in a system in which fewer children entered care, foster placements offered potential for greater stability, and almost all foster children could eventually be legally freed for permanent placement.

While there are specific differences in the ways that Britain and the United States provide protection and substitute care to children, comparison of the two approaches is helpful for those in either country who are looking for ways of dealing with the problems of child placement and the foster care trap.

---

[31]*New York has incorporated many child-centered and progressive provisions into its social services law. See Carrieri,* The Foster Child.

Deinstitutionalization
of Adolescents

KATHRYNE G. KOLAR

THE CHILD WELFARE field has struggled for decades to formulate a rational, comprehensive policy to regulate the development of services for youth in need of placement outside their own home. There are three major categories of youth who frequently require out-of-home care: (1) juvenile delinquents; (2) emotionally disturbed youth; and (3) dependent and/or neglected youth who concomitantly evidence serious social, behavioral and/or emotional problems. The long-standing controversy over what type of facility constitutes the most appropriate and effective form of residential care for those youth in out-of-home care is no longer merely a debate among child care professionals but has been codified. Public Law 94-142[1] requires that services provided to children, including residential treatment, be the "most appropriate" and "least restrictive" alternative. The amendments to Title XX of the Social Security Act as set forth in Public Law 93-647[2] favor the development of community-based services and do not support institutional care. Consequently, the concept of deinstitutionalization has, for all intents and purposes, become enacted as federal law. Moreover, the passage of Public Laws 93-647 and 94-142[3] has reinforced the prevailing view of institutionalization as an inherently injurious form of intervention while supporting the assumption that placement in an alternative community-based facility is not only a less restrictive, but also a more appropriate and effective treatment modality.

THE IMPACT OF DEINSTITUTIONALIZATION POLICIES
ON RESIDENTIAL CARE

The debate over the appropriate role of institutional care in the group care of children and youth has continued for over a century, and disputes in regard to this issue persist among professionals in the child care field. Currently the controversy has been embodied in the principles of deinstitutionalization.

KATHRYNE G. KOLAR is Program Director and Associate Professor, Social Work Program, Stephen F. Austin State University, Nacogdoches, Texas.

[1]Education for All Handicapped Children Act, U.S. Statutes at Large *(1974)*, vol. *89.*
[2]Title XX Grants to States for Services, U.S. Statutes at Large *(1973)*, vol. *88.*
[3]U.S. Statutes at Large, *vols. 88 and 89.*

Deinstitutionalization is defined as the philosophy of utilizing institutions as placement alternatives only after the resident has been unsuccessfully maintained in a foster home or group home and/or institutional settings are perceived as intrinsically inferior treatment modalities when compared to foster and group homes.[4] The term deinstitutionalization has become a value-laden concept that has several meanings. To some professionals deinstitutionalization indicates the need to eliminate all institutions, which implies, in effect, that the institution has no useful purpose in the spectrum of child welfare services.[5] These individuals generally advocate the development and use of community-based programs as alternatives to institutionalization.[6] Community-based care[7] is a form of residential placement in a facility that houses four to twelve residents in a single dwelling or cottage, simulates a family-type environment, and uses supportive services in the community, such as schools, rather than providing such services within the confines of the agency.[8]

An alternative connotation of deinstitutionalization is the gradual phasing out of certain types of institutions or institutional programs. Rather than calling for the elimination of institutional programs, advocates of this perspective suggest that institutional resources be modified in order to mitigate the potentially damaging aspects of this type of facility (total isolation, rigidity, and so forth). This view assumes that the institution has a function in the provision of child care services.[9]

These differing philosophies of deinstitutionalization raise two questions which are relevant to policy formulation: Should institutionalization be regarded as generally harmful for all people under all circumstances? Or should modified forms of institutional settings be utilized as a part of child care services? These questions and the responses to them are substantive, not academic, issues since the resolution of the debate will have significant ramifications in the child care field. Determination of the optimal setting for residential care will dictate funding patterns, the availability of treatment modalities and types of facilities, and the investment of professional involvement and expertise in the delivery of services.[10]

[4]*Leona L. Bachrach, "A Conceptual Approach to Institutionalization,"* Hospital and Community Psychiatry *(1978), 29 (9):573.*

[5]*Alfred Kadushin,* Child Welfare Services *(New York: Macmillan, 1980), p. 618.*

[6]*Robert D. Vinter, George Downs, and John Hall,* Juvenile Corrections in the States: Residential Programs and Deinstitutionalization *(Ann Arbor, Mich.: University of Michigan Press, 1975), p. 49.*

[7]*The term "community-based care: may have a multiplicity of meanings, denoting a range of therapeutic services such as preventive programs, supportive in-home services, and so on. In this study the term applies only to residential group care facilities (group homes) that function as alternatives to institutionalization.*

[8]*Vinter, Downs, and Hall,* Juvenile Corrections, *p. 49.*

[9]*George Thomas,* Is Statewide Deinstitutionalization of Children's Services a Forward or Backward Social Movement? *(Champaign, Ill.: University of Illinois, 1975), p. 7.*

[10]*Alex Weintrob, "Changing Populations in Adolescent Residential Treatment: New Problems for Program and Staff,"* American Journal of Orthopsychiatry *(1974), 44(4):606.*

In fact, not only the answer to the question of which is the optimal setting for residential child care, but merely the formulation of the issue has had an impact on the child care field. The debate over the concept of deinstitutionalization has entered the legislative and judicial arenas. The result has been that community-based care is regarded by the advocates of deinstitutionalization as preferable to institutional care for most, if not all, people. Thus, community-based care is perceived as the more therapeutic alternative and the treatment of choice in most instances.

Legislative policies and judicial decisions provide substantial support for the perspective of deinstitutionalization that favors the elimination of institutional settings. Although there have been numerous pertinent judiciary and legislative determinations, these all have several elements in common. Deinstitutionalization has been codified as a process that involves two concomitant components: the eschewal or avoidance of traditional institutional settings and the concurrent development and expansion of community-based residential facilities.[11] This movement is based on the assumption that the functions performed by the institutions can be effected equally well, if not better, by the community-based facilities. For example, the amendments to Title XX of the Social Security Act provided in Public Law 93-647[12] are not neutral with references to institutional settings, but are decidedly biased in favor of funding the development and expansion of community-based facilities while being nonsupportive of institutional care.[13]

Another common element in the judicial decisions and legislative enactments is that concepts of the "most appropriate alternative" and "least restrictive alternative" are treated as if these were synonymous terms. For example, during the hearing of the case of *Gary W. v. The State of Louisiana*[14] a class action suit in which the plaintiffs charged that institutional placement violated their civil rights, one of the major premises was that the least restrictive alternative is invariably the most appropriate alternative to treatment. In this and other judicial cases, the effort for necessary and appropriate social and institutional reform has resulted in a definition of deinstitutionalization that focuses on the physical properties, the locus and structure of residential care, rather than on the focus and substance of the services being provided.[15]

The controversy over which type of facility is inherently better has fostered the continuation of viewing the concept of the least restrictive alternative as the quintessence of deinstitutionalization. It may be an error to assume that any specific category of facilities is either more or less restrictive than another. The error occurs in presuming that restrictiveness is in the locus of service rather than a multivariate, a correlate of many variables. The use of a single

[11]Bachrach, "Institutionalization," p. 575.
[12]U.S. Statutes at Large, *vol. 88.*
[13]Kadushin, Child Welfare Services, p. 594
[14]Gary W. v. State of Louisiana, *622 F. 2d 304, C.A. La. (1976).*
[15]Weintrob, "Changing Populations," p. 607.

criterion such as the class of facility to define the degree of restrictiveness may be inappropriate.[16] Concentration on the locus of service obscures the relevant concerns with what the programs do and what they accomplish.[17]

For some youth institutional care, while not the least restrictive alternative, may be the most appropriate or, at minimum, the least detrimental.[18] When it is used cautiously, conceived properly, and implemented appropriately, institutional care may be a valuable and supportive resource.[19] Numerous authors have noted on a clinical, but not empirical, basis, that institutions would seem to be better equipped than community-based alternatives to serve the needs of impulsive, aggressive, or acting-out youth.[20] Some types of youth may require the external control and structure provided in the institutional setting in order to achieve socialization.[21] However, due to the prevailing bias in favor of community-based care, the institution is more frequently used as a placement of desperation or last resort than as a selective treatment of choice.[22] If one is willing to acknowledge that no single type of treatment may be capable of serving the needs of all children,[23] then consideration should be given to the relative effectiveness and differential utilization of all types of child care facilities in the group care of children and youth. However, with the community-based program being perceived as preferable to institutional placement, many youth may, in fact, be denied access to what could be the most effective and appropriate service. Therefore, efforts should be made to refine methods of matching the potential resident to the most suitable type of facility and program.

In the current age of accountability and diminishing resources, child welfare services, like all social services, are facing increasing demands to operate effectively and efficiently. Continuing debates among professionals concerning the intrinsic value of differing types of facilities need to be replaced by reasoned analyses of how to employ most effectively all residential treatment resources, including institutions. The concept of deinstitutionalization, which is founded upon values more than empirical knowledge, proposes the systematic elimination of an existing resource. This appears to be an irrational course of action in an age of scarcity. The number of youth being referred for residential placement has continued to increase while funding for residential

[16]*Jerry D. Mitchell and David L. Cockrum, "Positive Peer Culture and a Level System: A Comparison in an Adolescent Treatment Facility,"* Criminal Justice and Behavior *(1980),* 7(4):405.

[17]*Alan J. Burnes and Leon J. Raczkowski, "Interactive Program Applications in a Residential Center for Juvenile Offenders: A Position Paper,"* Child Care Quarterly *(1972), 1(4):275.*

[18]*Kadushin,* Child Welfare Services, *p. 594.*

[19]*James K. Whittaker,* Caring for Troubled Children *(San Francisco: Jossey-Bass, 1979) p. 8.*

[20]*Burnes and Raczkowski, "Interactive Program Applications," p. 274.*

[21]*Morris F. Mayer, Leon H. Richman, and Edwin A. Balcerzak,* Group Care of Children: Crossroads and Transitions *(New York: Child Welfare League of America, 1977), p. 22.*

[22]*Anthony N. Maluccio, "Problems and Issues in Community-Based Residential Services as Alternatives to Institutionalization,"* Journal of Sociology and Social Welfare *(1979), 6(2):199.*

[23]*Whittaker,* Caring for Troubled Children, *p. 4.*

treatment has become increasingly restricted.[24] Community-based group home programs can provide care for fewer residents at a per diem cost equal to, or higher than, the costs for institutional care; thus, the increasing impetus toward community-based care may exacerbate the difficulties of having fewer funds for more youth.

EXAMINATION OF DEINSTITUTIONALIZATION POLICIES

Deinstitutionalization is, in essence, a social reform movement that may have several different connotations. In the literature, deinstitutionalization refers to institutional reform, avoidance of institutional placement whenever possible, and the development of alternatives to institutionalization.[25] A review of the judicial and legislative decisions reveals a different interpretation. The judicial decisions and legislative enactments appear to support elimination of the institutional setting from the continuum of care more strongly than the differential utilization of the institution as a placement alternative. From this perspective, deinstitutionalization is basically a protest movement that is best understood as the obverse of institutionalization.[26]

In broad terms there are two sources that contribute to the impetus for deinstitutionalization of residential care for children and youth. One source of pressure is the concern about the negative effects of institutionalization on the psychological and social development of youth. The second origin of support for the deinstitutionalization movement is the concern with improving the delivery of social, administrative, and judicial justice for groups of citizens who traditionally have been denied their rights and freedoms.[27] The preference for deinstitutionalization through the use of community-based programs is based on several operational premises: (1) community-based programs are more humane and less damaging than institutional placements;[28] (2) community-based facilities are less restrictive and more closely approximate "normal living";[29] and (3) community-based group care is a more appropriate form of treatment.[30]

Although virtually no one in the child care field would dispute the desirability of the stated goals of deinstitutionalization policies, there is little systematic data that examine the implementation and outcomes of these policies. The preference for community-based care and most policies and practices in regard to deinstitutionalization are based on value judgments and assumptions.

---

[24]*Weintrob, "Changing Populations," p. 606.*

[25]*Maluccio, "Community-Based Residential Services," p. 200.*

[26]*Bachrach, "Institutionalization," p. 576.*

[27]*Thomas,* Statewide Deinstitutionalization, *p. 12.*

[28]*Martha M. Dore and Karen G. Kennedy, "Two Decades of Turmoil: Child Welfare Services 1960–1980,"* Child Welfare *(1981), 60(6):379.*

[29]Ibid., *p. 380.*

[30]Ibid.

Since 1970 there has been a movement away from institutional care and a commitment to community-based care, but there is little or no empirical evidence in the literature that demonstrates the superiority of one type of facility over the other as justification for such a change.[31] The arguments that support community-based care over institutional care are based primarily on the fact that the community-based programs have not been proved as ineffective as the institutions, rather than on the demonstated effectiveness of the alternative forms of care.[32] It cannot be assumed that because the institutions have not worked that the community-based programs will.[33]

The effectiveness of community-based residential facilities has been assumed but not verified. Furthermore, the issue of the suitability of residential placements has concentrated on whether the institutional placements have an appropriate use. There has not been similar concern with establishing the appropriateness of the community-based facilities. The institutional placements are assumed to be unsuitable unless there is sufficient justification; however, the community-based programs are considered appropriate placements unless the youth cannot be maintained in the facility for some reason (acting-out, running away). Thus, there is an unequal application of the concept of the most appropriate alternative. Although "most appropriate" and "least restrictive" are frequently used conjointly in discussions of residential placement, in practice the two terms are often separated with the least restrictive alternative predominating. In order to achieve both the most appropriate and the least restrictive alternative residential placement, the differential use of facilities, both institutional and community-based, must be determined.

COMPARISON OF MEDIATORY INSTITUTIONS AND COMMUNITY-BASED CARE

The underlying philosophy of the concept of deinstitutionalization and its ramifications is that residential institutions do more harm than good,[34] and that "any home is better than an institution."[35] While no one would argue the desirability of large, impersonal, isolated institutions that do little more than warehouse children, some advocates of community-based care have overstated the case: all institutions are bad; all community-based programs are good, or at least less harmful.[36] However, it is difficult to find empirical support for the contention that community-based facilities are more advantageous than a well-run, mediatory institution. Mediatory institutions are residential facilities that serve twenty-five or more youth in dormitories on a campus which is

[31]*Thomas*, Statewide Deinstutionalization, *p. 7.*

[32]*Vinter, Downs, and Hall*, Juvenile Corrections, *p. 49.*

[33]*Joseph Reid, "On 'Deinstitutionalization,'"* Child Welfare *(1975), 54(4):296.*

[34]*Whittaker*, Caring for Troubled Children, *p. 5.*

[35]Ibid.

[36]*Reid, "On Deinstitutionalization," p. 295.*

partially or fully separated from the surrounding residential neighborhood, but the institution is oriented to, and interacts with the external community, and performs the role of mediator between the residents and the external environment.[37].

Until more conclusive data are available, it seems likely that the question of what forms of group care have what effects on children and youth will continue to be a major issue.[38] This has been the primary formulation of the problem, virtually to the exclusion of other hypotheses. The statement of the problem in this manner has had significant consequences in establishing the parameters for developing theories and policies as well as conducting empirical research in the area of group care for children and youth. The focus of deinstitutionalization issues and policies continues to be on which type of facility is inherently superior. The statement of the problem in this manner excludes the possibility that institutions can perform a useful function in the spectrum of child care services. Consequently, it would seem to be more advantageous to evaluate the differential utilization of institutions in the treatment of certain types of youth exhibiting particular symptomatology rather than to persist in the attempt to eliminate institutions through the use of group homes or similar community-based alternatives, since these may not be the most effective or appropriate for modifying certain symptom behaviors of the residents.

The premises of deinstitutionalizaton are interrelated and contribute to the conclusion by advocates of deinstitutionalization that community-based residential facilities are inherently superior to institutional settings. The assumption that institutional placements are dehumanizing and stigmatizing suggests that these facilities are not only essentially undesirable, but also highly restrictive. Because community-based group care facilities are considered less restrictive than institutional placements, the advocates of deinstitutionalization conclude that the communty-based programs are universally the most appropriate placement alternative. If it is true that greater restrictiveness of institutional settings causes dehumanizing and stigmatizing effects, community-based facilities are, indeed, more appropriate alternatives than institutions. However, the crucial variable in this issue is whether the premises are substantiated facts or unverified assumptions. The author conducted a study to evaluate the differential uses of institutional and community-based residential placements based on the relative effectiveness of the two types of facilities. The study examined the validity of the premises of deinstitutionalization.

Sixty residents in nine group homes and five institutions in the state of Louisiana were used as subjects. Thirty-one resided in groups homes, and twenty-nine were in institutional settings. Comparisons between the baseline and outcome scores for the residents in the two types of facilities served as a measurement of the relative effectiveness and as conjunction of the programs

---

[37]*Kadushin*, Child Welfare Services, *p. 618.*
[38]Ibid.

in modifying behavioral problems. In addition, variables other than type of facility that might have influenced the placement selection and the outcome of treatment were investigated. Furthermore, the similiarities and differences in the two of facilities were analyzed.

RESULTS OF THE STUDY

The preference for community-based care frequently has been founded on the premise that institutional settings are more restrictive and less humane than community-based facilities. There have been numerous clinical observations that the group home, as compared to the institution, better approximates a normal way of life.[39] However, the empirical evidence in the literature fails to support the conclusion that community-based facilities are less restrictive than mediatory institutions.[40] The findings of previous research that, in many respects, a large percentage of the group home programs are distinguished from the mediatory institutions only by size and location, not by relevant programmatic variables such as staffing patterns, attendance in public schools, and the use of treatment modalities were replicated in this study. Two primary factors contributed to the facilities having been functionally equivalent: the group home programs demonstrated variables that imply that these facilities are as restrictive as the institutional settings; the institutions evidence a pattern of community integration and interaction that is similar to the group homes.

Restrictiveness of the group homes. One of the intended advantages of the group home setting is that the family-style atmosphere created by live-in houseparents results in a less restrictive environment than the use of shift workers. Shostack's[41] survey of group home facilities showed that 40 percent of the programs used shift workers rather than live-in houseparents. In this study, the percentage of the group homes (56 percent) that used shift workers was even higher than Shostack's findings.

The group homes had fewer residents per facility as compared to the institutions. The mean number of residents per group home was fifteen while the average number of residents per institution was twenty-nine. However, the apparent difference in the number of residents in the two types of facilities may have been mitigated by the facilities' ratios of staff to residents. The group homes had a ratio of one child care worker to every twelve residents while the institutions had a ratio of one child care worker to every fifteen residents. Even though the group homes had only half the number of residents per facility, the group homes demonstrated only a slightly lower child care worker-to-resident ratio as compared to the institutions. Thus, the group homes

---

[39]*Whittaker,* Caring for Troubled Children, *p. 6.*

[40]*Paul Lerman, "Trends and Issues in Deinstitutionalization of Youth in Trouble,"* Crime and Delinquency *(1980), 26(3):289.*

[41]*Albert L. Shostack, "Staffing Patterns in Group Homes for Teenagers,"* Child Welfare *(1978), 57(5):309.*

presumed advantage of providing a less restrictive, "normalized" environment may have been reduced by the ratio of child care workers to residents as well as the use of shift workers.

Lerman[42] found that the majority of the group homes surveyed employed recreational directors and provided recreational activities within the facility. The findings of this study were similar to those of Lerman's research: 33 percent of the group homes and 40 percent of the institutions employed full-time recreational directors. All of the group homes and institutions provided both on-grounds and community recreational activities. Furthermore, the analyses revealed that the institutions actively sought community recreational activities for the residents rather than confining them to on-grounds recreation. This finding replicated Handler's[43] study of institutions which demonstrated that institutional residents were encouraged to participate in local activities and events. The group homes and the mediatory institutions in this study did not differ in regard to the group recreational programs for the residents.

The implication of the findings in regard to the child care staff and recreational programs of the group homes is that instead of creating a family-style, normalized environment, the group homes replicate the features that traditionally have been found in institutions. Institutions historically have used shift workers, have relatively high staff-to-resident ratios, and provide organized recreational activities, and many of the advocates of deinstitutionalization object to these characteristics because the restrictiveness of the placement is increased and normalization decreased. The findings of this study indicated that the creation of smaller group home facilities did not result in a concomitant change in less restrictive patterns of child care or a more normalized environment. The treatment program components of the two types of facilities were remarkably similar. The group homes used a behavior modification treatment approach and incentive systems with about the same frequency as did the institutions. A behavior modification program and the use of formal incentive systems challenged the premise that the group homes provide a family-style, less restrictive environment than the institutions.

The group homes and institutions had similar types of treatment staff (social workers, psychologists, counselors). If the group homes had created a family-style way of life in order to normalize the environment and enhance the residents' socialization, one would have expected that the child care workers would have been the primary change agents. Thus, one would have anticipated that the group home facilities would have demonstrated different therapeutic staffing patterns than the institutional facilities. However, the evaluation of the facilities' therapeutic staffing patterns indicated that there was no difference between the group homes and institutions.

---

[42]Lerman, "Trends and Issues," p. 289.
[43]Ellen Handler, "Residential Treatment Programs for Juvenile Delinquents," Social Work (1975) 28(3):221.

The similiarity of the treatment modalities and therapeutic staff used by the group homes and institutions implies that rather than creating a family-like, normalized environment, the group homes, like the institutions, were "treatment-oriented." The group homes in this study did not create a milieu that was substantially different from that of the institutions. The therapeutic components of the group homes were consistent with traditional treatment modalities commonly used in institutional settings.

One of the advantages frequently claimed for the residents in a group home is attendance in public school rather than a facility school because attending public school is considered a "normalizing" experience. However, the group homes and institutions in this study did not differ in their use of public schools, and all of the facilities permitted community school attendance for some or all of the residents. Thirty-three percent of the group homes employed on-grounds teachers, and one home used the facility school instead of the public schools. Eighty-nine percent of the group homes and 80 percent of the institutions used the public schools.

One of the study questions explored the residents' perceptions of, and resistance to, the staff. The premise of this question was that the smaller, more intimate environment of the group homes should have produced a different type of resident-staff interaction than the larger institutional settings, and the difference should have been reflected in the residents' perceptions of the staff as change agents. The vast majority of the residents (90 percent) perceived the staff as helpful even though 48 percent disagreed with and resisted some staff-recommended changes in behavior.

These findings indicated that the institutional residents were able to form positive perceptions of the staff. Even though the institutional settings were larger and had a greater number of residents than the group homes, these factors did not necessarily produce negative, depersonalized staff-resident relationships. Thus, the results of this study challenge the assumptions of many advocates of deinstitutionalization that the institutional settings are less effective than the smaller programs, such as group homes, because the institutions inherently produce negative interactions between residents and staff. The findings support the literature, which notes that the internal structure of the institutions has been modified so that institutional settings are not as socially isolating, dehumanizing, and impersonal as previously thought.[44] Furthermore, the findings concerning the relationships between the residents and the staff indicated that the interactions between residents and staff may not be a result of the size of the facility or the number of residents but also involves other factors. For example, the similarity between the group home and institutions regarding the child-care worker-to-resident ratios may have influenced the interactions between the residents and staff in both types of facilities.

---

[44]Weintrob, *"Changing Populations,"* p. 607.

The data revealed that the purpose, structure, and functioning of the group homes and institutions coalesced so that the marked similarities in the programs rendered them functionally equivalent. It was previously noted that the group homes had many features generally associated with institutional settings so that these facilities functioned as "mini-institutions." Conversely, the mediatory institutions demonstrated relatively high degrees of interaction with the community and, in essence, operated as community-based institutions. Thus, in many respects, the two types of facilities were functionally equivalent.

One of the assumptions of the study was that the group homes and mediatory institutions evidenced fundamental differences in the nature and functioning of their programs and that this diversity would be reflected in the residents' behavior control and socialization outcome scores. However, rather than evaluating two distinctive types of programs, the data were collected in two overlapping and poorly defined entities, and this phenomenon may have accounted for the lack of difference in the residents' outcome scores. For all intents and purposes, the data were collected in homogeneous types of programs with the primary differences having been whether the facilities were large or small, based on the number of residents in the facilities, and which type of housing unit—house or dormitory—was used by the agency.

Since both types of facilities produced positive change in the residents' behavior control and socialization problems, one implication is that the modification of these types of behavioral problems is not a function of the size of the program. These findings challenge the assumptions of many advocates of deinstitutionalization that institutionalization is an inherently injurious form of intervention while the smaller programs, such as group homes, are more appropriate and effective treatment modalities.[45] The results of this study demonstrate that the outcome of treatment in residential care is more likely associated with the functional rather than the structural characteristics of the programs.

A review of the deinstitutionalization literature revealed that the definition of deinstitutionalization focuses primarily on the physical properties, the locus and structure of residential care, rather than on the focus and substance of the services provided.[46] The results of the study reiterated the need to reformulate the question of which type of facility is the optimal setting for residential care. The controversy over which type of facility is inherently better has obscured the relevant issue of what forms of group care have what kinds of effects on the youth residing in the facilities. In relation to the deinstitutionalization process, the findings of this study emphasized the need to examine the institutions and alternative forms of group care on a functional as well as structural basis.

The preference for community-based alternatives frequently has been founded on the assumption that the alternatives to institutionalization are more

---

[45]Bachrach, *"Institutionalization,"* p. 575.
[46]Ibid.

therapeutic and effective placements than the institution. Furthermore, the underlying philosophy of the concept of deinstitutionalization is that residential institutions do more harm than good,[47] and that any form of care is better than an institution.[48] The results of the study indicated that the mediatory institutions accomplished the same service objectives as effectively as did the group homes; consequently, the prejudice for alternative forms of group care on the basis of a presumed superiority in terms of therapeutic effectiveness was not supported by the empirical evidence.

In addition to presuming that the alternatives to institutionalization were more effective and appropriate, the controversy has fostered the continued view of the least restrictive alternative as the quintessence of deinstitutionalization. The study results supported the concept that it is an error to assume that any specific category of facilities is either more or less restrictive than another. The error in this formulation of restrictiveness occurred as a result of the advocates of deinstitutionalization assuming that restrictiveness is in the locus of service rather than a multivariate—a correlate of many variables. Mitchell and Cockrum[49] noted that the use of a single criterion, such as the type of facility, to define the degree of restrictiveness is inappropriate. The data from this study concerning the functional nature of the group homes and institutions supported the conclusion that restrictiveness is best defined and measured as a multivariate.

The results indicated that placement in a residential facility is not actually selective, based on what is the "most appropriate" alternative, but that the type of facility in which a youth is placed frequently is the result of extraneous variables. It was demonstrated that three factors—race, sex, and income—influence whether or not a youth is institutionalized regardless of other variables that indicate that a community-based placement may be more appropriate. The racial distribution within the facilities was disproportionate, with black residents being overrepresented in the institutional placements and underrepresented in the group home programs while the converse was true for the white residents. These findings imply that race acts as a determinant in placement decisions. Furthermore, the black residents had a greater probability of institutionalization while the white residents appeared to have been given preferences in the group home placements.

The data from this study supported the conclusion that males are more likely to be institutionalized. The facilities were gender-segregated so that placement decisions were, at least in part, determined by gender. Although males composed over 60 percent of the total facility populations, only 40 percent of the potential group home placements were for males. Conversely, females composed 40 percent of the residential population, but only 14 percent

[47]*Whittaker,* Caring for Troubled Children, *p. 5.*
[48]*Ibid.*
[49]*Mitchell and Cockrum, "Positive Peer Culture," p. 405.*

of the female placements were in institutional settings. Sixty percent of the group home placements were for females. Due to gender segregation, the potential placement options for males were predominantly institutional while the female placements were primarily in group home settings. These findings indicated that males had less of a chance than females to be deinstitutionalized.

Although the sample was almost equally divided between group home and institutional subjects, the highest income category included more than three times as many group home subjects compared with the institutional residents. Furthermore, the lowest income bracket was composed of twice as many institutional as group home residents. It was reasonable to conclude that the institutional subjects were overrepresented in the highest income categories.

Deinstitutionalization policies are intended to enhance justice in the delivery of social services; however, this research indicates that this may not always be true. In fact, promoting the use of community-based facilities may create instances of institutionalized discrimination with certain populations of youth having unequal access to community-based resources, depending upon the factors of race, gender, and economic status. When analysts evaluate the effects of deinstitutionalization policies, it may not be sufficient to consider only the appropriateness of the placement based on the reasons for placement. In order to assess properly the impact of deinstitutionalization policies, analysts should collect data that could be used to ensure that one form of social injustice is not being supplanted by another, including institutionalized discrimination.

The findings of this study demonstrated that the purpose and function of the group homes and institutions coalesced so that the marked similarity of the programs rendered them functionally equivalent. The group homes functioned as "mini-institutions" while the institutions were, in many respects, community-based facilities. The primary differences between the facilities were whether the programs were large or small based on the total number of residents and if they used dormitories rather than a house in a neighborhood. The research findings reiterate the need to reformulate the policy question of which type of facility is the optimal setting for residential care and to focus on the functional rather than the structural components of residential facilities. The concept of deinstitutionalization, which is founded more upon value judgments and assumptions than empirical knowledge, proposes the systematic elimination of an existing resource. This appears to be an irrational course of action in an age of scarce resources. If one is willing to acknowledge that no single type of treatment modality may be capable of serving the needs of all youth, then consideration should be given to the differential and selective use of all types of child care facilities in the continuum of residential care. Further investigations of the functional aspects of the facilities—what the programs do, what they accomplish, and what forms of group care have what kinds of effects on the youths residing in them—need to be conducted in order to provide an empirical basis for deinstitutionalization policies and service delivery in residential care.

Mobilizing Services
for Homeless People

MARSHA A. MARTIN and JANE W. HAUSNER

In recent years many urban areas have begun to experience a dramatic increase in the number of men, women, and children who are isolated from, and are in need of, basic mental health and social services. The New York City Department of Mental Health, Mental Retardation, and Alcoholism Services, using special state funding, has developed a mobile outreach service model which is designed to offer those isolated, alienated people greater access to the human service system.

Many of those served by the outreach programs are homeless, a group whose numbers and needs have gained national concern as their ranks have increased. For purposes of this discussion we will focus on outreach services to homeless people, although the model is and will be shown to be more broadly applicable.

Homelessness is not a new phenomenon. Traditionally, the worldwide causes of homelessness have been war, famine, and social upheaval. In America today these are obviously not the causes. The causes are more subtle and are indicative of the ills of contemporary society. The five primary causes of homelessness are hospitalization policy, shortage of low-cost housing, unemployment, breakdown of the family unit, and the failure of the human service system to respond adequately to need.

Deinstitutionalization is a frequently cited factor. Over the past twenty years the population of state psychiatric centers has decreased, with many former patients living in their communities of origin, often without adequate resources and supports. Perhaps more significant than deinstitutionalization is the recent hospitalization policy which severely limits access to state, municipal, and voluntary hospitals, decreased average length of hospital stay,

MARSHA A. MARTIN is Program Director, Midtown Outreach Program, Manhattan Bowery Corporation, New York.

JANE W. HAUSNER is Westside Community Support System Coordinator, New York City Department of Mental Health, Mental Retardation, and Alcoholism Services.

The authors thank James C. Rice, Edward I. Geffner, Richard Riedy, and the Outreach Program staff at Manhattan Bowery Corporation and Goddard Riverside Community Center, New York, for their help and support.

and insufficient or inappropriate community aftercare services. Certainly high census and limited facilities must not be overlooked as contributing factors to current hospitalization policies.

In New York City, the decrease in low-cost housing, particularly the decrease in single room occupancy (SRO) hotel rooms, has contributed to the problem of homelessness. What was once an important resource for the city's poor and low-income people is no longer available to many. The number of SRO rooms had dropped from approximately fifty-thousand in 1975 to less than fourteen thousand by 1981.[1]

Many men and women who apply for shelter at the municipal shelters in New York City have indicated that the primary cause of their homelessness was the recent loss of a job, or a long-standing inability to find work. In 1982, over 25 percent of the applicants at the Men's Shelter reported that they were unable to find employment.[2] The women, many of whom had worked as housekeepers, waitresses, and in other types of employment without security or pensions, find that employment opportunities are severely limited.

The breakdown of the American family has been widely documented. Many women have been abandoned, divorced, or widowed with nowhere to go and no means of social and financial support. Many men, often out of desperation and a sense of hopelessness, have elected to leave their family, perceiving that action as their only option. Elderly people are often rejected by family members, or feel that they are burdensome to the family and elect to "be on their own." Young people are often expelled by families which are unable or unwilling to care for them, or leave voluntarily, seeking an idealized life of independence and excitement.

While the causal factors of disaffiliation are multiple, the need for comprehensive care and service is a constant. The integrated functioning of a full spectrum of public services—among them transportation, housing, employment, education, health care, and social services—is basic to the provision of maximal benefits to all members of society. When service integration is poor, all services become less accessible, resulting in increased isolation, alienation, desperation, and antisocial reactions.

These factors, along with a sense of powerlessness and a fear of victimization, produce a disorganized, "hard-to-reach, hard-to-work-with, hard-to-rehabilitate client." The present public service network, through its categorically organized, nonintegrated delivery of services, has failed to respond adequately to the needs of those who cannot negotiate a complex, sophisticated, highly bureaucratized system. Consequently, many people are unable to utilize any aspect of the existing system without considerable support and assistance in

---

[1] Michael Goodwin, "S.R.O. Hotels: Rare Species," *New York* Times *November 20, 1981, p. B1.*

[2] See *Human Resources Administration, Family and Adult Services reports, "New Arrivals, First Time Shelter Clients" (November 1982) and "Chronic Situational Dependency: Long Term Residents in a Shelter for Men" (May 1982).*

orchestrating the services of the community to meet their most basic needs.

In 1979 New York State Community Support Systems funding became available to provide services to chronically mentally ill people living in the community. While this funding was initially designated for individuals who met specific prior psychiatric hospitalization criteria, it was agreed that homeless people were sufficiently at risk of needing mental health intervention to warrant the use of this funding for the development of outreach services to them without regard to hospitalization history. The New York City Department of Mental Health, Mental Retardation, and Alcoholism Services developed the program concept, identified provider agencies in the community, and contracted with those agencies to offer outreach services. Outreach programs were established first with Goddard Riverside Community Center and then with the Manhattan Bowery Corporation.

Due to the presence on the streets of a large and visible group of people who appeared to be isolated, disorganized, and without resources and supports, as well as a high concentration of SRO hotels in which many former state hospital patients resided, the initial outreach effort began on the Upper West Side of Manhattan.

The Upper West Side is an ethnically and socioeconomically mixed community. The presence of two universities, several museums and cultural centers, and well-developed commercial areas has made this a highly desirable residential area. This has resulted in increasing gentrification, and the consequent threat of displacement of people and services. The service area is fifty blocks long and six blocks wide, bounded by Central Park and the Hudson River. The earliest design relied on outreach workers traveling through the area in vans and approaching people with the expectation of assessing and referring them to service providers within the community. With experience, it became evident that many people were so isolated or dysfunctional that much fuller advocacy and interim case management services were essential.

Over the past four years the success of this model for reaching and engaging people had led to its expansion, with additional outreach teams working in Central Park and in the Midtown-Times Square area. While it has been found that there are some variations in the needs and conditions of the individuals in these three areas, the basic philosophy and method for delivering service have remained consistent. It is important to note that in each of these areas community groups have been interested and active in the initiation of the services and have offered their continued support. Effective liaisons have been developed with other public service systems, including police precincts, the Parks Department, the Public Library, and the Department of Transportation, as well as local merchants and the business community. All of these groups have acted as nontraditional collaborators with the outreach teams as well as often functioning as referral sources.

There is no single social or psychological profile of homeless people. Some stand out in a crowd with tattered and mismatched clothes, swollen and ulcerated legs, or an unusually large collection of bundles and bags. Others blend in with the stream of passersby, noticeable only because they remain in one spot with no apparent business over a period of time. Homeless people include those who simply have no source of income, or have minimal funds but cannot find affordable housing. They include people with alcohol and substance abuse problems, mentally ill people, the runaways and the unemployed, and the otherwise disenfranchised. Because of the wide variety of people and needs, there is no catchall solution to the problems of homelessness and no single resource that will work for all.[3] The situation is further compounded by the fact that services designated specifically for homeless people are scarce. Many of these men and women have tried to make use of the traditional social service, health, and mental health systems without success. These are systems fraught with eligibility and documentation requirements, with rules and regulations difficult to negotiate under the best of circumstances. In response to the multiple needs of homeless men and women and the paucity of appropriate services the outreach model has evolved.

The outreach model seeks to identify men and women who appear to be in need of assistance and to introduce and connect those individuals to appropriate community resources. The program director is responsible for the overall program operation, the negotiation of systems, the development of the service network, the continued informing of the outreach teams of changes in services and client status, and the maintenance of relationships with concerned agencies, organizations, and individuals in the community.

Outreach teams of two or three workers are staffed with trained social workers and experienced paraprofessionals. The social worker's training and professional experience in engaging people and assessing their needs, coupled with a broad knowledge of the community resources, are vital. The paraprofessional staff brings a range of backgrounds and experience, lending a diversified balance to the team. Each outreach team drives through its service area in a readily identifiable van, looking for men and women who appear to be in need of service as well as maintaining contact with people known to them. The hours of operation vary from program to program depending on the presence of prospective service users in their areas. For example, it has been found that many people are reached in Central Park during early morning hours, while in Midtown there is a need for late evening availability.

Once the team sees someone in distress, they will park the van, approach the individual on foot, identify the program and its services, and invite the person to make use of those services. The team carries simple food, beverages, and clothing in the van in order to respond to immediate needs as well as to initially engage individuals in the least threatening manner. The team members, based on an on-the-spot assessment, may also make suggestions as to other basic services needed, such as "a hot meal," "a shower," or "a bed," and

---

[3]*See* Helping the Homeless: A Guide to Services *(New York: Manhattan Bowery Corp., 1982).*

inform the man or woman that there are places where such services are available on a regular basis.

If interest in services is expressed, the team will offer to escort the individual to the service provider. If this occurs at an hour when services are closed, arrangements will be made to escort the client there at a suitable time. If the person is not immediately interested in assistance, the team will offer a flyer which describes the program and includes a telephone number to call if assistance is needed at a later time. Even though aid may be refused, the outreach teams will continue to encourage the use of their services and alternatives to living on the street.

All of the work with clients is performed in the community. Clients are not seen at the outreach office. The voluntary nature of the outreach service is basic and is stressed. Friendly persuasion and encourgement are frequently utilized when people are frightened or reluctant to accept service.

Once an individual begins to respond to the outreach team and their offers of assistance, efforts are made to connect the person to the appropriate service network. At this point outreach ends and a three-tier service program begins.

The first tier of service is limited to the provision of services to meet immediate needs, offering access to emergency medical and psychiatric care, hot meals, temporary shelter, and socialization. The focus of the second tier is on connecting individuals with appropriate service systems such as welfare and Supplementary Security Income, rehabilitation, and community care facilities. The third tier is aimed at establishing a permanent residence for the person and maximal use of community supports and aftercare services. In addition, the team may formally or informally manage a client's finances until a clear indication of the person's ability to manage independently is evident. The length of service is variable, depending upon the time needed to develop a relationship of trust, and thereby engage an individual; the range of services needed; and the time required to gain access to those services and assure the person's connection to them.

It is important to note that while housing may at first glance seem to be the most critical need, there are other supports which must be in place in order to help sustain the individual in a room or an apartment. In the outreach program socialization and rehabilitation programs have been found to be a critical factor in successfully helping someone to remain "living indoors." While the team seeks to arrange for housing, efforts are also being made to link the client to appropriate medical and mental health services. Advocacy and case management are critical at this stage.

While the established service providers of the community by and large rely on the knowledge, willingness, and ability of individuals to find and make use of their services, the outreach model redefines the boundaries of service provision. By establishing effective relationships with agencies and other resources in the community a base is developed from which service can be initiated. Through active advocacy and interim case management on behalf of each client in relation to each appropriate agency and resource, reengagement in the broad service system becomes possible. This role is sustained by the team either until the client is involved in community services where case management responsibility is taken over, or until the client is able to manage and negotiate independently, or until it is mutually decided that the services of the team can no longer be of benefit.

An essential step in the development of each outreach team was the exchange of reciprocal letters of agreement with all relevant service providers in the community. The letters introduced the outreach team and its clients and requested that the community programs offer full access to service to all eligible individuals. While the letters served to introduce the outreach program, in fact, a rigorous and sustained effort to develop and maintain access to services for homeless men and women was necessary. Community agencies were often reluctant to offer services for a variety of reasons, including: unfamiliarity with the homeless population and their multiple needs; concern about possible increased demands on already overtaxed services; and concern about prospective dumping or abandonment of homeless people whose needs range far beyond the scope of services of any single agency in the community. With full recognition and appreciation of these concerns, the outreach program director and staff met with community program directors to share information and initiate a liaison for ongoing communication. In some agencies all staff participated in these meetings. Once the liaison was established and referral processes agreed upon, outreach program staff began to assess and refer clients to community agencies. During the initial period when both clients and agencies are tentative and skeptical about their "match," outreach program staff accompany clients to the agency and also are available for consultation at any time. As an individual becomes more involved with the service provider or providers, the team's role becomes less active, although they remain available for consultation and support.

While the outreach team does not offer ongoing mental health or social services, interim case management provides a necessary bridge to those services. The outreach team, with its knowledge of, and familiarity with, each person served, often participates in the treatment-planning process of the agency which assumes responsibility for primary care. This ongoing commitment to follow each individual until he or she is engaged in service provides an important sense of support and continuity to the client, to the agency, and to the outreach team.

Men and women on the street have been isolated from the human service system for varying lengths of time and for a variety of reasons. Some are recently unemployed and have never had occasion to seek access to, or knowledge of, public services. Many more have long histories of involvement with a variety of "service" agencies which were, or which they felt to be, unresponsive to them. This, combined with the process of alienation and adaptation to life on the street, has led them to become reluctant seekers and users of the services of the community. The structure, the consistency, and the concerted effort to be as unthreatening and respectful of privacy and dignity as possible make the outreach model a significant first step in reestablishing the relationships between people in need and the services of their community.

While the outreach model was developed to extend services to those who were isolated, alienated, and potentially "at risk," the need for service has been found to reach well beyond that population. In its ability to assess individual needs readily and use the resources of the community creatively, the outreach program model reaches individuals who might otherwise go unnoticed and unserved, eventually needing more intensive intervention. Ideally, each service agency should have the capacity to reach out to and serve all who are in need. However, in the absence of such availability, the mobile outreach service model provides a viable conduit to care.

Advocacy Organizations for Nursing Home Residents

JORDAN I. KOSBERG and LARRY C. MULLINS

IT IS, NO DOUBT, unnecessary to repeat the litany of findings on abuse, exploitation, and maltreatement within long-term care facilities for the aged in the United States. Such books as *Tender Loving Greed,*[1] *Too Old, Too Sick, Too Bad,*[2] and *Unloving Care*[3] effectively point out the potential and actual existence of negligence, physical abuse, lack of sanitation, poor food preparation and nutrition, theft, overmedication, improper use of restraints; understaffed medical, nursing, and rehabilitation departments and insufficent resources; failure to provide social and psychological stimulation; and complete denial of individual worth and dignity. It is true that the better nursing homes are "damned by association" with those inferior facilities which come to public attention through periodic exposés and investigations. Although it is unfortunate, concern must be directed to all nursing home residents, regardless of the reputation of the facility, for "the aged in institutions are perhaps the most powerless, voiceless, invisible and uncared-for group in this country."[4] In a seven-year study by the U.S. Senate of 23,000 nursing homes, more than half were found to be substandard. Only 5 percent were considered "good."[5]

What are some of the reasons for the tragic paradox of pervasive poor care of the frail elderly in nursing homes? Among other explanations are those

JORDAN I. KOSBERG is Professor, Department of Gerontology and Suncoast Gerontology Center, University of South Florida, Tampa.

LARRY C. MULLINS is Associate Professor, Department of Gerontology, International Exchange Center on Gerontology, University of South Florida, Tampa.

The study reported here was funded by a grant from the Retirement Research Foundation.

[1]*Mary Adelaide Mendelson,* Tender Loving Greed *(New York: Vintage Books, 1974).*
[2]*Frank E. Moss and Val J. Halamandaris,* Too Old, Too Sick, Too Bad *(Germantown, Md.: Aspen Systems, 1977).*
[3]*Bruce C. Vladek,* Unloving Care: The Nursing Home Tragedy *(New York: Basic Books, 1980).*
[4]*Jordan I. Kosberg, "The Nursing Home: A Social Work Paradox,"* Social Work, March *1973, pp. 104–10.*
[5]*Peter Stathopoulos, "Consumer Advocacy and Abuse of Elders in Nursing Homes," in Jordan I. Kosberg, ed.,* Abuse and Maltreatment of the Elderly *(London, England, and Littleton, Mass; John Wright-PSG Publishing Col, 1983).*

pertaining to the preponderance of proprietary facilities; the fact that between 80 percent and 90 percent of patients' care in nursing homes is provided by undertrained, overworked, and often ill-suited aides and orderlies; and the absence of physicians in these health care settings. In addition, nursing home visitors (generally family members) are unknowledgeable about differentiating between good and bad nursing homes and are often limited in their appraisals to the appearance of a nursing home, the friendliness of administrators, odors and sights, and plaques and certificates hanging in the lobby or waiting rooms. In addition, these visits are generally limited to daytime hours, and thus do not include more "telling" periods, such as evening or early morning hours, weekends, and holidays.

NURSING HOME CONTROLS

Given the dependency of the institutionalized elderly residents, potentials for abuse and maltreatment, and naïve and unknowledgeable visitors, what mechanisms are there to safeguard the rights (if not the lives) of the institutionalized aged? Geriatric facilities must meet a variety of local, state, and federal requirements (those of state health departments, Medicare, and so forth). Often such requirements focus upon physical features related to safety and sanitation rather than on residents' care and treatment. Often deficiencies continue indefinitely, when there are lengthy "periods of grace" to upgrade facilities and rectify the inadequacies and deficiencies. But even when requirements are met and licensure is approved or renewed, continued enforcement is necessary. Trained inspectors are vital. As Kosberg and Tobin (1972) have stated: "It is imperative that inspectors be sufficient in number and adequate in training to see beyond the superficial, side-step rhetoric and promises and be above reproach for ignoring deficiencies."[6]

Inasmuch as nursing homes, unlike other institutions such as prisons and mental hospitals, are usually located in the community, they should be subject to community surveillance. Kosberg has pointed out that there are mechanisms to permeate the "closed doors" of geriatric institutions and has discussed formal policies, community organizations, professionals, and friends and families.[7]

OMBUDSMAN PROGRAM

One response to the need for the surveillance of nursing home residents by outsiders, the Long-Term Care Ombudsman Program, was begun in 1971. In 1972 five demonstration projects were funded, and in 1975 all the states

[6]*Jordan I. Kosberg and Sheldon S. Tobin, Variability Among Nursing Homes,"* The Gerontologist (Autumn 1972), 12 (3, Part I):218.
[7]Jordan I. Kosberg, "Methods for Community Surveillance of Geriatric Institutions," Public Health Reports, *March–April, 1975, pp. 144–48.*

were invited to submit proposals to the Administration on Aging (now in the Department of Health and Human Services). Under the 1978 amendments to the Older Americans Act, every state is required to have an ombudsman program providing for: complaint resolution; monitoring the development and implementation of laws, regulations, and policies affecting long-term care; disseminating information, and training volunteers and involving citizen organizations in ombudsman efforts. Each state has the freedom to devise its own system of ombudsman activities.

Generally speaking, in each state, the ombudsman programs have been reactive (responsive to complaints and violations) rather than proactive (seeking to discern maltreatment of residents and unreported adverse conditions). Although hardly a panacea, the ombudsman program has done a great deal in providing some surveillance over conditions in nursing homes. But the program has also been widely criticized:

"There is no reason to hope than any new units of state government will be any less corrupt, indolent, or callous than the existing bureaucracies. . . . there is no shortage of state officials with whom to register complaints—there is only a desperate shortage of officials who will respond to the complaints they already get."[8]

AOA's attitude towards its ombusdman program has run the gamut from mild support to total indifference. . . . In most states, the ombudsman's offices are only paper tigers."[9]

For a thorough assessment of a sample of ombudsman programs, pointing out the diversities and shortcomings of the programs, one should read the forthcoming Monk, Kaye and Lewin study, *Resolving Grievances in the Nursing Home.*[10]

Moreover, recent trends—plus only the partial effectiveness of the ombudsman program—may well exacerbate the vulnerability of the elderly within institutional settings. First, it is quite possible that the current administration's policies might result in reducing ombudsman program funding. Second, the current administration, in its policy of limiting federal influence in social and health programs, is considering deregulation of the nursing home industry which will delete certain standards believed to be "burdensome, costly, and duplicative."[11] However, it seems that not everyone agrees with this approach: "HHS Secretary Richard Schweiker seems reluctant to risk embarrassment over any proposal that would make the Administration appear to favor *action potentially damaging to nursing home residents*" (emphasis added).[12] Third, there is some suggestion that the Department of Health and Human Services believes that it has no legislative mandate for maintaining patients' rights.

---

[8]*Mendelson,* Tender Loving Greed, *p. 236.*

[9]*Vladek,* Unloving Care, *p. 200.*

[10]*Abraham Monk, Lenard W. Kaye, and Howard Lewin,* Resolving Grievances in the Nursing Home *(New York: Columbia University Press; in press).*

[11]Aging Services News, *January 15, 1982.*

[12]Ibid.

ADVOCACY ORGANIZATIONS

"Those who are responsible for managing institutions and the government officials who are regulating them must be held accountable to the patients and the consumers in the community."[13] It seems as if the responsibility for seeking this accountability falls to local nursing home advocacy organizations. Unofficially, there are about two hundred such organizations (generally privately funded) across the nation that are engaged in a variety of advocacy activities: monitoring care, complaint resolution, community and state lobbying, and community education. A sample of such groups includes: Illinois Citizens for Better Care (Chicago), Kansans for the Improvement of Nursing Homes, Concerned Relatives of Nursing Home Patients (Cleveland), Consumer Advocates for Better Care (Fitchburg, Mass.), Committee for the Improvement of Nursing Homes (Seattle), and Citizens for Better Care (Detroit).

These advocacy organizations vary extensively. Some organizations focus upon nursing home residents in a neighborhood or community and train volunteers to visit the residents on an ongoing basis. Some organizations are engaged in lobbying activities to upgrade the care provided in nursing homes around the state. Other organizations attempt to form coalitions of community agencies, relatives, and local professionals to work for the improvement of nursing home care through community education and publicity of adverse conditions found within local nursing homes. Some organizations take on adversary relationships with nursing homes; others seek to work with the nursing home industry to improve care of the elderly.

Although the Washington-based National Coalition for Nursing Home Reform serves as an informal mechanism for interaction among these organizations, there has been no systematic effort to describe these advocacy groups, their activities, and effectiveness in maintaining a quality level of care in long-term care facilities for the elderly. While Horn and Griesel's work[14] does describe a few efforts around the country, their focus is on encouraging the organization and planning of advocacy efforts on behalf of nursing home residents. It is for this reason that the study reported here was undertaken. In systematically collecting data on nursing home advocacy groups, findings will be of importance for local organizations, state-level policy-makers, national organizations, and the federal government.

METHODOLOGY

Inasmuch as advocacy groups for nursing home residents can be small, informal, and exist for limited periods of time, the determination of the universe of these organizations was especially problematic. Lists of advocacy organizations for nursing home residents were obtained from the National Citizens

[13]*Linda Horn and Elma Griesel,* Nursing Homes—A Citizen's Action Guide *(Boston: Beacon Press, 1977).*

Coalition for Nursing Home Reform, from a survey of the Coalition's *Newsletter*, from discussions with knowledgeable individuals throughout the country, and from the staff of the ombudsman program in the Administration on Aging. Over two hundred organizations were identified which were either private or originally private in sponsorship (as opposed to totally publicly sponsored ombudsman programs). The study was focused not upon ombudsman programs but on advocacy groups that were not a part of the ombudsman system. Unfortunately, the dichotomy between advocacy groups and ombudsman programs was neither clear nor simple.

A questionnaire was developed to obtain information on these organizations regarding: (1) geographic/political scope of activities; (2) types of legislation or agreements permitting entry into nursing homes; (3) historical development of the organization; (4) membership structure; (5) use of volunteers; (6) size of paid staff; (7) relationship to ombudsman programs; (8) current financial support; (9) organizational governance; (10) advocacy activities; and (11) present and future concerns regarding the effectiveness of advocacy activities in behalf of nursing home residents.

A total of 215 questionnaires was sent to all private advocacy organizations for nursing home residents and a purposive sample of quasi-public organizations. Excluded from the study were ombudsman programs which were totally public in auspices (county, state, or sponsored by a public area agency on aging). Two telephone follow-up calls were made to each organization in order to ensure a high response rate. The questionnaires were sent to the director/administrator of each organization; 20 indicated that their organizations were not actually involved in nursing home resident advocacy. Of the 195 eligible organizations, 16 refused to participate in the study, and 47 have not responded in any manner. Thus, the data base is composed of responses representing 132 advocacy organizations, a response rate of 67.7 percent.

FINDINGS

LOCATION AND SCOPE OF ACTIVITIES

The 132 organizations covered a total of 39 different states and 12,101 nursing homes. Nursing homes covered by these organizations ranged from one facility to 1,500 facilities. The average number of nursing homes within the area of the organization was 94, with 17 facilities being the most common (for 6 organizations). The respondents were asked whether enabling state legislation existed which permitted (if not mandated) advocacy organizations access to nursing homes. Of 128 responses, 88 (68.8 percent) indicated that such legislation did exist in their states. It was learned that 80 (63 percent) of the organizations were designated ombudsman programs.

HISTORICAL DEVELOPMENT

The first year in which an advocacy group was founded was 1945, and 55 percent of the organizations were founded between 1975 and 1979. The major reason for the formation of an organization was the organization's designation by the state as an ombudsman program. The next most common reason for a group's formation was as a result of the attempts of local citizens and professionals to improve the quality of nursing home care. The third most frequent reason was the efforts of area agencies on aging to form advocacy groups in the area.

The great majority of advocacy groups were initially funded by public sources (Older Americans Act, state monies), but 30 percent of the organizations were funded mainly by personal or private donations. The initial financial support ranged from $1,000 or less (fifteen organizations—11.6 percent) to $100,000 or more (five organizations—3.9 percent). Sixteen (12.4 percent) of the advocacy organizations received no initial funding. For those organizations which had originally received funding, the average amount was $1,850.

CURRENT ORGANIZATION

The advocacy groups differed greatly as to the use of volunteers, members, and paid staff. The number of members (mainly those who paid dues) varied from 3 (two organizations) to 300 (one organization). Interestingly, 46 organizations had no active members. In some cases, the members were non-dues-paying elderly nursing home residents. In other cases the members paid dues and were either actively involved in advocacy activities or merely received literature from the organization. For those organizations without members, the use of volunteers served the same purpose, and for the 107 organizations that indicated the availability of volunteers, there were a total of 9,010 volunteers, an average of 84 per organization.

It was found that 56 percent of the advocacy organizations had either no paid staff (N = 25) or only one paid staff person (N = 46). Five organizations had six salaried staff members. The majority of the organizations had at least some nonpaid staff. Of those administrators/directors who responded to the question about their education (N = 81), 42 percent had at least a master's degree, and 90 percent had at least a baccalaureate degree.

For 104 organizations represented in the responses, current financial support ranges from under $1,000 per year (N = 9) to over $500,000 per year (N = 3), with an average of $21,500, a median of $17,000. The modal range was the $15,000–$25,000 per year category (32 organizations). Sources of funding include Title III of the Older Americans Act (44 percent), personal and private donations (29 percent), and private foundations (27 percent).

The three most important nursing home issues seen by respondents, in descending order, were Medicaid discrimination and cuts, maintenance and enforcement of regulations, and the quality of care. The three most important ways that the organizations were seen to be effective as advocate groups, in descending order, were community education, complaint resolution and investigations, and legislative activities. The three most frequent current issues being worked on, in descending order, were enforcement of state and federal regulations, self-empowerment of residents (resident councils), and discrimination against Medicaid recipients.

The great majority of non-ombudsman program advocacy organizations had friendly, cooperative working relationships with the local ombudsman program. Only a few organizations admitted relationships which were adversarial or competitive with the ombudsman program.

CONCLUSIONS

This exploratory survey of advocacy organizations for nursing home residents has led to the conclusion that these organizations are staffed mainly by highly motivated volunteers with a very small group of committed employees. Most organizations are receiving public funds; most are designated as quasi-public ombudsman programs. With few exceptions, good cooperation exists between private advocacy groups and ombudsman programs, and the impression is that most advocacy groups, both public and/or private, do not seek an adversarial relationship with the nursing homes in their areas; instead, they seek to influence by persuasion and cooperation.

Advocacy organizations engage in a variety of activities ranging from community education to complaint resolution, to lobbying on behalf of upgrading nursing home standards. Variations in these activities seem related to the priorities of the organizers or directors of organizations, the background of key staff or board members (lawyers or social workers), and size of staff which permits division of labor for advocacy activities.

Many advocacy groups have banded together with organizations representing other dependent populations to form coalitions. In other cases, advocacy groups from around a state have formed coalitions of nursing home advocacy groups. This statewide effort ensures a broader-based lobbying effort for influencing state legislators and policy-makers.

The survey of nursing home advocacy groups is being supplemented by personal site visits to selected organizations representing different models of advocacy activities, different geographical locations, and different-sized organizations. Qualitative information will add to the picture of variations in nursing home advocacy activities and permit conclusions to be reached regarding effectiveness of activities and the quality of care within nursing homes. Suggestions will also be made to assist in the development of advocacy groups for nursing home residents in areas where such activities are needed.

All of us share in extending gratitude to those working in the nursing home residents advocacy field; for these committed and dedicated individuals help provide surveillance over perhaps the most powerless, voiceless, invisible, and dependent population in our nation.

United Way at the Crossroads

ELEANOR L. BRILLIANT

IN RECENT years it has become apparent that the formerly sharp dividing line between the institutions of the voluntary sector and those of the business world has increasingly become blurred as organizations in the non-profit sector have begun to act more like businesses.[1] Indeed, even before the Reagan administration focused attention on the role of private-sector initiatives in meeting human service needs, the impact of the business ethos on the human services was evident. Until recently, however, there was only limited debate about the desirability and extent of this development. The use of management techniques such as management by objectives had been gradually accepted as part of the route toward greater accountability. Even the moment of social welfare professionals closer to the world of work and back into industrial settings, is greeted with enthusiasm.[2] Greater involvement of the corporate world in community activities has been a deferred agenda; it appeared to be happening but not in significant amounts—with one notable exception, and that was through the United Way system.[3]

ELEANOR L. BRILLIANT is Assistant Professor, Columbia University School of Social Work, New York.

Research on this paper was supported in part by grants from the Exxon Corporation, the Johnson's Wax Fund, and Thomas J. Lipton, Inc., and is part of a larger study. I also wish to express my appreciation to the United Way of America and local United Way ogranizations for their cooperation with this research.

For their valuable comments on an earlier draft of this article, I want to thank Russi Sumariwalla and Professor Esther Wattenberg, and also Rowland Todd who chaired the panel in which it was presented.

[1] See Eleanor L. Brilliant, "Private or Public: A Model of Ambiguities," Social Service Review (September 1973), 47(3):384–96; Sheila B. Kamerman, "The New Mixed Economy of Welfare," Social Work (January–February 1983), 28(1):5–10; Dennis Young, "Motives, Models and Men: An Exploration of Entrepreneurship in the Non-Profit Sector" (Yale University Program on Non-Profit Organizations, Working Paper #4, 1978).

[2] See Paul A. Kurzman, "Ethical Issues in Industrial Social Work Practice," Social Casework (February 1983), 64(2):105–11; Rino J. Patti, "Applying Business Management Strategies in Social Agencies," in Sheila H. Akabas and Paul A. Kurzman, eds., Work, Workers, and Work Organizations: A View from Social Work (Englewood Cliffs, N.J.: Prentice-Hall,1982), pp. 147–75.

[3] There are approximately 2,100 local, autonomous United Ways, of which somewhat under 1,200 are dues-paying members and therefore formal supporters of the national organization, the United Way of America (UWA), which does not itself raise funds. I use the terms United Way and United Way system generally to refer to the nearly 1,200 dues-paying local organizations and the UWA. The United Way system also includes state and regional organizations, but these are less relevant to the present discussion.

In the past decade, questions have been raised frequently about the effect of the United Way's close relationship with the corporate sector. Scholars, journalists, and members of the social welfare community have expressed concern about possible conflicts between values of the profit-making world and those of the social welfare arena and their impact on practices of the United Way.[4] Because the United Way has occupied a key position at the crossroads of the corporate world and the voluntary sector, the public policy implications of this analysis are significant.[5]

DISTINGUISHING CHARACTERISTICS OF NONPROFIT AND
PROFIT-MAKING ORGANIZATIONS

Nonprofit organizations are generally defined by three major characteristics: (1) the absence of a profit motive, or prohibition against distribution of profits (surpluses) made by the organization to individual members or shareholders, or for purposes other than those for which the corporation was established; (2) the clear presence of a public purpose or collective goods for which they were established, that is, expected public benefits; (3) their capacity to fill in gaps in the marketing system that relate to the distribution of goods or services. The public purposes for which the human services exist are related, of course to meeting human service needs, such as day care and mental health services. In any case, following from these major characteristics, nonprofit agencies have been considered relatively immune to competition in the marketplace, and consequently difficult to change. Since products are intangible, control systems are also vague. Finally, failure to achieve vaguely defined goals is generally not attributed to weaknesses of the organization, but as requiring a doubling of organizational efforts.[6]

In contrast with the voluntary or nonprofit agency, profit-making corporations are defined by the following characteristics: (1) they are in business to satisfy the profit motive; owners and shareholders expect satisfactory returns on their capital investment, and products are manufactured and sold within

---

[4]*All sources for this are too numerous to list, but see for example, Natalie Wexler, "Corporate Charity,"* New Republic, *April 5, 1980, pp. 19–22; David Horton Smith, "The Role of the United Way in Philanthropy,"* in Research Papers, *sponsored by the Commission on Private Philanthropy and Public Needs, the Filer Commission (Washington, D.C.: Department of the Treasury, 1977), II, pp.1353–82; Ron Chernow, "Cornering the Goodness Market: Uncharitable Doings at United Way,"* Saturday Review, *October 28, 1978, pp. 15–18; Chester W. Hartman and Thomas Lynn, "Sweet Charity Gone Sour,"* Society, *November–December 1974, pp.54–58; Timothy Saasta, "Octopus of Benevolence; United Way—Cornering the 'Charity Dollar,' "* The Nation, *September 29, 1979, pp. 261–71; David J. Blum, "Donor's Backlash; Many Workers Oppose Employers' Pressures to Give to Charities,"* Wall Street Journal, January 12, 1982, p. 1.*
[5]*This paper is an initial presentation of issues discussed in my in-depth study of United Way to be published by Columbia University Press, New York, in 1984.*
[6]*See Henry Hansmann, "The Role of Non-Profit Enterprise,"* Yale Law Journal, *April 1980, pp. 855–901; Burton A. Weisbrod,* The Voluntary Non-Profit Sector *(Lexington, Mass.: Lexington Books, 1977).*

that constraint; (2) products ·are distributed via the market mechanism to consumers for private purposes and private uses; (3) survival of the organization is explicitly related to demand for its product and efficiency; inefficiency in production or decreases in demand will lead to fewer sales or less profit and the expectation of a change in the product. Consequently, business organizations have developed procedures and techniques to ensure effective and efficient performance, including strategic planning, management by objectives, and extensive training programs.[7]

Although there is some blurring of the lines between the sectors, and heterogeneity even within them, nonetheless it seems evident that the conceptual model for each sector remains as described, and different ideologies and purposes have generally prevailed until recently.

THE UNITED WAY AS A BUSINESS

In 1957 John Seeley suggested that the conflict between business success and community organization was one of the central value conflicts of the local federated fund-raising organization (in this case, the Community Chest in Indianapolis).[8] Nearly twenty years later, in a paper prepared for the Filer Commission, David Horton Smith concluded that the United Way is in many respects more like a business organization than a nonprofit organization; he referred particularly to governance and fund-raising activities but stopped short of a full analysis.[9] In more recent years "the Business of Charity" has been denounced in the journals and in the newspapers, but the implications of this characterization have still not been fully explored.[10]

In what respects does the United Way function as a business organization and what are the consequences of this functioning? In order to answer this question we will look at three main aspects of the United Way: purpose and function; product and marketing; and reactions to competition.

[7]Ibid.; see also Peter Drucker, Management: Tasks, Responsibilities, Practices *(New York: Harper and Row, 1974), pp. 558–98; Robert B. Anthony and Regina E. Herzlinger,* Management Control in Non-Profit Organizations *(rev. ed.; Homewood, Ill.: Richard D. Irwin, 1980), pp. 31-76.*

[8]*John R. Seeley et al.,* Community Chest: A Case Study in Philanthropy *(Toronto: University of Toronto Press, 1957).*

[9]*Smith, "The Role of the United Way in Philanthropy;" see also David Horton Smith,"* United Way is the Name—Monopoly is the Game," *Business and Society Review (Spring 1978). For a somewhat more technical analysis, see Susan-Rose Ackerman, "United Charities: An Economic Analysis,"* Public Policy *(Summer 1980), 28(3):323–50.*

[10]*Even* Forbes, *an exponent of the business point of view raised the question. See James Cook, "Is Charity Obsolete?"* Forbes, *February 5, 1979, pp. 45–51; Chernow, "Cornering the Goodness Market"; Hartman and Lynn, "Sweet Charity Gone Sour."*

The Purpose and Function

It is frequently stated that since earning profits, or raising more money than last year, is the purpose of the United Way, the United Way is like a business. Although it is current practice in United Way circles to talk of a full-service local United Way that will deal with planning, allocations, fund-raising, and a variety of other functions, such as technical assistance and volunteer services, fund-raising, the bottom line for United Way, remains the dominant theme. In internal discussions among staff and volunteers, the critical questions asked are: How much did you raise this year? Did you make your goal? How much more did you raise than last year? By definition, competition in the fund-raising arena is a prominent concern of professionals in a philanthropic organization; and even the national United Way organization, the United Way of America, included in their Program for the Future (1976) a national goal of raising $3 billion by 1985.[11] Local United Way organizations, however, are now beginning to feel that they have become the victims of their own goal displacement, and are reassessing their preoccupation with the dollar goal. In recent documents, the United Way of America (UWA) has promulgated a new concept which states that the mission of the United Way is "to increase the organized capacity of people to care for one another."[12] Professionals at United Way conferences now start discussions with concerns about raising more funds but conclude that it is services to people and people involvement which are the determining factors. Some progressive United Ways are dropping the concept of one goal, and many are focusing on new activities of the United Way organization in the community.

The attempt to deemphasize dollars raised while focusing on community service activities and new services is a complicated response to a changing environment. The environment is difficult for raising money; there is increasing competition for the voluntary dollar as cutbacks occur in governmental funds for human services. And yet United Way is talking about funding more agencies, increasing its own activities, and engaging in greater community involvement, with a concomitant increase in the cost of its own services, at a time when funds for human services generally are decreasing. What is happening to the bottom line?

The apparent paradox in the United Way position will be further analyzed in relation to strategies and techniques. At this point, however, it may be well to remember that while theoretical economists may talk of profits as the

[11]*Although the UWA does not itself raise funds, it does have a prestigious board of directors, including corporate executives of companies such as Exxon, J. C. Penney, and Aetna Life and Casualty, and it provides leadership in corporate fund-raising as well as in other services for local United Ways.*

[12]*Included in remarks of William Aramony, national executive of the UWA, and in material distributed at the Volunteer Leaders Conference, 1982, and also presented at the United Way Southeast Regional Staff Conference, 1983.*

purpose of business, pragmatic conceptualists such as Peter Drucker have described the purpose of business differently: in terms of satisfying customers. Profit then becomes a constraint under which business operates, but the purpose of a given business lies in the nature of the product it delivers to the customer. United Way organizations are indeed being businesslike: they are focusing on the consumer and on the nature of the product they are offering the consumer. To the extent that they can define their product and target their consumer (or customer), they are therefore developing a market strategy.[13] "Because the purpose is to create a customer, the business enterprise has two—and only these two—basic functions: marketing and innovation. Marketing and innovation produce results: all the rest are "costs."[14]

Marketing the Product

Marketing has been defined generically as an exchange of values, with specific reference to the exchange of resources (values) between an individual and the business or organization which offers a product or service. Marketing thus enables a business to distribute a product which is effective in meeting customers' needs at a price which is congruent with demand for the product and profit for the company. Marketing is not the same as sales; it is concerned with the relationship between the product and consumer orientation, and utilizes market research.

The United Way system has utilized a sales approach for a long time, both at the local and the national level. In the report of the UWA Program Evaluation Committee (1981) considerable attention is given to the United Way communications program, which includes a variety of sophisticated films, television spots, and video materials. While some of the materials covered in this evaluation report relate to marketing research, many of the techniques listed, such as National Football League public service announcements and video materials, resemble "commercial sell."

Since the first national United Way survey in 1976, and the 1978 establishment of a communication/marketing research program under the National Communications Advisory Committee, the UWA has been encouraging local United Ways, particularly in larger communities, to develop a comprehensive marketing approach. At a recent regional staff conference, there was considerable discussion about efforts to institutionalize a systematic approach to

---

[13]*Marketing, however, is increasingly becoming a strategy of nonprofit corporations as well as businesses. See Philip Kotler,* Marketing for Nonprofit Organizations *(Englewood Cliffs, N.J.: Prentice Hall, 1975); Patrick J. Montana, ed.,* Marketing in Nonprofit Organizations *(New York: AMACOM, 1978).*

[14]*Drucker,* Management, *p. 61.*

marketing the United Way product in local communities.[15] But the attempt to do so system-wide suggests some very basic dilemmas in relation to definition of the product, delineating target publics or consumers, and costs for hiring staff with the appropriate training and expertise.

THE UNITED WAY PRODUCT

Funded Agencies

What is the United Way product? Traditionally, the United Way has gone to the public with a list of agencies that it funds and on which it has based its campaign appeals. Community chests, and later even the United Funds through the early 1970s raised money for a group of agencies well known to the public (Girls Scouts, Boy Scouts, YMCAs and YWCAs, Red Cross, family service agencies). The community knew what it was getting for its money, since these agencies had generally been there a long time, and were frequently visible as well as well established.

The winds of change in the 1960s, however, included criticism about the irrelevance of many of the established organizations, and led to a proliferation of new agencies, which were often supported by government funds, through the war on poverty or model cities programs.[16] In response to pressure, many local United Way organizations added a few of these agencies as part of their funded agency package. By the early 1970s, for example, in Westchester County, New York, local community chests were funding minority-oriented agencies in White Plains, Port Chester, and Mount Vernon; funding was increased county-wide for the Urban League, and simultaneously other traditional agencies were being encouraged to direct their services to underserved, disadvantaged populations. A study by the Yale University Program on Non-Profit Organizations found that 174 new agencies were admitted between 1970 and 1981 by the eight local United Ways studied, and a UWA allocations report documents that most of the larger United Ways added several new agencies each year from 1979 to 1982.[17] The dollar amount allocated overall,

[15]*Workshops and discussion groups at the Southeast Regional Staff Conference, 1983. See also Memorandum to Selected United Way Professionals Regarding the Design of a Marketing Plan for Campaign, from Thomas J. Walker, Vice-President, Fund Raising Development Division, February 24, 1980. Marketing is a key aspect of the United Way, "New Horizons for People" program and is included in the 1982 program description.*

[16]*Smith, "The Role of the United Way in Philanthropy": Stanley Wenocur, "The Adaptability of Voluntary Organizations: External Pressure and United Way Organizations,"* Policy and Politics *(June 1975, 3:3–23; Ralph Kramer,* Voluntary Agencies in the Welfare State, *(University of California Press, 1981), pp. 67–76.*

[17]*Deborah K. Polivy, "A Study of Admissions Policies and Practices of Eight Local United Way Organizations" (Yale University Program on Non-Profit Organizations, Working Paper #49, 1982); also according to the UWA, new agencies in 1981 accounted for 4 percent of all agencies receiving United Way support. See* Local United Way Allocations to Agencies and Program Services, Metros I–VIII, *United Way of America Research and Development Division (Alexandria, Va.: UWA, 1981), pp. 2–3.*

however, has not been large and generally seems to come out of new funds or venture grants rather than out of the base funds the United Way allocates to its traditional agencies.

In the late 1970s and early 1980s, challenges to the United Way federated fund-raising organization increasingly developed from other fund-raising groups. In 1978, after a ten-year agreement had ended and a two-year battle occurred ("the charity wars"), the Association of In-Group Donors, known as AID, settled a law suit out of court and was eventually merged with the United Way in Los Angeles. Other major types of alternative funds can be identified currently: the National Combined Health Appeal and local Combined Health Appeal organizations the National Black United Fund and its affiliates; arts councils and funds; and social action/public interest funds, some of which are reported to be incorporating as the National Coalition to Increase Charitable Giving.[18] Other organizations, such as the International Service Agencies are grouped together in the Combined Federal Campaign (which raises funds from civilian as well as military employees), but these are not actually organized as alternative funds.

United Way's success in raising money at low cost through payroll deduction, together with decreased government funds and increased costs of community fund-raising, have resulted in greater pressure from new groups for access to the workplace. After a series of skirmishes in the courts, some employers may also be concerned about potential law suits or bad press, as well as employee relations. Thus, it is not surprising that in July 1981 the New York Black United Fund was included among the list of agencies which may be designated in IBM employee campaigns in the New York Metropolitan area, and that Bell Laboratories in New Jersey allowed solicitation by the Black United Fund.[19] Some other companies also allow various formats for multiple designations or combined federated fund-raising drives for their employee campaigns.

Although United Way is a nonprofit organization with 501 (c) 3 charitable status under Federal Internal Revenue Service (IRS) regulations, and not a business, it is sensitive to charges of monopoly practice. In 1976, the concept of inclusiveness became an official part of the United Way of America long range plan, and was interpreted to mean inclusion of branches of national health agencies, as well as new services to subgroups that had typically been underfunded by the United Way, such as minorities and women. After more than twenty years of separation, many local United Ways have made successful attempts to bring the American Cancer Society (ACS) into the package of their funded agencies and also, to a lesser extent, the American Heart Association (AHA). The move toward more inclusiveness in funding was framed with some degree of ambiguity, but was certainly a response to a variety of

---

[18]*National Committee for Responsive Philanthropy, "Big Change in Workplace Fund-Raising as the Alternative Fund Movement Grows,"* Bulletin for Members Agencies, *July 22, 1982.*
[19]Ibid., *3–4.*

outside pressures on the United Way, including the research of David Horton Smith and the papers of the donee group which developed arguments critical of the mainstream position of the Filer Commission.[20]

In any case, by the mid-1970s the UWA recognized the need to change the United Way mix of agencies, and to develop a new inclusiveness, perhaps far more than most of the 2,100 independent local United Ways did at that time.[21] Local organizations may have worried that adding ACS and AHA to the United Way agency list would cause a problem with the other agencies they funded. Moreover, since neither ACS nor AHA provides extensive services locally, they would run counter to a major selling point used with United Way contributors—community services—and neither agency could be subject to the local citizens' review process. On the other hand, "heart" and "cancer" were believed to have popular appeal at the workplace, where workers seem to identify with health problems and to respond emotionally to requests for support of agencies that provide services or do research in this area. Thus, local branches of the national ACS and AHA are generally brought into local United Ways as partners in the campaign rather than as funded agencies, and their fund-raising capacity is "bought out" through a fixed formula or agreed-upon annual payment which appears to average somewhat less than 5 percent of the gross funds raised by local United Ways. As of March 1982, at least 80 local United Ways had contracts with local branches of the American Cancer Society, using some variation of a fairly standard formula-based contract.[22]

United Ways Services

While small nontraditional agencies and "cadillac" health agencies, such as ACS, are being added to the United Way package mix, another significant development is occurring in the United Way marketing program. The use of service groupings in United Way literature occurs significantly as campaign materials across the country are developed with reference to "services funded." Indeed, the UWA allocation data collection system gathers data by program service categories, such as employment training or housing services, in line with the UWA established data classification schema, United Way of America

---

[20] See the Donee Group Report and Recommendations, "Private Philanthropy: Vital and Innovative? Passive and Irrelevant?" in Research Papers, compiled by the Filer Commission (1977), Vol. I.

[21] "American Cancer Society-United Way Contract Definitions and Process" (mimeo.; 1982), distributed to local United Ways by the UWA. for discussion of inclusiveness, see "Long Range Planning Report on Critical Issues Confronting Local United Ways: Inclusiveness" (UWA, 1978).

[22] Internal United Way memorandum to interested United Ways, from Robert Beggan, on United Way/American Cancer Society Relationships, UWA, March 1982. This memorandum also states that in 1980 new United Way/American Cancer Society agreements averaged 3.64 percent of total funds raised by United Ways.

Services Identification System (UWASIS) as well as by agency name.[23]

In addition to the category of agency services which are funded by United Ways, however, there is also a new and increasing group of services that are provided by the local United Way organizations themselves, and which can be conceived of as part of the United Way product. These services may be classified in two ways: (1) those which are essential to the United Way purpose and mission; and (2) those which are add-ons, and that appear to be responses to environmental pressures. Among the services which fall into the first category is certainly the allocations process by which available funds are distributed to agencies. This process is characterized by extensive volunteer participation and is proclaimed as the citizen review process. Complementary to this process are service and demographic data collection conceived as part of the operational planning function of the allocations program.

United Way's definition of services to the community, however, is in the process of changing. The old concept of community organization and community planning is apparently re-emerging, with United Way defining a critical role for itself as the lynch pin between the business world and the social welfare sector. Indeed, over the past fifteen years local United Way organizations have defunded or absorbed formerly independent community councils at such a rate that of the forty-five operating councils in large cities in 1970, only twenty-seven currently remain in existence. Among the most recently defunded councils is the Planning Council in Toledo, which is now trying to form a community human service coalition including the United Way and public-sector funding sources.

United Ways are also trying to reach out to meet emergency needs created by the cutbacks in federal funding and mounting unemployment. In Seattle, which is noted for a responsive United Way leadership, this is not a totally new role. In 1971 the United Way was instrumental in developing a community employment referral and resource center for Boeing employees facing extensive layoffs. In 1981, the United Way took the community-wide lead in developing a special public-private partnership, Project Transition, which raised money, largely from corporate sources, to help meet the emergency needs of the unemployed. Over $1.5 million was raised through this special fund for a variety of services, including emergency shelter and food, day care, chore services, and medical services,[24] provided by both United Way agencies and non-United Way agencies.

---

[23]UWASIS II: A Taxonomy of Social Goals and Human Service Programs *(Alexandria, Va.: UWA, 1976)*.

[24]*Information gathered from interviews in Seattle, August 1982; see also "Start-Up" report of the Project, Service to Add Reinforcement to Unemployed People, Seattle, 1974; "Project Transition," report of the Project Transition Committee, Seattle, 1982. The UWA and local United Ways are also deeply involved in the program for distribution of funds to meet emergency food and shelter needs, under Public Law 98-8 (the Job Stimulus bill) with the UWA serving as a fiscal agent for the national program.*

It is not, however, just in Seattle that United Ways are adding a range of ancillary roles to their formerly central functions of fund-raising and fund allocation. New functions are inevitably connected with broader definitions of accountability, and relate to community planning and community services. Specific activities of local United Ways now include evaluation of agency performance; needs assessment and priorities-setting; community development with other public and private agencies in the human services; and such other miscellaneous activities as information and referral, volunteer training, and technical assistance to emerging community agencies and new groups. All of these were delineated in the *Standards of Excellence* promulgated by the United Way of America in 1972, but they are currently receiving renewed emphasis.[25]

These activities may be laudable, but will the public or the donor pay for them? Traditionally, local United Ways' own activities were advertised as costing less than 10 percent of total funds raised. The United Way in short, was considered an extremely efficient way to give money. Corporate leaders spoke with pride about the efficiency of United Way operations; currently they are being asked to join the United Way national executive in recognizing a need to accept additional costs for the United Way system.[26]

Donor Option

One last function of United Ways returns the wheel almost full circle. Among the options which local United Ways are now exploring is the function of collecting funds for any defined health and welfare organization that is a 501 (c) 3 registered charitable organization. As of September 1982, forty-five local United Ways had some form of donor option in place. For funds designated to agencies under this plan, the local United Way organization essentially serves as a conduit only.[27] The funds collected are turned over directly to the recipient organization, with generally a charge made for the cost of collecting the funds. This form of contribution, under donor designation, may be highly responsive to individual donor preference, but it does not relate to the needs of the recipient nor is it controlled by any community priority-setting or citizen accountability process.

What product, then, is the United Way marketing? Is it marketing the agencies it funds (Red Cross, the YMCA), or the services that it funds, by categories such as health, employment services, and day care? Is it marketing the "full service" United Way which includes funded services provided by a

---

[25]Standards of Excellence for Local United Way Organizations; A Program for the Future Publication *(Alexandria, Va.: UWA, 1972; amended 1977).*

[26]*Remarks by Donald Seibert and William Aramony at the Volunteer Leaders Conference, 1982; also remarks by William Aramony at the Southeast Conference, 1983.*

[27]*"Donor Option Resource Packet," UWA, June 25, 1982, and "Donor Option: A Consideration" (UWA, 1982).*

group of agencies, together with the United Way community services component previously described and the option of donor designation? And what
difference does it make?

UNITED WAY MARKETS AND COMPETITION

If the United Way is like a business, then the test of its product will be in
the profit it makes, primarily through new funds raised in the campaign. In
that case, the mix of services provided should be considered a local option,
and there need not be one universal United Way model. The message about
the United Way product can be planned to satisfy segments of the market or
groups of donors, so long as the donor knows what he is buying with his
contribution.[28]

It is evident however, that local United Way organizations face a double
dilemma. They must develop greater understanding of their various market
groups in order to function effectively and they must determine who is the
client they are serving. These may or not be the same. For example, their
market includes groups as diverse as blue-collar workers, professionals in
high-tech industries, self-employed professionals, owners of small businesses,
and corporate leaders. Some or all of these groups may be the United Way's
client group, but clients may also be the unemployed and the disadvantaged,
or the client may be the community as the whole. Certainly, the actual service
needs of the groups described are different, and their perception of philanthropy
is not the same. The United Way, therefore, has to develop a product and a
message appropriate to various market segments, and at the same time has
to serve a client which may ultimately be defined as the whole community.

In any case, it seems evident that local United Ways will increasingly be
competing in the market (and specifically in the workplace) with other groups
seeking funds. It may even be that this competition will have some benefits
for the United Way itself in terms of organizational change and innovation.
It seems certain to bring some benefits to the community. While the United
Way has used good business strategies in trying to absorb, merge, or co-opt
attractive agencies and competitive funds, evidence suggests that such efforts
may not always serve the general welfare. To begin with, competition or,
more benignly, choice among philanthropies, appears to result in larger overall
contributions to voluntary social welfare agencies, at a time when this group
of agencies has generally been receiving a declining share of the charity
market.[29] It is too soon to reach definitive conclusions, but the National
Committee for Responsive Philanthropy reports that for independent alterna-

---

[28]*Marketing strategies are discussed extensively in* Listening to the Community: 1979 United
Way National Marketing Survey, *Communication Resource Handbook III (Alexandria, Va.:
UWA, 1980).*

[29]Giving and Getting: A Chemical Bank Study of Charitable Contributions through 1984 *(New
York: Chemical Bank, 1981), p. 15.*

tive funds for which "hard figures" were available, a sizeable 34.0 percent increase in contributions was registered from 1980 to 1981, compared with a 10.3 percent increase for United Ways across the country.[30]

Evidence seems to indicate that as new federated groups collect payroll deductions, they raise the total amount contributed generally, although the United Way share increases less rapidly than that of the new groups. It should also be pointed out that health rather than social welfare agencies may be among the larger beneficiary group in new monies.[31] It seems likely, therefore, that United Way is, on the one hand preparing a marketing strategy so as to be more competitive in an open charity market, and on the other hand, promoting donor option to diminish the growth of multiple and competing solicitations by alternative funds.

SOME FINAL OBSERVATIONS

Considerable research has been undertaken concerning the reason that corporate leaders allow United Way access to the workplace and give a corporate donation to the United Way. Among the factors which influence corporate donations are the amount that a corporation has given in the past and the corporate leader's belief that United Way is efficient and cost-effective in carrying out its functions, the conviction that local needs are served through the United Way, and the amount of pretax profits available.[32] Corporate leadership also appears to believe strongly in the United Way as the American Way. In my interviews with corporate leaders across the country, they continually reaffirm their belief that United Way exemplifies the capitalist system, and that voluntarism is allied with industry. Services provided by the voluntary sector in the local community are resources that remain in the community, and are infinitely preferred to those that may result from sending taxes to Washington.[33]

Finally, with all the discussion about the United Way product, and elaborate communication aids, the United Way knows that a large segment of the public and the business community does not give to the United Way. The reasons

[30]*National Committee for Responsive Philanthropy, "Big Change in Workplace Giving"; see also Deborah C. Brown, "The United Way of South Eastern Pennsylvania: The Philadelphia Story" (unpublished manuscript; n.d.).*

[31]*Data from national United Way surveys indicate that 68 percent of nongivers would cotibute to United Ways if more health services were included. See* Listening to the Community: 1979 United Way National Survey, *pp. 63–64.*

[32]*Dennis J. Murphy, Corporate Contributions: Understanding the Decision-Making Process (Alexandria, Va.: UWA, 1981);* Annual Survey of Corporate Contributions: An Analysis of Survey Data for the Calendar Year 1980 *(New York: the Conference Board, cosponsored with the Council for Financial Aid to Education, 1982).*

[33]*Interviews held with corporate executives in Seattle, San Diego, and Boise in June–August, 1982; interviews in Toledo, November, 1982; in Springfield, Mo., and Corpus Christi, Texas, in January, 1983.*

are complex, but local and national market surveys have revealed that the United Way name is frequently not recognized, and there is less general awareness of United Way functions in the community, even of such a basic function as the citizen review process, than might have been anticipated.[34] Increased marketing and community activity are expected to address this concern. Nevertheless, the United Way may still have to deal with the problem of its internal confusion over the nature of its product, which could result in a critical loss of identity, and a potential loss in the marketplace due to intense competition from a range of single-purpose or sharply defined advocacy organizations.

SUMMARY

United Way organizations work closely with the corporate community, and not surprisingly they have adopted the style, strategies, and technologies of the business organizations with which they associate. In this respect the United Way can certainly be considered in the forefront of a rapidly developing movement in the human services, as agencies are more and more assuming businesslike practices to deal with declining resources and increased competition. The United Way system is, however, particularly complex in terms of structure and function. Thus, our research suggests that as the United Way becomes more businesslike, it is facing difficult dilemmas in the definition of its market and product, along with increased competition from other organizations in the environment. In order to deal with the strains caused by these dilemmas, the United Way system will have to show even greater flexibility in its approach to fund-raising, while it persists in developing both a broader base of market support in the community and a more clearly delineated concept of the clients that it serves.

[34]See Listening to the Community, p. 29.

Index to *the Social Welfare Forum*, 1982/1983